Introduction to Sport Management

Jordan R. Bass

University of Kansas

second edition

Kendall Hunt
publishing company

Kendall Hunt
publishing company

www.kendallhunt.com
Send all inquiries to:
4050 Westmark Drive
Dubuque, IA 52004-1840

Published in the United States of America

second edition

Table of Contents

Chapter 1

Introduction to Sport Management

Jordan R. Bass • *University of Kansas*

KEY TERMS

Sport Management

Program Requirements

Program Resources

Professional Society

1

When students choose to attend the University of Kansas, they have a wide range of majors from which to choose. From Math to Sociology to Exercise Science, KU provides a plethora of opportunities students can take advantage of to advance their knowledge and prepare for their future careers. One major that has exploded in popularity over the past two decades is Sport Management. You are reading this textbook because you are enrolled in the Introduction to Sport Management course at the University of Kansas, or something has gone terribly wrong in my career and you found this relic in a used bookstore. Either way, you at least have some interest in the sporting field if you are reading this chapter. Whether you are enrolled in this course to fulfill the prerequisite for the Sport Management Major, Minor, or just saw the word "sport" in the course title and thought, "Cool!" I'm happy you are enrolled.

If you are interested in working in sports, you have chosen wisely by attending the University of Kansas. As you likely already know (and will read in Chapter Three), KU has a storied sporting history on the field and in the locker room. But more importantly for your education and future career, the front offices and administrative ladders of thousands of sport organizations in the United States and world are filled with Jayhawk graduates. Better yet, our graduates are incredibly proud of their alma mater and have selflessly given their time and knowledge back to the Sport Management program to help current Jayhawks. Throughout this book, you'll read interviews I conducted with Jayhawks who work in sport and in class you'll have an opportunity to hear from alums who work in the area and graciously agree to come back as guest speakers and lecturers. In previous semesters, Jayhawks graduates who work for the Kansas City Royals, Kansas City Chiefs, University of Kansas Athletics, Special Olympics Kansas, Kansas Speedway, Sporting KC, and a number of other organizations visited HSES 289 and imparted their wisdom to future Jayhawk graduates.

The graduates you will hear from all started the same way you are this semester: with skills, goals, uncertainty, desire, and ambition. This Introduction to Sport Management class is designed to provide students with a broad overview of the sporting field and a snapshot of the different topical areas that will be covered if you choose to apply to the Major or Minor in Sport Management at the University of Kansas. If you look at the Table of Contents for this textbook, you'll see a wide variety of topics and emphasis areas that we will touch on throughout the class. By no means will we have the time to cover these topics on a substantive level; instead, we hope to stoke your interest in the field and help you preliminary identify areas of the sport management field you'd like to get experience in during your undergraduate career to help your future job search process (scary and exciting to think about,

Courtesy of the Department of Health, Sport, and Exercise Sciences at the University of Kansas

right?). Each topic will also be paired with interviews and guest speakers to help connect the theory you'll read in this text with the cutting-edge practices Jayhawks are engaged in throughout the industry.

Major in Sport Management

The Sport Management Major at the University of Kansas is part of the Department of Health, Sport, and Exercise Sciences within the School of Education. Incoming freshman at KU can indicate an interest in Sport Management but cannot officially apply (or be admitted) to the Major until they have taken the required prerequisite classes and have a Grade Point Average (GPA) above the required level. The current requirements for admission can be found by visiting https://soe.ku.edu/students/admission-to-school-of-education and clicking on "Sport Management." Along with other general requirements, students must have a 2.75 Grade Point Average to be considered for admission. Finally, the program offers admission for both the fall and spring semester. Once students are admitted to the major, they will take a number of required program classes including Sport Marketing, Sociology of Sport, and Sport Finance. Additionally, students have the choice of a minor in Business, Journalism, or Psychology. The major program concludes with a 15-credit hour internship. See the program sheet below for more detailed information.

Minor in Sport Management

In January 2017, the program added a Minor in Sport Management open to all students at KU who have completed 40 hours with a cumulative Grade Point Average of 2.5. Students must also complete HSES 289 (this course) before or during the first year of declaring the minor. The 18-credit hour minor has four required classes and two electives that must be completed with a 2.5 Grade Point Average. The minor pairs well with a number of majors, including School of Business offerings, Journalism, and other Health, Sport, and Exercise Science majors like Community Health and Exercise Science. More information on the minor and directions on how to declare are located at http://hses.ku.edu/academics/sport-management/minor/curriculum. See the program sheet below for more details:

Master's Degree in Sport Management

The University of Kansas also offers a Master's of Science degree with a Sport Management emphasis. The degree consists of 36 (or 30 if the student chooses the thesis option) credit hours of coursework, an internship, and comprehensive exam. This interdisciplinary graduate program trains professionals who are seeking administrative positions within all sectors of the sports industry. Students are required to submit three letters of recommendation, scores from the Graduate Record Examination (GRE), undergraduate transcripts, and a personal statement detailing their motivations for completing the graduate degree. On average, 25 students are enrolled in the Master's program at one time and students typically complete the degree in 18 months to two years. More information about the degree program can be found at hses.ku.edu/academics/sport-management/masters-degree/overview-benefits.

KU School of Education
Sport Management Major
Bachelor's Degree Program Guide

Program Admission Requirements

☐ ENGL 101 & 102
☐ MATH 101
☐ COMS 130
☐ PSYC 104
☐ ECON 104, 142 **or** 144
☐ PHIL 160

☐ BIOL 100/102
☐ ELPS 250
☐ HSES 244
☐ HSES 260
☐ HSES 289
☐ Humanities Requirement

General Education Requirements

☐ Natural Science Lecture & Lab
  Requirement
☐ Upper Division Requirement #1
☐ Upper Division Requirement #2

☐ Upper Division Requirement #3
☐ Approved Elective #1
☐ Approved Elective #2

Sport Management Program Requirements

☐ HSES 380
☐ HSES 381
☐ HSES 382
☐ HSES 384
☐ HSES 440
☐ HSES 483

☐ HSES 485
☐ HSES 486
☐ HSES 487
☐ HSES 488
☐ HSES 499

Courses Required for Selected Minor

☐ Business Minor (18 credit hours)
☐ Journalism Minor (18 credit hours)

☐ Psychology Minor (18 credit hours)

Requirements for the Sport Management bachelor's degree program fulfill the KU Core Goals
kucore.ku.edu

Sport Management Major

Freshman Year

Fall Semester

☐ Composition (ENGL 101)
☐ College Algebra (MATH 101)
☐ General Psychology (PSYC 104)
☐ Speaker-Audience Comms (COMS 130)
☐ Intro to Ethics (PHIL 160)

Spring Semester

☐ Principles of Biology & Lab (BIOL 100/102)
☐ Education & Society (ELPS 250)
☐ Introduction to Economics (ECON 104)
☐ Personal & Community Health (HSES 260)
☐ Critical Reading & Writing (ENGL 102)

Sophomore Year

Fall Semester (Apply for SOE admission)

☐ Intro to PE & Sport Studies (HSES 244)
☐ Intro to Sport Management (HSES 289)
☐ Natural Science Lecture & Lab Requirement
☐ Humanities Requirement
☐ Upper Division Requirement #1

Spring Semester

☐ Sport Ethics (HSES 381)
☐ Sport Facilities & Event Management (HSES 382)
☐ Upper Division Requirement #2
☐ Critical Thinking Requirement
☐ Global Awareness Requirement

Junior Year

Fall Semester

☐ Sociology of Sport (HSES 380)
☐ Sport Law (HSES 384)
☐ Upper Division Requirement #3
☐ Approved Minor Course #1
☐ Approved Minor Course #2

Spring Semester

☐ Applied Sport & Performance Psych (HSES 440)
☐ Sport Marketing (HSES 486)
☐ Approved Minor Course #3
☐ Approved Minor Course #4
☐ Approved Minor Course #5

Senior Year

Fall Semester

☐ Pre-Internship Seminar (HSES 488)
☐ Communication in Sport (HSES 485)
☐ Sport Finance & Economics (HSES 483)
☐ Personnel Management in Sport (HSES 487)

Spring Semester

☐ Internship in Sport Management (HSES 499)

Learn more:
hses.ku.edu/sport-management

121 credit hours (min.)
soeadvising@ku.edu

Please note: This is only a sample plan of study. Please consult with your academic advisor before enrolling.

Courtesy of the Department of Health, Sport, and Exercise Sciences at the University of Kansas

BOX 1.1

Minor in Sport Management

Requirements to Declare
1. Completed 40 cumulative credit hours before beginning the minor coursework
2. Completed coursework with 2.5 cumulative GPA
3. Completed HSES 289 before beginning the minor coursework OR in the first semester of the minor
To declare, complete the form at http://tinyurl.com/SportMinor

Sport Management Minor Coursework
Pre-requisite or co-requisite
(Completed before or during first semester of minor)
HSES 289/Introduction to Sport Management

Required Minor Coursework (12 Hours)
HSES 380 Sociology of Sport (3 Hours)
HSES 483 Sport Finance and Economics (3 Hours)
HSES 486 Sport Marketing (3 Hours)
HSES 487 Personnel Management in Sport (3 Hours)

Elective Coursework (6 Hours)
(Students may choose any two of the following courses)
HSES 384 Sport Law
HSES 484 Sport in Film
HSES 485 Sport Communication
HSES 381 Sport Ethics
HSES 382 Sport Facilities and Event Management
HSES 598 Special Topics (Including Experiential Learning)

In order to be awarded the Minor in Sport Management, students must complete the minor coursework with a minimum GPA of 2.5

Date: October 2016

Program Resources

Being a Jayhawk interested in the sport industry affords you a number of unique and useful resources. First, you have access to the *KU Sport Management Professional Society,* a group of over 300 Jayhawk alumni who work in the sport industry and related fields. The continually updated list of members can be found by visiting http:// tinyurl.com/JayhawksInSport. You can also view a number of talks, interviews, and guest lectures by subscribing to the KU Sport Management Professional Society YouTube channel at www.youtube.com/channel/UCWBi03Xqt1ZkqxlZUoetEaQ. Additionally, you can read updates about the sport management program and Professional Society on the program website at www.medium.com/sportmgmtku. Finally, as a member of this class you have access to our private Facebook group where I post volunteer/internship/and job opportunities that are sent to me to advertise to KU students. Ask to join at www.facebook.com/groups/KUSMGTJobs.

A list of other important departmental links to visit, to subscribe, and to follow is below.

Department of Health, Sport, and Exercise Sciences (HSES)
Homepage: www.hses.ku.edu
HSES Facebook Page: www.facebook.com/KUHSES/

Jayhawks in the Field

Henry Wear

Lecturer at Deakin University in Melbourne, Australia

Hometown
Portland, Oregon

Education
UG 2012 – University of Oregon (Economics)
Masters 2014 – University of Kansas (Sport Management)
Doctoral 2017 – University of South Carolina (Sport and Entertainment Management)

1. At what point did you decide you wanted to go into academia and what were your motivations? Was there someone who had a big influence on you?

My parents are both educators, and had always placed an important value on education. They have also always been incredibly passionate about what they do as teachers and as lifelong learners. My mother might be the most overqualified sixth-grade science teacher in the world with a Ph.D. in economics. So working in academia had always been in the back of my mind as a potential career path. However, academia and sport didn't become a reality for me until I enrolled in sport marketing and sport research classes at the University of Oregon. I remember talking to my professors at the time, and having them explain to me that there was an entire world of academia in which you were able to research and teach sport management. While I was amazed that such an opportunity existed, I really wanted to see what it was like to work in the sport industry. When I arrived at KU for my Masters, I was truly able to experiment and try several different sport-related passions. I worked in academic services with Dr. Scott Ward and was able to get some first-hand college athletics experience. I was lucky enough to work for the Kansas City Royals in Media Relations and finally achieved my dream of making it to the big leagues. Ultimately, it was the work opportunities as a teaching assistant in the HSES department and the research project opportunities supported by Dr. Clopton and Dr. Bass that I was the most passionate about. I loved being in the classroom and working with students, and also loved conducting research about why sport fans do what they do. Being able to experience academia and the sport industry simultaneously allowed me to understand what it was I was really passionate about. Following this revelation, I knew I had to continue to get my Ph.D. and was part of the very first cohort at the University of South Carolina. There, I was fortunate enough to have worked with

Dr. Bob Heere, a leader in sport management research, who helped me develop and hone my research skills and guided me through what it meant to be a professor of sport management. There were many people along the way that encouraged and supported me, and I'm grateful that I have the opportunity to do something I love for living.

2. Oregon to Kansas isn't exactly a common path. What about KU and the program attracted you to Lawrence?

As soon as I knew that I wanted to continue on work toward my Master's degree in sport management I set off on a road trip to visit campuses and programs across the country. My wife (fiancé at the time) was nice enough to join me and we drove East from Oregon and stopped at many campuses along the way. As soon as we stopped in Lawrence, we were blown away. We immediately fell in love with the town, the people, and KU. I met with Dr. Clopton and got a great feel for the program. After returning back to Oregon, I was still considering several programs, but something about KU stuck out and I kept coming back to it. As soon as I found out I had the opportunity to work in the department as a teaching assistant heading to Lawrence was an easy decision. I still have great memories, friends, and colleagues from my time at KU and in Lawrence, and still reminisce about eating barbeque at Biemer's, hanging out at Free State Brewery, and spending game day in Allen Fieldhouse.

3. During your academic travels, you lived in three very different areas and now live outside the United States. How would you compare and contrast the "sporting culture" in the different areas?

Each place has been quite different. In the Pacific Northwest, we are a bit removed from the rest of the country and the sporting landscape. I'm sure there is some portion of sport fans that probably think we're all bearded lumberjacks, which isn't far from the truth. Sport in the Pacific Northwest is fantastic, it's filled with passion, and since the area isn't overflowing with teams, much of that passion gets funneled into the few local teams and the fan culture is outstanding. Kansas and the Kansas City area were somewhat similar, smaller market areas with fewer teams, but loyal and passionate fans. Sport in general seemed to be a bigger priority in Kansas and Kansas City, and you couldn't go too far without having a conversation about a team or game. The South was quite different. There seemed to be a more direct focus on one particular sport at a time rather than several, and the influence of the SEC was never far away. I would encourage everyone to experience SEC football at least once in their lives; it's pretty unbelievable. Living abroad has been quite a different experience, but Australian sport has many similarities with the United States. Overall, I would say the sporting culture here has been much more inclusive in regard to fandom and participation. People enjoy sport because it is sport, not because it is a particular team, league, or code. Due to the population distribution in the country, many of the larger cities will have many teams competing in the same league, and often for the same fans. The membership culture that exists for professional teams seems to do a great job of making fans feel as if they're part of the organization and not just consumers. Ultimately, I would encourage anyone who wants to work in this industry to travel and see sport from as many different states, regions, and countries as possible. It provides a wonderful perspective to why this industry is so great, and so valuable to our society.

4. If you only had two hours in Lawrence, what would you do?

I would probably head to the heart of KU and take a quick stroll around campus, making sure to snap a few photos of Fraser Hall, The Campanile, and end with a quick visit of the Booth Family Hall of Athletics. I'd head straight for Mass Street after that and make sure to duck in and out of some of my favorite shops and cafes. Finally, I'd be sure to end with a trip to Free State Brewery and bring one of my favorites home. Ideally, this trip would be during November or December and I would head to Allen Field House at the end of the day to cheer on the Jayhawks.

5. When you teach undergraduate students, what makes exemplary students stand out from the crowd?

Passion, passion, passion. Students who are passionate and willing to do the work required are ones that I think will be successful in the long run in this industry. I think students very early on need to come to the realization that this industry is incredibly competitive, and that it takes some time to rise through the ranks to achieve their dream job. I also believe students who are able to recognize that working in this industry is about more than being a fan and watching ESPN stand out amongst the crowd. These students recognize that the study of sport management is focused on the industry from both a business and cultural perspective. Students who not only embrace the work, but also are truly passionate about the role of sport in our world, will be quite successful.

6. Describe the favorite parts of your job and give some specific examples if possible.

I feel fortunate to have the type of job where I get to focus my energy in to several different areas. I love being able to conduct research and contribute to the knowledge of the sport industry. I've always been curious, and in my research I'm able to harness my curiosity into projects regarding sport branding, fandom, and community development. I'm also able to engage with students on a daily basis, and love the time I spend in a classroom. I think more than anything being able to interact with students one on one and help them reach their career goals is why I wanted to work in academia.

Name: _____   Section: _____   Date _____

HSES 289
Introduction to Sport Management

In-Class Quiz and Activity Sheet

Name (or names if done in a group)

Answer #1

Answer #2

Answer #3

© Denis Zyatkov/Shutterstock.com

Chapter 2

Why Sport Management?

Jordan R. Bass • *University of Kansas*

KEY TERMS

Program Requirements

Jayhawks in Sport

Job Perks

Motivation

Passion and Desire

Icon Sportswire/Getty Images

Throughout this class, you'll hear me say many things I believe can make you stand out when you enter the sport management job market after you graduate from the University of Kansas. You'll also hear me say that you should never begin a cover letter or job interview with some variation of "I love sports!" or "Sports have always been a big part of my life." Even though these statements may be true, they are implied for the vast majority of professionals whom choose to dedicate their lives to working in sport. So, that leads to the question . . . how do you express your passion and love for sport in a way that will both indicate your interest and show you know working sport is so much more than just being a fan?

One way is to develop an understanding of why those who currently work in sport enjoy their positions. In the pages that follow, you will do just that by reading what over a dozen Jayhawks who work in sport responded when I asked them their favorite part of their job. While reading, take special note of those professionals in positions or organizations that interest you and the language they use to describe why they enjoy their job. Do their motivations match up with the reasons you believe you want to work in sport? What phrasing and information from their answers could you use to better describe your passion and desire to be in the field? Do their answers make you want to work in sport more or less? Consider all of these questions as you hear from Jayhawks who work outside the Kansas City area (those in the area are not included as they may be in class to answer this question in person!)

Describe Your Favorite Parts of Your Job?

Danielle Dasht, Compliance Coordinator, Georgia State University

Watching student-athletes compete and grow as individuals throughout their tenure while knowing my role assists in the process. Working in compliance, my responsibilities include various tasks pertaining to student-athletes from their recruitment through their collegiate career. For example: I do evaluations on recruits' transcripts to ensure they are academically eligible; then I approve and audit their campus visits; once they commit, I have a hand in the (National Letter of Intent) process; prior to their start at school I ensure they have completed compliance forms we need before they can engage in team activities; once they are on campus as a student-athlete, I provide daily support and assistance as needed. Seeing them play and win on the field and in the class room is a very rewarding experience.

It is always gratifying to be able to assist coaches and staff. Particularly, it's a good feeling when I'm able to give them the answer they are looking for or provide them a solution to a potential problem. My personal favorites revolve around recruiting.

Daily, I enjoy the amount of detail and research my job entails. It is highly detail oriented and focus is crucial as even a little mistake, such as a one digit difference when inputting a (Grade Point Average) can bare significant consequences. Providing interpretations and creating rules education for coaches and support staff is also a key function of my job I have come to like. While at first the extent of information and knowledge needed was overwhelming, I am now able to use resources to successfully deliver the necessary material.

Will Hoven, Events and Operations Coordinator, Valero Alamo Bowl

First, I'd say the people I get to work with. I wanted to get into sports for the chance to work on projects I am passionate about, and for the prestige working in this industry can bring (though I can assure you it is not a glamorous industry when you're starting out). When you get in, however, you meet people with the same enjoyment and passion for what they do. Getting to work with a group that shares your enthusiasm for what you do makes the work so much more enjoyable and rewarding.

I was fortunate enough to work at the Valero Alamo Bowl during a year where they were hosing an additional neutral site game (the Notre Dame "Shamrock Series"). These types of unique opportunities are not uncommon in the bowl industry, and are a nice added benefit that most people don't think about. For instance, the Final Four will be hosted in San Antonio at the Alamodome in 2018; the bowl staff will get to assist with that event in some capacity. Another example would be the college football national championship; depending what city the game is played in, such as Phoenix or Atlanta, the local bowl game (Fiesta and Peach) staff will more than likely get the opportunity to assist in the production of those games. If you love working in large-scale events, this is a great way to get more exposure and experience, even if it is in more of a support role than a lead role.

It's not all about game day and large-scale events. The smaller events (coaches' dinner, team pep rallies, luncheons, sponsor mixers) allow you to make a strong impression on a small group of people that is more immediately felt. For the average fan, they may perceive their experience at the actual bowl game a poor one if the game is a blow out, but at say a coaches dinner, where you control the venue, food selection, and entertainment (we had a modern violinist at our most recent coaches' dinner, who was a big hit with our guests), you can tell right away if you hit the mark or not, and it's always a great feeling when you do. That's really why I've come to love working in sport events; it gives you the opportunity to create memorable, lasting experiences for guests and fans via a platform that already brings so many people together.

Olivia Kinet, Customer Support, CaptainU

My absolute favorite part of my job is when I hear from an athlete or parent that I have been working closely with that they have committed to a university and athletic program of their choice. I love engaging with the athletes and parents throughout their recruiting process and providing them with some insight from my personal experiences as a college student-athlete and coach.

Life is a journey, not always straight up. There are ups and downs. Sports teach many of life's lessons and if I can help an athlete on his or her journey toward personal fulfillment, then it makes it all very worthwhile.

John Mallory, Assistant Director of Video, Seattle Seahawks

My favorite part of the job when I first started as an intern in still my favorite part all these years later. I love road games. I have visited every NFL city and been to every NFL stadium. Getting to experience different cities, even briefly, is such a great experience. When I began at the Chiefs, the only states I had been to were Kansas, Missouri, Colorado, and Florida . . . now I've been to almost every state. What I've learned from visiting all these places is that each city offers something unique and I have fun being a part of that. Road games are also a fun experience because it's just our small group of guys against a whole stadium. You really see the closeness and brotherhood of the team come out on the road.

I also enjoy being part of such a great organization that has had a lot of success during my time in Seattle. I've been fortunate enough to receive two NFC championship rings and a Super Bowl champion ring. The Seahawks have been very generous giving football staff the same rings the players receive which is really a dream come true. What little boy growing up playing football doesn't dream of receiving a Super Bowl ring or holding the Lombardi Trophy? The success of the team is great, but even just being a part of the team is rewarding. Knowing that I'm trusted to carry out so many important tasks that are vital to our players, coaches and scouts being more prepared and informed is a great feeling.

© Smith Sights/Shutterstock.com

Matt McDonough, Assistant Director of Athletics Development, Missouri State University

The relationship building with donors. I love seeing and hearing what motivates them philanthropically and then finding an avenue for them to exercise that motivation. Also, seeing the impact that our donors make on the lives of student-athletes currently and in the future.

The ever-changing landscape of the job is something that keeps me going. We are always looking for new and innovative ideas to fundraise and engage donors. I love being able to get those creative juices flowing and coming up with ideas that will benefit the Bears Fund and Missouri State University in the long run. Working in college athletics is a privilege and I feel fortunate to come to work every day and be involved in the business of sport.

Jacob Petty, Athletic Academic Advisor for Men's and Women's Track and Field/Cross Country, University of Oklahoma

My favorite part about my job is that I can wake up every day and go to work impacting the lives of others. Not a day goes by that work feels like work. I'm so fortunate to work in a place like the University of Oklahoma and work with the student-athletes that I work with. Knowing that you maybe played a small role in the educational process of a student is an extremely rewarding experience.

One example in particular, when I was a graduate assistant Academic Mentor with the Football team, I was working with the student all semester that historically struggled in English. Through our weekly sessions and possibly tips and time management skills that I taught him he received a "B" in the class. Once we found out his grade, this 6" 4' 250 lbs. football player cried and gave me a hug because he was so happy this was his first "B" in English in his life.

It is instances like that I keep you going. It is instances like that that make what you do all worth it. Knowing that you can make a positive impact on someone else's life and having the ability to reach new heights with them is immeasurable.

I have no doubt that the faculty and staff in the KU sport management program will provide you all with the education, experience, end in sight to excel in the field of sport. Good luck to you all and Rock Chalk!

Kayla Shirey, Events Coordinator, Arizona State Athletics

One part of my job I enjoy is being involved with the entire event and having a hand in the planning process. Coordinating a large-scale event takes months (sometimes years), many meetings, walk-throughs, and checklists. Being involved in each part of the process makes having a successful event worth the time and effort.

Another aspect of my job I enjoy is being a part of a team, and knowing you are important to the success of program (obviously not on the field but their program in general). For example, I oversee all home softball events, everything from umpires to guests to parking. Making constituents, want to attend the games and have a positive experience regardless of the results on the field are an important part of any successful program. My job is to make sure everyone leaves wanting to come back.

© Arthur Eugene Preston/Shutterstock.com

Justin Stucky, Football Scout, Dallas Cowboys

The favorite parts of my job include working for the NFL and the Dallas Cowboys organization, the competitive atmosphere and traveling. Sports and football have always been a major part of my life so to be able to find a job that is solely based around the sport on a day-to-day basis, and at the highest level possible, is a dream come true. The Dallas Cowboys have been one of the premier organizations in the sports industry since they were created in 1960 and with the help of the Jones family they continue to raise the bar for not only NFL organizations but also sports organizations across the world. Being able to work for a Hall of Fame owner in some of the best facilities in the country is a privilege many people don't get to experience.

Every new season and every week we get a chance to pursue a victory and strive for the ultimate goal of winning a championship. As a former athlete who can no longer participate on the field, this job is a great avenue for allowing my competitive nature stay alive. When it comes to traveling, being away from family and friends on a regular basis is difficult, but being on the road has allowed me to see over half of the country and waking up in a different city and going to a different school every day keeps the job from getting monotonous.

Justin Bauman, Director of Basketball Operations, Wake Forest Men's Basketball

I am very fortunate to work for someone that trusts me/believes in me to do my job and run the program. This is always the most difficult question for me to answer because I deal with so many different areas on a daily basis. I truly do enjoy all parts of my job. There are not any items that annoy me, I do not like, wish I did not have to do, etc. I am very lucky. This job really does not feel like a job to me. I enjoy the interaction with athletic department personnel, fans, media, parents, campus representatives, etc.

If I had to choose one of my favorite parts is planning for senior day. This is because I know how special it is to a player and their parents. This is the final time a player will step on their home court. The final time, they will "likely" be in the spotlight. The player and parents have accomplished something great over 4 years. It is great to see the happiness on the parents and players faces during this moment. Both parties sacrificed so much over their lives to get to that moment of accomplishment (4 years of a player career and usually a 4-year college degree).

Matt Gardner, Senior Director of Promotions and Digital Strategy, St. Louis Blues

Sports and technology are two of my biggest passions in life. So, having the opportunity each and every day to join these passions together as my career is truly a blessing. In two different professional sports team settings now, I've been able to help build and shape a Digital Media department. Technology helps change our world and those experiences begin to take shape within sports all the time. Finding ways of integrating innovation into the product we deliver to our fans becomes more and more important as days past by. Just in the last 10 years, we've gone from a website

© Rawpixel.com/Shutterstock.com

and email-focused digital environment, to embracing social media, adapting to a smartphone-first mentality and now all of those strategies are starting to emerge into the venue experience. The look forward to watching evolve how technology will next help shape the relationship between sports teams and their fan bases.

One of the favorite parts of my job is Opening Night and the first home game of the Playoffs. You put a ton of work into those events in particular. To go out on the concourse as fans file into the arena and see their excitement is what makes all that hard work worth it. Often times, I try to imagine myself as the fan when working on a strategy. I think about those moments when you still feel like a little kid when something gets you excited. I think about the moments that make me the happiest when I'm attending an event for my favorite teams. The chill you feel when that opening video plays or you hear that amazing rendition of the National Anthem. Those are moments you want to capture with each fan that walks through those doors. Those are the moments that make you pinch yourself.

But to do something you love every day and call it "work" is something that will never get old.

Chris Huey, Graduate Assistant, St. John's Men's Basketball

There are so many great parts of my job, one of the coolest being the opportunity I have every day to be around guys like Chris Mullin and Mitch Richmond. Coach Mullin was a great college player here at St. John's back coaching at his alma mater. He's a three-time Big East Player of the year, played 16 seasons in the NBA, 5 time NBA All Star, and a gold medalist with the 1992 Dream Team. Mitch played a junior college before being one of the best players ever at Kansas State, and yes Jayhawks and Wildcats can get along. Mitch's career in the NBA lasted 14 seasons and included being NBA Rookie of the Year, 6 time NBA All Star, 5 Time All-NBA team, and Gold Medalist in 1996 and NBA champion with Kobe and Shaq in '01-'02. Learning the game from guys like these two and hearing stories from their playing days makes everyday enjoyable. Who can say they've watched part of the documentary on the Dream Team with a member of the Dream team? Or heard about the playing days in the Big 8 when Kansas, Kansas State, Missouri, and

Oklahoma were all making deep runs in the NCAA tournament in the late 1980s? It's pretty cool stuff.

Here at St. John's, we play half of our home games on campus at Carnesecca Arena and the other half at Madison Square Garden. On campus, the arena is small which creates a great atmosphere, and named after Coach Mullin's Head Coach Lou Carnesecca, who took the school to the only final four appearances in school history. Coach Carnesecca is 92 years old and still around the program today, that makes it even more special. Playing home games in the "World's Most Famous Arena," Madison Square Garden for 7 home games out of the year, you really can't beat that. We go into Manhattan the night before the game and stay across the street from Central Park. The bus ride into the game includes seeing Central Park and driving through Times Square. To me this is one of the coolest things about a career in sports, the places basketball has taken me and the things I have been able to see in a few short years pushes me for the future.

James Kocen, Fan Development Representative, Nashville Predators

Working for a professional team has a lot of benefits. I really enjoy being able to watch games in between my game day duties and your fandom is just different working for a team. Beyond that, I have amazing coworkers and I think a lot of that has to do with the fact that we are all bought into advancing our careers past our current entry-level jobs and we all understand what it means to work in sports. Having people like that to share the peaks and valleys with is much needed during a long season. Lastly, I really enjoy being able to talk with people about our team. Whether it is a waiter at lunch or someone I bump into around town, people love talking about sports and having a unique perspective of working in sports, they love talking with me about my job and our team.

Hunter Lochmann, Senior Vice President for Marketing and Brand Strategy, Monumental Sports

What I love about my job is the creativity that comes with marketing. We can roll out marketing campaigns, sales ideas, etc. and sometimes they work and sometimes they don't. This constant feedback loop – especially with social media – not only keeps you honest and on your toes – but also makes you better. But my favorite part of my job is at the end of the day, I work for properties that people care very passionately for. What we take for granted – working in an arena – others find so interesting and want to read about us and consume everything about our brand every day. Not every brand can say that. And it never fails – when you surprise a fan with something small (e.g. a seat upgrade at a game) the looks on their faces and the memories you are making is what makes the hard work and long hours satisfying.

Sean Norris, Elite Account Manager, Hudl

I really enjoy working with people to solve a problem and building relationships with those people throughout that process. One example is working with a client from the initial discussions about renewing their account to when that account is paid. This process can include everything from reminding them of the value they're getting out of the product, working with them to better utilize the product, and working with their billing department to make sure we receive the money. Often coaches agree to purchase something, then it's out of their hands as they're not the people writing the checks. At this point, I've done the work to build a relationship and we're in good light in the coach's mind; it's important to not risk that by making it easy on them from this point forward.

The other favorite part of my job is just the people I work with. I have some great coworkers who bring good energy every day and have taught me a ton about a variety of topics. I appreciate emphasis on sharing ideas and challenging each other in the office, I think it helps us reach our potential.

Jim Small, Vice President of Asia Pacific Region, Major League Baseball

My favorite part of the job is the diversity—of food and language and culture—that comes with international business. In any given month, I could be in Tokyo, Beijing, Shanghai, Seoul, Taipei, Sydney, or New York. I still love the rush that comes with traveling to those places and dealing with the business culture there. They are all so different and it is up to me to adapt to the business culture there if I am to achieve MLB's business goals. That is really, really fun to me.

Connor Terry, Manager of Business Development, Billiken Sport Properties

I love meeting with people in person and building relationships. In addition, because all sorts of companies sponsor sports organizations, I enjoy learning more about different industries I don't work in: Banking, telecommunications, home improvement, insurance, law, etc. At the end of the day, its most rewarding to see how I can help these individuals drive their business through a partnership in college sports.

© f11photo/Shutterstock.com

Henry Wear, Lecturer, Deakin University

I feel fortunate to have the type of job where I get to focus my energy in to several different areas. I love being able to conduct research and contribute to the knowledge of the sport industry. I've always been curious, and in my research I'm able to harness my curiosity into projects regarding sport branding, fandom, and community development. I'm also able to engage with students on a daily basis, and love the time I spend in a classroom. I think more than anything being able to interact with students one on one and help them reach their career goals is why I wanted to work in academia.

Colin Zvosec, Assistant Director of Marketing and Promotions, Creighton University

One of the most rewarding parts of this job is the opportunity to interact with our student workers. At Sam Houston, I was responsible for the hiring and leading of an athletics promotions team to work all of our marketed events. In two years there, I had the chance to work with some really amazing kids that wanted to play a role in improving our game atmospheres. Specifically, I remember a game toward the middle part of our baseball season in 2016 that still stands out as a personal favorite of mine. Before every event, I would meet with the team to go over the day's events and delegate tasks. Our promotions and contests typically stayed the same on a day-to-day basis, so the promotions team will usually know by the time they get there what they want to do, however, they'll still wait for me to go through each one. On this day, our workers showed up, divvied up the tasks themselves, and took care of everything without my having to say a word. It was exactly the kind of initiative and team attitude I had been trying to get out of the group all year.

Of all the sports I've worked, football and baseball are definitely the top two when comes to favorites. Running football games, specifically the second year at Sam Houston when we had a new state-of-the-art video board, is an experience second to none. There are so many moving pieces, that you have to be really in-tune to everything going on in the moment and up ahead. There was a game in my second year where we ended up with one less timeout than originally planned, and I had to coordinate with about 10 individuals a brand new game plan on the fly. We ended up getting every element (which were all sponsored and had to be included) into the game, and I still remember our Assistant AD for Sponsorships asking me after the game how we pulled it off.

Conclusion

As you can see, there are a plethora of reasons that Jayhawk graduates enjoy working in the sport industry. From college sport, to professional sport, to recreation and technology, Jayhawks have enjoyed success in a number of areas. Hopefully this chapter will help you answer the ever elusive question of, "Why do you want to work in sport?"

Name: _____ Section: _____ Date _____

HSES 289
Introduction to Sport Management
In-Class Quiz and Activity Sheet

Name (or names if done in a group)

Answer #1

Answer #2

Answer #3

Source: Jordan R. Bass

Chapter 3

"Crimson and the Blue" An Era of Athletic Achievement

Francis B. "Bernie" Kish • *University of Kansas*

KEY TERMS

Jayhawks

Basketball Dominance

National Championships

Billy Mills

Tradition and History

Transforming the University of Kansas: A History 1965-2015, edited by John L. Rury and Kim Cary Warren, published by the University Press of Kansas, © 2015. www.kansaspress.ku.edu. Used by permission of the publisher.

THE past 50 years for Kansas Athletics have been marked by a tradition of excellence in sports competition and also changes in the gender equity and racial makeup of its student-athletes and teams. In addition, its athletics program has become a big business, in line with other major universities. It has also been characterized by a loyal and enthusiastic legion of fans, both locally and across the country. KU athletics stands today as one of the great institutions in collegiate competition, proudly looking forward to the future.

The story of KU's athletic tradition begins with men's basketball and football, the university's principal revenue sports, but it has assumed many other dimensions in this period. Beginning in the early 1970s, with the implementation of Title IX, women's athletics have become a vital, respected, and highly visible aspect of the KU athletics program. The Jayhawks now have ten women's sports, and these teams have represented the university with distinction nationally and in conference play. Many female athletes have earned All-American and All-Conference honors, and one track and field athlete won an Olympic gold medal.[1]

A notable change also occurred in the racial makeup of athletics at KU. In the 1960s, very few student-athletes or coaches were African American. That has changed over the years, with African American athletes playing a vital role in almost every sport at KU, both men's and women's. During this period, Kansas also hired African American head coaches for its football, women's basketball, and track and field teams. There has been a marked increase in black assistant coaches, particularly in football, men's basketball, and track and field. This has been a very positive development, for both KU athletics and the institution as a whole.

Since 1965, the athletics program at KU has steadily progressed toward becoming a big business, with the budget growing from about $9 million in the early 1990s to almost $80 million in 2014. The salaries of coaches, particularly in the two revenue sports, basketball and football, have been major contributors to the escalating budget, along with a facilities arms race.[2] Beginning in the early 2000s, KU built a new football complex and practice fields, a rowing boathouse, and a state-of-the-art facility for its track and field, soccer, and softball programs.

In the early 1990s, changes began to take place in the composition of athletics conferences nationwide. Several schools bolted conferences, lured mostly by the financial gain from television contracts. KU stayed true to its roots. In 1965, Kansas was a member of the Big Eight, and since 1996, when that conference expanded, it has been in the Big 12 Conference. Its loyalty has paid off, with enhanced conference revenues being instrumental in funding its athletics programs.

Ten men have served as athletics director since 1960, and there were also five acting or interim athletics directors. Four earned degrees on Mount Oread. All of them enjoyed success, some greater than others, and all faced challenges associated with managing a big-time athletics program.[3] As a matter of comparison, from 1911, when the position of athletics manager/athletics director was instituted at Kansas, until 1950, there were only four athletics directors and one interim director. This difference clearly reflects how the responsibilities of the job have expanded, especially with regard to balancing the athletics budget, maintaining winning programs, and negotiating public scrutiny.[4]

The major focus of this chapter is on the coaches and student-athletes in each of the sports and the exemplary reputation they have collectively earned for KU athletics. Kansas is known, and rightfully so, as a "basketball school." In this chapter, however, readers will note that every KU sport has enjoyed its day in the

© SITTHIGO/Shutterstock.com

sun. National and conference championships, NCAA postseason play, All-American and All-Conference honors, Olympic athletes, and coaches of the year in many different sports are all part of the Crimson and Blue, Rock Chalk Jayhawk, history of athletic distinction.

Kansas Basketball: A Tradition of Excellence

The University of Kansas has a long heritage of basketball excellence. It is arguably the most storied program in America. The inventor of the game, Dr. James Naismith, taught physical education at KU from 1898 until 1937 and was the Jayhawks' first basketball coach. Dr. Forrest C. "Phog" Allen, often called the "Father of Basketball Coaching," coached at KU for 39 years and is its winningest coach. Historic Allen Fieldhouse, opened in 1955, is generally considered to be among the most iconic venues in college basketball.[5]

KU's list of basketball accomplishments is undeniably impressive. Among them are the second-most wins in the history of the game (2,126 through the 2013–2014 season); 5 national championships and 14 Final Four appearances; 17 players and coaches selected for the Naismith Memorial Basketball Hall of Fame; and 21 players selected as first-team consensus All-Americans.[6]

Since 1964, Kansas basketball has continued to maintain its place of honor in college basketball lore. There has been head coaching stability: only five men have occupied the position, two of whom are Naismith Hall of Fame inductees. The Jayhawks have won 26 Big Eight and Big 12 Conference titles, including ten straight from 2004 until 2014. There have been nine Final Four appearances and three NCAA championships. At Allen Fieldhouse, the site of 212 consecutive sellout crowds through the 2013–2014 season, the Jayhawks have won over 95 percent of their games since 2003.[7] Finally, in 2014, Kansas was selected by the International University Sports Federation to represent the United States in the 2015 World University Games in Korea, the first time that a university team rather than all-stars would represent the country.[8]

This remarkable period began with a coaching change. In the summer of 1964, following the resignation of Dick Harp, 34-year-old Oklahoman Ted Owens, who had been Harp's assistant since 1960, became the Jayhawks' head basketball coach. Harp had led the Jayhawks for eight seasons, posting a record of 121–82, winning two conference titles, and advancing to the NCAA tournament twice.[9]

Owens, who came to Mount Oread following a highly productive coaching stint at Cameron College in Oklahoma and a stellar playing career for the Oklahoma Sooners, was an instant success at KU. His first squad posted a 17–8 record and a second-place finish in the Big Eight. During the remainder of the decade, his teams had four 20-win seasons and won two conference titles and four Big Eight Holiday tournament championships. Center Walter Wesley from Fort Myers, Florida, and Jo Jo White of St. Louis, Missouri, were named first-team All-Americans. The 1965–1966 and 1966–1967 teams advanced to the NCAA tournament.[10]

The 1966 NCAA tournament is forever etched in the memory of the Jayhawk faithful. KU was optimistic going into the tournament, having a talented team led by a solid group of stalwart performers: White, Wesley, Al Lopes, Riney Lochmann, Delvey Lewis, and Rod Franz. The regionals were played in Lubbock, Texas. After defeating Southern Methodist in the regional semifinal, 76–70, Owen's squad faced Texas Western in the regional final. It was an epic clash. Jo Jo White hit a 35-foot jump shot at the buzzer of the first overtime that seemingly won the game, but an official ruled that he had stepped out of bounds. Texas Western prevailed in the second overtime, 81–80, and went on to defeat Kentucky for the national title.[11]

The 1966–1967 squad also enjoyed a banner year, finishing with a 23–4 record and capturing the Big Eight title with a 13–1 record before losing to Houston in a first-round NCAA tournament game in Allen Fieldhouse. Owens's 1967–1968 and 1968–1969 teams were selected to play in the National Invitational Tournament in New York City. The 1967–1968 team advanced to the championship game, losing to Dayton. Outstanding performers on these teams, in addition to White, were forwards Franz and Rodger Bohnenstiel, plus sophomore center Dave Robisch.[12]

The success Ted Owens and his Jayhawks experienced in the 1960s continued in the next decade. During the 1970s, Kansas earned four berths in the NCAA tournament, reached two Final Fours, won four Big Eight titles, and had three players named first-team All-Americans.[13]

KU's 1971 and 1974 Final Four teams were both outstanding. The 1971 edition was led by All-American Robisch, along with Isaac "Bud" Stallworth, Roger Brown, Pierre Russell, and Aubrey Nash. The Jayhawks lost to Coach John Wooden's UCLA Bruins in the NCAA semifinal game in Houston. The 1974 team posted a 23–7 record and tied for first place in the Big Eight. The Jayhawks were led by five juniors, Danny Knight, Roger Morningstar, Dale Greenlee, Rick Suttle, and freshman Norm Cook. KU was defeated by Al McGuire's Marquette Warriors in the NCAA semifinal game in Greensboro, North Carolina.[14]

KU also made it to the Big Dance in 1975 and 1978, when both teams won Big Eight championships. The 1978 men's team was sparked by freshman guard Darnell Valentine, who had a spectacular career at Kansas and earned first-team All-American honors as a senior. Owen's other All-American in the 1970s was Stallworth. The Hartselle, Alabama, native was also an Academic All-American and set a KU scoring record for a conference game, with 50 points against Missouri in 1972 in Allen Fieldhouse.[15]

Ted Owens's career at KU came to a close following the 1982–1983 season. He had a sparkling 348–182 record and is KU's third-winningest coach, behind Phog Allen and Roy Williams. Owens was the Big Eight Coach of the Year five times and Basketball Weekly's National Coach of the Year in 1978.[16]

Owens's successor, Larry Brown, also had a remarkable run in his five years at KU. His teams posted a 135–44 (.754) record, appeared in five NCAA tournaments, made it to the Final Four in 1986, and won the national championship in 1988.[17]

The 1985–1986 edition of the Jayhawks is considered one of the very best teams not to win a national title. Paced by brilliant sophomore Danny Manning, sensational shooters Ron Kellogg and Calvin Thompson, center Greg Dreiling, and point guard Cedric Hunter, the Jayhawks posted a 35–4 record and won the Big Eight regular season and tournament titles. The Hawks suffered a heartbreaking 71–67 loss to Duke in the NCAA semifinal in Dallas.[18]

In the spring of 1988, Larry Brown and his Jayhawks, a team eventually dubbed "Danny and the Miracles," were crowned national champions. "The Miracles" were a talented group who epitomized teamwork. The team also included Kevin Pritchard, Milt Newton, Chris Piper, Jeff Gueldner, Scooter Barry, Clint Normore, Keith Harris, Lincoln Minor, and Mike Maddox. KU had an up-and-down season, finishing the campaign 21–11, and were considered a "bubble" team for the NCAA Tournament. Kansas received an at-large bid and proceeded to make a dramatic run to the title game with wins over Xavier, Murray State (a 61–58 nail-biter), Vanderbilt, and, in the regional final, Kansas State.[19]

The 1988 Final Four, the 50th, was played at Kemper Arena in Kansas City. The Jayhawks prevailed in the semifinal game, defeating Duke, 66–59. In the championship game against Big Eight rival Oklahoma, KU defeated the Sooners, 83–79, with Danny Manning scoring 31 points, snagging 18 rebounds, and icing the win with four clutch free throws.[20]

Kansas became the first unranked team and the first with double-digit losses to win a national championship. Manning, not surprisingly, was named the tournament's

© Alexander Sviridov/Shutterstock.com

Most Valuable Player. A few months after winning the national title, Larry Brown resigned to become the head coach of the NBA's San Antonio Spurs. He had a spectacular career in the NBA and was inducted into the Naismith Memorial Basketball Hall of Fame in 2002.[21]

In early November 1988, the NCAA informed the university that it was being placed on probation for violations that had occurred in 1986.[22] Penalties included "loss of three scholarships; being banned from the NCAA tournament in 1989; and not being able to bring recruits on campus for a year."[23]

In July 1988, Roy Williams, an unheralded assistant for Dean Smith at North Carolina, became the seventh head coach in the storied history of Kansas basketball. Williams led the Jayhawks to an extraordinary 418–101 record (.805) in 15 years and won more games in this time than any other coach in Division I history. Kansas made it to four Final Fours under Williams, playing in championship games in 1991 and 2003. He also won nine conference titles; his 2002 squad became the only team in Big 12 history with a perfect conference slate, 16–0.[24]

Williams produced a bevy of outstanding players, four of whom were selected as first-team consensus All-Americans: Nick Collison, Drew Gooden, Raef LaFrentz, and Paul Pierce. Ten of his players were first-round NBA draft selections. Williams's record of excellence was recognized with several coaching awards, including the Naismith Coach of the Year three times and the 2003 John R. Wooden Legends Coaching Award. In 2007, he was enshrined in the Naismith Memorial Hall of Fame.[25]

All of Williams's Final Four teams (1991, 1993, 2002, and 2003) were sources of great pride for Jayhawk fans. The 1991 KU team, sparked by Mark Randall, Terry Brown, Adonis Jordan, Richard Scott, Alonzo Jamison, and Mike Maddox, went all the way to the championship game in Indianapolis, where it was edged by Duke. Two years later, KU advanced to the NCAA semifinal game in New Orleans before coming up short against North Carolina. One of Williams's best Kansas teams was the 1996–1997 Jayhawks. Sparked by a superb cast that included guards Jacque Vaughn and Jerod Haase, forwards Paul Pierce and Raef LaFrentz, and center Scott Pollard, KU finished the campaign 34–2. Kansas's only two losses came at the hands of Missouri in Big 12 play and of Arizona in the NCAA Sweet 16.[26]

The 2002 and 2003 teams were true powerhouses. The 2002 team, led by Nick Collison, Drew Gooden, and Kirk Hinrich, finished the season with a 33–4 record, and the 2003 squad completed the campaign with a 30–8 record and another Big 12 title before falling to Syracuse in the NCAA championship game. In addition to Collison, Gooden, and Hinrich, sharpshooting Jeff Boschee and Wayne Simien were key members of the 2002 team; and Simien, Keith Langford, and Aaron Miles were valuable contributors in 2003.[27] In early April 2003. Williams returned to his alma mater, the University of North Carolina, to become the Tar Heels' head coach.

Within a week of Williams's departure, Drue Jennings, KU's interim athletics director, hired Coach Bill Self away from the University of Illinois. Over the last 11 years, Self has clearly established himself as one of the elite coaches in college basketball with a splendid overall record of 325–69 (.825). His Jayhawks have captured one national championship, ten straight Big 12 Conference titles, and six league tournament championships and have reached two Final Fours, five Elite Eights, and seven Sweet 16s. He has been selected the Big 12 Coach of the Year on three occasions, and in 2008 he won eight National Coach of the Year honors.[28]

Several of Self's players have achieved recognition as well. Wayne Simien, Marcus Morris, and Thomas Robinson were Big 12 Players of the Year. Mario

Chalmers, Cole Aldrich, and Jeff Withey were Big 12 Defensive Players of the Year, and Sherron Collins earned the Big 12 Sixth Man Award in 2008. Sixteen Jayhawks were All–Big 12 first-team selections, and 16 student-athletes were also NBA draft selections.[29]

All 11 of Self's KU teams have been a competitive force nationally. Six of his teams have won 30 or more games. In addition to the 2008 national champions, the 2011–2012 Jayhawks also were spectacular, finishing the season at 32–7 and making a run all the way to the NCAA championship game against Kentucky. Tyshawn Taylor, Elijah Johnson, Jeff Withey, and Thomas Robinson were standouts on this team.[30]

Bill Self's 2007–2008 Jayhawks had arguably the best season in KU's storied basketball history, culminating with a dramatic victory over Memphis in the NCAA championship game. KU set a school record for wins in a season with a 37–3 record. They won both the Big 12 regular season and tournament titles and earned a number-one seed in the NCAA tournament for the second consecutive year.[31]

KU's road to the Final Four at the Alamodome in San Antonio included victories over Portland State, UNLV, Villanova, and Davidson. The Davidson game in the regional final went down to the wire, with the Jayhawks holding on for a 59–57 win. In the national semifinal, KU defeated Roy Williams's North Carolina Tar Heels, 84–66. This victory set up a meeting with Memphis, the number-one team in the tournament, coached by former Kansas assistant John Calipari.[32]

In one of the most memorable comebacks in NCAA tournament history, the Jayhawks rallied from a 60–51 deficit with 2:12 remaining in regulation. Kansas tied the game in the final seconds and won it in overtime, 75–68, for its third NCAA title and fifth national championship. KU was paced by the gritty play of Brandon Rush, Darnell Arthur, Mario Chalmers, Sasha Kahn, Sherron Collins, and Darnell Jackson. Chalmers hit the biggest shot of the game (known as "Mario's Miracle"), a contested three-point shot that tied the score at 63 and sent the game into overtime. Mario was named the Final Four's Most Outstanding Player.[33]

© CLS Digital Arts/Shutterstock.com

Self has continued to recruit top players and win conference titles, going to the NCAA tournament annually. The KU tradition of excellence in basketball, reflecting the genius of Dr. Naismith and Phog Allen, continues to flourish in the twenty-first century.

KANSAS FOOTBALL

If basketball has been KU's athletic calling card, football has offered Jayhawk fans a heritage with moments of pride also. Football at KU since 1960 has been marked by occasional periods of success and noteworthy accomplishments by outstanding student-athletes. There have been 11 head coaches during the past 53 years, with teams posting a record of 251 wins, 349 losses, and 14 ties for a .408 winning percentage. The Jayhawks have participated in 11 bowl games, winning six. KU's dramatic victory over Virginia Tech in the 2008 Orange Bowl was a special highlight. KU won one conference title, sharing the Big Eight championship with Oklahoma in 1968. Stellar players like John Hadl, Gale Sayers, Bobby Douglass, John Zook, David Jaynes, Bruce Kallmeyer, Aqib Talib, and Anthony Collins earned first-team All-American honors.[34]

The 1960s began with the successful teams of Coach Jack Mitchell, led by such stars as All-Americans John Hadl and Gale Sayers, posting winning seasons for four of the first five years of the decade. Two subsequent disappointing seasons, however, led to Mitchell's departure and the arrival of Pepper Rodgers, who came to KU from UCLA. His four years at KU were highlighted by a Big Eight championship, a trip to the Orange Bowl, and All-American honors for Bobby Douglass and John Zook.[35]

Led by quarterback Bobby Douglass of El Dorado, Kansas, the first edition of Rodgers's Jayhawks finished in a tie for second in the Big Eight with a 5–2 record and defeated Border War rival Missouri, 17–6. Rodgers's second year at KU proved to be even more magical. The Jayhawks posted a 9–1 regular season record with the only loss coming to Oklahoma in Norman, 27–23. KU finished the season with wins over its archrivals, a 39–29 defeat of Kansas State and a 21–19 victory over Missouri in Columbia. KU lost to undefeated Penn State in the Orange Bowl, 15–14, after a penalty for 12 men on the field permitted the Joe Paterno–led Nittany Lions to succeed on a two-point conversion attempt. Rodgers was named the Big Eight Co-Coach of the Year.[36]

Rodgers's final two seasons were disappointing, with a combined 6–15 record. Highlights were John Riggins rushing for 1,131 yards in 1970 and becoming the KU career rushing leader with 2,706 yards. Pepper resigned to take the head coaching job at UCLA and was replaced by longtime KU assistant coach and former KU player Don Fambrough.[37]

At this time, the Big Eight was one of the strongest and most competitive conferences in the country. Fambrough would serve two stints as the KU head coach, 1971–1974 and 1979–1982. The first edition of his Jayhawks won 19 games, and his 1973 Liberty Bowl team, led by All-American quarterback David Jaynes, was one of KU's finest. He also defeated KU rivals Kansas State and Missouri in three out of four games. Fourteen players from the Liberty Bowl team, which lost to North Carolina State, 31–18, went on to NFL careers. The 1981 edition of Fambrough's Jayhawks posted an 8–3 regular season record and earned an invitation to play Mississippi State in the Hall of Fame Bowl in Birmingham. They lost 10–0, playing without injured quarterback Frank Seurer. The Jayhawks were led throughout the season by Seurer and several All-Conference players: offensive guard and co-captain David Lawrence, wide receiver Wayne Capers, linebacker Kyle McNorton, and kicker Bucky Scribner.[38]

Bud Moore, an assistant coach and former player for the legendary Paul "Bear" Bryant at Alabama, replaced Fambrough in 1975. He installed a wishbone offense and found the perfect quarterback to direct it, Nolan Cromwell, from Ransom, Kansas (a defensive back originally). That first season was a huge success, and Moore was named Big Eight Conference Coach of the Year. Cromwell came out as a wishbone quarterback in the third game of the season. The Jayhawks defeated Oregon State, 20–0, as Cromwell set an NCAA record for quarterbacks by rushing for 294 yards, including a 79-yard touchdown scamper. One of the most notable victories in KU football history came against the undefeated Oklahoma Sooners in Norman. KU dominated, 23–3, as Cromwell sparked the offense, while the Jayhawk defense completely shut down the Sooners, ending their 28-game winning streak and 37-game unbeaten string. Oklahoma did not lose another game in 1975 and eventually was crowned national champion. The Jayhawks won seven games and were selected to meet the Pitt Panthers in the Sun Bowl in El Paso, coming up short, 33–19, against a team led by All-American Tony Dorsett.[39]

Moore's 1976 team won six games, despite a season-ending knee injury to Nolan Cromwell. His Jayhawks won just three games in 1977, including victories over Kansas State and Missouri, and only one game in 1978. After a terrific start, Bud Moore's Jayhawks slipped conspicuously. He posted a 17–27–1 career record and Fambrough stepped in again.[40]

In October 1983, the NCAA announced the results of an inquiry into football recruiting irregularities that had occurred at KU in 1980 and 1981.[41] Also during this period, 1983–1985, 26 players were declared academically ineligible, a situation that prompted considerable consternation on campus.[42]

Fambrough was replaced after his second tour with KU by Mike Gottfried, the 38-year-old head coach at the University of Cincinnati. His tenure as the Jayhawks coach lasted for three seasons, during which his teams won 15 games. In addition to a victory over nationally prominent Southern California, Gottfried's Jayhawks also upset highly ranked Oklahoma and won five of six games against Missouri and Kansas State. Two of his outstanding players were All-American placekicker Bruce Kallmeyer and linebacker Willie Pless. Following the 1985 season, Gottfried resigned to become head coach at the University of Pittsburgh.[43]

Following two disappointing seasons with former KU assistant Bob Valesente at the helm, Jayhawk fans were ready for another change. In December 1987, KU hired Glen Mason, the energetic 37-year-old head coach from Kent State, who had played for Woody Hayes at Ohio State. Mason remained on the Jayhawks sidelines for nine seasons, posting a 47–54–1 record.[44]

In 1991, Kansas had its first winning football season in ten years, with a 6–5 record. That year also saw Mason's gritty running back, Tony Sands, gain nationwide attention by rushing for 396 yards against Missouri in Memorial Stadium, ranking second all-time in NCAA single-game history. Sands finished his career with 3,788 rushing yards, second only at KU to June Henley's (Henley played for Mason from 1993 to 1996) 3,841 yards.[45]

Mason led KU to two bowl games, the 1992 and 1995 Aloha Bowls, played in Hawaii. Surprising the prognosticators in 1992, KU posted an 8–4 record and finished third in the Big Eight Conference. KU's standout players were defensive linemen Dana Stubblefield and Gilbert Brown (both of whom went on to long NFL careers), quarterback Chip Hilleary, and placekicker Dan Eichloff. Mason's Jayhawks capped the season with a dramatic 23–20 victory over Brigham Young in Hawaii. Stubblefield was chosen the game's Most Valuable Player.[46]

In 1995, KU was a surprise team in college football. Picked to finish in the bottom half of the Big Eight, the Jayhawks finished the season with a 10–2 record and road wins over strong Colorado and Oklahoma teams. They then thrashed UCLA in the Aloha Bowl, 51–30. Quarterback Mark Williams passed for three touchdowns and was picked as the bowl's Most Valuable Player, and KU career rushing leader June Henley led the ground attack. Following the season, Mason was honored as the Big Eight Coach of the Year.[47]

Prior to the Aloha Bowl, Mason announced that he would be leaving for the University of Georgia, but he changed his mind and stayed at KU another year before departing for the University of Minnesota. He was replaced by Terry Allen, the highly successful coach of the University of Northern Iowa, who would lead the Jayhawks through five straight losing seasons, compiling a 20–33 record. That record included, however, three wins over Missouri and ten victories against Big 12 Conference competition. Chuck Woodling, sports editor of the *LJW,* noted that

© skyforger/Shutterstock.com

Allen was likeable, commenting that "Terry Allen is a good man who never had anything good happen to him at Kansas."[48]

KU moved quickly to replace Allen. In early December, Mark Mangino, the offensive coordinator at Oklahoma, was named the Jayhawks' head coach. His first season resulted in a 2–10 record, but the general feeling among fans was that KU was playing hard and becoming more competitive; football season ticket sales climbed to their highest point since 1969.[49]

In his eight seasons at KU, Mangino's teams posted a 50–48 record and played in the Tangerine, Fort Worth, Orange, and Insight Bowl games, winning three of those and producing several outstanding players. The 50 wins is the second-highest total of any coach in KU football history, behind only A. R. Kennedy (1904–1910). His 2007 season was arguably the best in KU football history, with a 12–1 record, a tie for first place in the Big 12 North, and the defeat of Virginia Tech, 24–21, in the Orange Bowl. Following that season, Mangino won all the National Coach of the Year Awards.[50]

The Orange Bowl victory, among the greatest in KU history, was sparked by the play of KU's dynamic quarterback, Todd Reesing, and the game's Most Valuable Player, Aqib Talib. Reesing threw for one touchdown and ran for another, while Talib's 60-yard interception for a touchdown set the tone for an inspired Kansas defense that had two more interceptions and three quarterback sacks. Following the season, two of Mangino's players received first-team All-American honors, Talib and offensive tackle Anthony Collins.[51]

Mangino's final year at KU, 2009, was full of promise. The Jayhawks won their first five games, but Reesing was injured in the Colorado game in Boulder and was hampered the remainder of the season. The Jayhawks lost the rest of their games and finished with a 5–7 record. Late in the season, the Kansas Athletics Department conducted an internal investigation of allegations that Mangino had physically and mentally abused players, which led to his resignation in December 2009.[52]

Mangino was replaced by former Nebraska great and University of Buffalo coach Turner Gill. The first African American head football coach at KU, he was given a five-year contract. Gill's teams struggled, however, and posted a two-year 5–19 record. The day after a season-ending loss to Missouri, KU announced that Gill had been fired. Athletics Director Sheahon Zenger commented that "new leadership was necessary to place us on the path to championships in the Big 12 Conference" and that he had "the utmost respect for Turner Gill as an individual."[53] Less than two weeks later, Charlie Weis was introduced as KU's new coach. A protégé of legendary NFL coaches Bill Parcells and Bill Belichick, Weis had been the Notre Dame head coach from 2005 to 2009 and more recently offensive coordinator for the Kansas City Chiefs and the University of Florida Gators.[54]

Weis immediately began to mold a new football culture at KU. He stressed to his players the non-negotiable values of accountability, academic responsibility, discipline, and conditioning. Weis's team competed hard and won four games in his first two years, including the Jayhawks' first victory over a Big 12 Conference opponent since 2010.[55] However, following the fourth game of the 2014 season, a 23–0 loss to Texas, Athletics Director Zenger dismissed Weis, commenting: "I normally do not favor changing coaches in mid-season. But, I believe we have talented coaches and players in the program and I think this decision gives our players the best chance to begin making progress right away."[56] Clint Bowen, Weis's defensive coordinator, a former KU player, and longtime assistant coach, was named interim head coach.[57]

In early December, Zenger introduced David Beaty, an assistant coach and recruiting coordinator from Texas A&M, as the 38th head coach of the KU football team. Beaty received a five-year contract at a base salary of $800,000 annually plus incentives, which could total $1.5 million. The Texas native had previously served as an assistant at Kansas under Mark Mangino and Turner Gill.[58]

The Rise of Women's Athletics

Women's athletics has a long and rich history at the University of Kansas in both intramural and extramural competition. In the late 1960s.

Marlene Mawson, an associate professor in Health and Physical Education, became KU's first advocate for women's extramural sports, organizing and coaching sports such as field hockey, basketball, softball, and volleyball. This began to change, however, in 1972 with the passage of Title IX of the Education Amendments Act, which prohibited the exclusion of women from any educational activities at institutions that received federal funding. This included intercollegiate athletics. One of the objectives of the statute was to give women an equal opportunity to develop their skills and apply them competitively.[59]

In June 1974, Marian Washington was hired as assistant director of intercollegiate athletics/women's sports. She had dual responsibilities as an administrator and women's basketball coach. Washington, a graduate of West Chester State College in Pennsylvania, was a highly acclaimed basketball and track and field athlete. At the time of her appointment, she was a graduate student and physical education instructor at KU.[60]

In July 1974, the women's intercollegiate athletics program began with ten sports: field hockey, gymnastics, basketball, golf, tennis, swimming, volleyball, track and field, cross-country, and softball. The budget for the program grew steadily over the next several years, with funds coming from both the Kansas legislature and the KU Student Senate. In the spring of 1976, KU began providing scholarships for female student-athletes.[61]

During the first ten years following the passage of Title IX, KU women's student-athletes represented their school admirably. Washington's basketball team was consistently ranked nationally, the swimming and diving team won eight consecutive Big Eight championships, and several other sports were competitive in conference play. However, field hockey and gymnastics were dropped for financial reasons.[62]

Women's Basketball

For 31 seasons, Marian Washington was the face of Kansas women's basketball. She became KU's head coach in 1973 and served the university with distinction until her resignation in January 2004. During that span, her teams won or earned a share of seven Big Eight and Big 12 titles and advanced to NCAA postseason play 11 times, including two runs to the Sweet 16. She was named the Big Eight Conference Coach of the Year in 1992 and 1996 and the Big 12 Coach of the Year in 1997. Highly regarded nationally, Washington served as an assistant coach on the 1996 gold medal US women's Olympic basketball team. Among her many honors were selection for the Women's Basketball Hall of Fame and recognition by the Black Coaches Association with its Lifetime Achievement Award. In 1996, she received the William I. Koch Outstanding Kansas Woman of the Year award.[63]

Washington also mentored three Kodak All-Americans, Tameka Dixon, Angela Aycock, and Lynette Woodard. Dixon was a 1997 honoree and the Big Eight Conference Player of the Year in 1996 and snagged the same accolade from the Big 12 Conference the following year. Aycock, who was recognized in 1995, was a three-time All–Big Eight Conference first-team selection. Woodard, a Wichita native, who played at KU from 1978 to 1981, is perhaps the most outstanding student-athlete in the history of women's college basketball. She was a four-time Kodak All-American, a two-time Academic All-American, and the all-time leading scorer in women's collegiate basketball history, with 3,649 points. Woodard was co-captain of the 1984 US Olympics gold medal women's basketball team and the first woman to play for the Harlem Globetrotters. She has been enshrined in the Naismith Memorial Basketball Hall of Fame and the Women's College Basketball Hall of Fame.[64]

Washington's teams struggled in the twilight of her career; her last three teams won only five games in the rugged Big 12 Conference. Following her resignation, Athletics Director Lew Perkins saluted her achievements at KU, noting, "Marian Washington has been a pioneer—a leader—a mentor and a terrific basketball coach. It's not a business for her—it's a passion."[65]

The hiring of the highly regarded 40-year-old head coach Bonnie Henrickson in 2004 signaled a commitment to put Kansas women's basketball in the top echelon of the sport. Henrickson came to KU from Virginia Tech, where she had led the Hokies for seven years, to a 158–62 record, 7 postseason appearances, and 20 or more wins every season. In her ten years with KU, the Jayhawks have posted four 20-win seasons, advanced to postseason play seven times, and produced four first-team All–Big 12 selections and 29 Academic All–Big 12 honorees. Her overall record is 173–154.[66]

In the 2012 NCAA tournament, Henrickson's Jayhawks defeated Nebraska and number eight–ranked Delaware, before falling to perennial powerhouse Tennessee in the Sweet 16. A year later, they beat

Colorado and South Carolina prior to coming up short in the Sweet 16 against the eventual NCAA tournament runner-up, Notre Dame. Center Carolyn Davis and guard Angel Goodrich were the standouts for the Jayhawks' first Sweet 16 team, and Goodrich was a key player again the following year.[67]

Both Davis and Goodrich will be remembered as two of the finest players in KU women's basketball history. Davis earned first-team All–Big 12 Conference honors in 2011 and 2012 and was a second-team selection in 2013, when her season was cut short with a knee injury. Goodrich, whose electrifying point guard play thrilled Jayhawk fans for four years, was a first-team All–Big 12 selection in 2013. She became the second Henrickson player selected in the WNBA draft when picked by the Tulsa Shock. In addition to Davis and Goodrich, Crystal Kemp and Danielle McCray also were first-team All–Big 12 selections in 2006 and 2009, respectively. McCray was drafted by the WNBA Connecticut Sun in 2009.[68]

Track and Field

By the 1960s, the University of Kansas was very well known for the excellence of its track and field teams under legendary coach Bill Easton, whose Jayhawks won NCAA Outdoor championships in 1959 and 1960. He had coached 54 All-Americans and 22 national champions, as well as seven Olympic gold medal winners. The outstanding performers on those championship teams were distance runner and future Olympic gold medal winner Billy Mills, four-time All-American sprinter

Charlie Tidwell, NCAA champion and javelin record holder Bill Alley, and hurdler and future Olympic silver medal winner Cliff Cushman.[69]

In 1965, Bob Timmons replaced Easton, and his reign as the Kansas head track coach from 1965 to 1988 was equally as impressive. Coach Timmons's KU teams won 13 Big Eight Indoor and 14 conference Outdoor titles. Even more significant, his Jayhawks captured NCAA Indoor championships in 1966, 1967, and 1970. His 1970 Outdoor squad shared the NCAA title with Oregon, Brigham Young, and Drake, a remarkable fourth NCAA title in five years.[70]

Timmons's most notable protégé was Jim Ryun, a standout for the coach at Wichita East, who followed him to KU. However, several other of Timmons's Jayhawks were noteworthy performers in the late 1960s. John Lawson was the NCAA cross-country champion in 1965; Gary Ard won three All-American awards in the long jump in 1966 and 1967, and Ron Jessie won the NCAA long jump in 1969.[71]

Ryun arrived at KU in 1965 and began perhaps the most storied career in Jayhawk track history. From 1965 to 1969, he set world records in 880 yards, 1,500 meters, the mile, two- and three-mile runs, plus the 5,000 meters. He also snagged five NCAA titles (four Indoor and one Outdoor). In 1966, *Sports Illustrated* named him its Sportsman of the Year, and he also earned the prestigious Sullivan Award as the top amateur athlete in America. A three-time Olympian, he captured the silver medal in the 1,500 meters at the 1968 Olympic Games in Mexico City. In 1982, Ryun was inducted into the National Track and Field Hall of Fame.[72]

To close out the decade, KU won the 1969 NCAA Indoor championship and finished second in the NCAA Outdoor championship. A year later, the Jayhawks were even better, sweeping the Big Eight and NCAA Indoor and Outdoor championships. The 1970 NCAA champions were led by a splendid trio of shot-putters. Known as the "Pachyderms," Karl Salb, Steve Williams, and Doug Knop finished first, second, and third in the 1969 and 1970 championships, earning All-American honors. The following year, KU swept the Big Eight shot put event for the fifth consecutive time.[73]

During the 1970s, under the leadership of Coach Bob Timmons, KU continued as a dominant force in track and field, winning eight of nine Big Eight Outdoor conference titles and four Indoor championships. Individual Indoor national champions were

Terry Porter in the pole vault and Theo Hamilton in the long jump. The two-mile and one-mile relay teams also captured national Indoor honors. Outdoor national champions were Sam Colson in the javelin and Randy Smith in the high jump. The 440-yard relay team also earned national honors.[74]

The KU women's track program began in 1973 with Marian Washington as its first coach. Teri Anderson took over the program in the late 1970s and led the Jayhawks to second-place finishes in the Big Eight Conference Indoor and Outdoor championships, as well as a third-place finish in the Indoor national meet in 1979. Sheila Calmese, a sprinter, was an outstanding performer for KU. She was the first three-time All-American in KU women's track history and still ranks second all-time in the 100-meter dash in the KU women's Outdoor record book. Calmese won the Indoor national championship in the 300-yard dash in 1978. Two other performers, Charmane Kuhlman in the long jump and high jumper Shawn Corwin, earned All-American honors.[75]

Carla Coffey, Kansas's second African American head coach, replaced Teri Anderson as the women's track and field coach in 1981 and took KU to seven national championship meets during the decade of the 1980s. Under Coffey, Kansas achieved national recognition in the throwing events. Anne Grethe Baeraas and Denise Buchanan earned All-American honors in the javelin and shot put, respectively. A particularly noteworthy performer, Halcyon "Tudie" McKnight, earned All-American recognition in the long jump three times. In 1995, the Kansas Relays women's long jump event was named in her honor.[76]

Beginning in 1979 and through the 1990s, Kansas gained a national reputation for excellence in the jumping events. KU had 31 All-Americans in the pole vault, high jump, long jump, triple jump, heptathlon, and decathlon events. The chief architect of these accomplishments was Rick Attig, the vertical jumps coach from 1985 to 2000. The Jayhawks' notable All-American pole-vaulters during this period were Jeff Buckingham, Chris Bohanan, Scott Huffman, Pat Manson, Cam Miller, and John Bazzoni. Huffman participated in the 1996 Olympic Games, and Manson's vault of 18·8″ in the 1989 Big Eight Indoor championships remains a KU record. Rounding out those with All-American honors for KU men were Sanya Owolabi, the 1980 NCAA Indoor triple jump champion, Warren Wilhoite in the long jump, and high jumper Nick Johannsen.[77]

When the legendary Bob Timmons resigned in 1988, he was replaced by his former pupil Gary Schwartz, who assumed responsibility for both the men's and the women's programs. As a student-athlete, Schwartz had won a Big Eight championship in the discus throw and was team captain as a senior. In 12 years, Schwartz produced 41 All-Americans (men and women) and led the KU men to a fourth-place tie in the 1989 NCAA Indoor championships.[78]

Several KU women achieved national recognition with Schwartz as coach. All-Americans included Mary Beth Labosky in the high jump, Heather Berlin in the javelin, Cathy Palacios in the mile, Kristi Kloster in the 800 meters, Andrea Branson in the pole vault, and Candace Mason in multiple events. Kloster was the 1996 NCAA Indoor champion in the 800 meters. Mason, who earned five All-American honors in the pole vault, pentathlon, and decathlon, also was an Academic All-American.[79]

In May 2000, KU hired a head coach destined to restore the Jayhawks' track and field program to its glory days. Stanley Redwine, a former All-American middle-distance runner at Arkansas, came to Mount Oread after six years as the successful head coach at the University of Tulsa. Over the next 14 years, Redwine produced and mentored 145 All-Americans, 15 individual national champions, and four Olympians, earned three Big 12 Conference team titles, and captured the 2013 NCAA women's Outdoor championship.[80]

The finish line at the 2016
Dr. Bob Run at historic Rim
Rock Farm north of Lawrence,
Kansas.

Source: Jordan R. Bass

Four of Redwine's male athletes won gold medals in the Indoor and Outdoor NCAA championships. The Indoor champions were Scott Russell and Egor Agafonov in the weight throw and sprinter Leo Bookman in the 200-meter dash. Bookman was also an Outdoor champion in 200 meters, as was Jordan Scott in the pole vault. On the women's side, the Indoor champions were Amy Linnen and Natalia Bartnovskaya in the pole vault, Diamond Dixon in the 400-meter dash, and Andrea Geubelle in the triple jump and the long jump. Lindsey Vollmer captured an Outdoor title in the heptathlon.[81]

Redwine also mentored four Olympians: Charles Gruber (1,500 meters, USA, Atlanta-2004); Scott Russell (javelin, Canada, Beijing-2008); Nickesha Anderson (4x100 meter relay, Jamaica, Beijing-2008); and Diamond Dixon (4x400 meter relay, USA, London-2012). Dixon, who won four Big 12 Conference titles and four more All-American honors in 2012, brought home a gold medal from London.[82]

The 2012–2013 seasons marked the most successful stretch in Redwine's illustrious coaching career, capped by his women's team winning the NCAA national Outdoor championship. It was the first women's national championship in any sport at KU and also the first national Outdoor title for Kansas since 1970, when Bob Timmons's men's team was victorious.[83]

Of Coach Redwine's 13 entries in the meet, 11 picked up points for the Jayhawks. Superstar and multiple All-American Andrea Geubelle earned 16 points with second-place finishes in the long jump and triple jump. Lindsay Vollmer captured KU's first-ever individual gold medal for the women's program in the national championships by winning the grueling seven-event heptathlon. Natalia Bartnovskaya won silver in the pole vault, and Jessica Maroszek finished fourth in the discus throw. Kansas totaled 60 points, well ahead of runner-up Texas A&M's 48 points. Following this landmark season, Redwine was named the NCAA Women's Head Coach of the Year.[84]

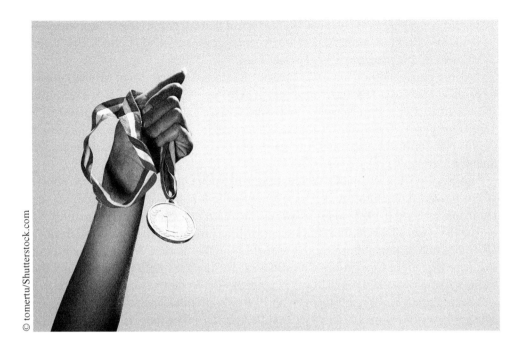

Cross-Country

Kansas has a rich and proud cross-country heritage. Legendary KU runners like Wes Santee, Al Frame, Herb Semper, Billy Mills, and Jim Ryun helped to shape this tradition of excellence. In 1965, John Lawson won the NCAA cross-country championship, and since Lawson's notable accomplishment, seven Jayhawk men and one woman have earned cross-country All-American honors. The men include Brent Steiner (1984), Michael Cox and David Johnston (1994), Benson Chesang (2004), Paul Hefferon (2006), and Colby Wissel (2006 and 2007). Chesang, a native of Kenya, was the Big 12 Conference champion in 2004 and 2005, KU's first back-to-back conference champion since John Lawson in the mid-1960s. Julia Saul, perhaps the greatest female cross-country runner in Kansas history, captured All-American recognition in 1992. And the KU women were crowned NCAA Midwest regional champions in 1993 and 1994. Kansas also boasts one of the nation's premier cross-country courses, Rim Rock Farm. Located north of Lawrence, it was purchased in 1970 by Coach Bob Timmons and his wife, Pat. They gifted the property to the university in 2006.[85]

Swimming and Diving

Kansas swimming and diving established a tradition of excellence that began in the 1960s and has continued to the present. Coaches like Dick Reamon, Bill Spahn, Gary Kempf, and Clark Campbell produced teams and individuals who were highly regarded within the Big Eight and Big 12 Conferences and nationally. Following his graduation from KU in 1962, Dick Reamon, a six-time Big Eight champion in the butterfly and individual medley, became the head coach of the Jayhawk men's swimming and diving team. Over the next 15 years, Reamon would set a standard for excellence, winning eight straight conference championships from 1968 to

1975 and compiling a sterling 90–36 dual meet record. Additionally, he produced 218 All–Big Eight swimmers, 107 conference gold medalists, six All–Big Eight Swimmers of the Year, and 15 All-Americans.[86]

At the conclusion of the 1977 season, Reamon stepped down as head coach to go into business. His individual event All-Americans included Kim Bolton (50-yard freestyle), Tom Kempf (1,650-yard freestyle), and Don Pennington (500-yard freestyle).[87] It was during Reamon's tenure, in 1967, that the new Robinson Center Natatorium opened, and it remains the home of the Kansas swimming and diving program.

Following Dick Reamon's resignation, Bill Spahn, the highly regarded mentor of the powerful Wichita Swim Club, became the KU head coach. Spahn served in this position until 1981 and won Big Eight championships in 1977 and 1979.[88]

In 1981, Gary Kempf, the highly successful KU women's swimming coach since 1976, became responsible for both the men's and the women's programs. Kempf, a former Big Eight Conference Swimmer of the Year, led both the men's and the women's programs, for 18 and 24 years, respectively. Kempf's head coaching record was exemplary. His women's teams won 13 Big Eight titles, including a remarkable nine straight titles from 1976 to 1983, and he posted a dual meet record of 124–33, winning 79 percent. He was named Big Eight Women's Coach of the Year five times, Men's Coach of the Year four times, and the NCAA Women's Coach of the Year in 1983. His women's teams finished in the top 25 of the national championships ten times.[89]

During Kempf's tenure, two KU women won NCAA titles, Tammy Thomas and Michelle Rojohn. Thomas, competing from 1980 to 1983, set American records in the 50- and 100-yard freestyle, finished first in the 1983 NCAA championships in those events, and earned All-American honors 17 times in individual events and relays. She was the Big Eight Co-athlete of the Year in 1983. Rojohn was the 1996 NCAA champion in three-meter diving.[90]

One of Kempf's outstanding male swimmers was Ron Neugent, a Wichita native who transferred from Southern Methodist. He earned All-American honors in 1983 by finishing 11th in the NCAA 1,650-yard freestyle and set five KU and two Big Eight individual records.[91]

In 2002, Clark Campbell became KU's swimming and diving team head coach. Campbell, a Kansas graduate and former swimmer, returned to Mount Oread after serving as the head coach at the University of Evansville, in Indiana. During his 12 years at KU, he has posted an impressive 83–49 meet record and his swimmers and divers have been recognized with All-American, Big 12 Conference, and academic honors. In 2014, the team had its best year ever under Campbell, finishing second in the Big 12 championship. Campbell was honored as the Big 12 Coach of the Year.[92]

Two swimmers and one diver have earned All-American honors over the past 12 years: Julia Kuzhil in the 100-yard backstroke, Chelsie Miller in the 400-yard individual medley, and Erin Mertz in three-meter diving. Campbell's swimmers hold almost half of the 21 pool records at the Robinson Natatorium. They include Maria Mayrovich in the 50- and 100-yard freestyle, Miller in the 1,000-yard freestyle and the 400-yard individual medley, Kuzhil in the 100- and 200-yard back-stroke, and Danielle Hermann in the 200-yard individual medley plus the 200-yard freestyle relay and 200-yard medley relay teams.[93]

Baseball and Softball

Baseball traces its roots at KU back to 1880 and enjoys a rich history of varsity competition. In the 1960s, it was headed by Floyd Temple, an icon whose name would become synonymous with the sport for the next 28 years on Mount Oread. Temple lettered in football and baseball and became the Jayhawks' baseball coach in 1954. While serving as the coach, he recorded a .500 or better record in 14 of those 28 years and won the Big Eight Conference tournament in 1976. Hampered in the early years by having only four scholarships, he fared much better in his last six seasons. When the number of grants in aid was increased to 13, Temple won 171 games, for a .629 winning percentage. He coached four All-Americans and seven future major leaguers, including Steve Renko, Bob Allison, and Chuck Dobson.[94]

A highlight of the 1990s was the performance of the KU baseball team under the tutelage of Coach Dave Bingham. Bingham, who had enjoyed success at Emporia State, was hired in 1988. Over the next eight years, he posted 249 wins, including 30- and 40-win seasons. In 1993 and 1994, Bingham's Jayhawks registered the best back-to-back seasons in KU history. The 1993 edition won 45 games, a KU record, and advanced to the College World Series in Omaha.[95]

The journey to Omaha was spectacular. After being eliminated by Oklahoma State in the Big Eight tournament, KU played in its first-ever NCAA regional tournament in Knoxville, Tennessee. The Jayhawks lost the first game to Fresno State and then defeated Tennessee, Rutgers, Clemson, and Fresno State in 10 innings to dramatically capture the championship and earn a trip to the Series. Although coming up short against Texas A&M and Long Beach State, the team had earned the respect of the college baseball community. It was paced by five All-Americans: pitchers Jim Walker and Jamie Splittorff (a freshman and 1994 selection), second baseman Jeff Berblinger, catcher Jeff Niemier, and outfielder Darryl Monroe.[96]

The 1994 season saw KU win 40 games, post a 17–9 Big Eight record, and once again move on to NCAA regional tournament play. This time, after defeating number four–ranked Ohio State, the team was eliminated after losses to Jacksonville and Brigham Young. In addition to the All-Americans on the 1993 and 1994 teams, pitcher Curtis Shaw also earned All-American recognition in 1990. Two other noteworthy baseball players in the 1990s were All-Americans Josh Kliner and Isaac Byrd. Kliner and Byrd both played in KU's final Big Eight season in 1996. Kliner, a second baseman, led the Big Eight with a .438 batting average and was named a first-team All-American by the American Baseball Coaches Association. Byrd, an outfielder, who also starred for the football Jayhawks, batted .393 and was named a third-team All-American.[97]

In July 2002, Ritch Price was hired as KU's new baseball coach, replacing Bobby Randall. Price a native of Oregon, came to Lawrence from Cal Poly in San Louis Obispo, California. Known as a player's coach and an excellent recruiter, he has had six 30-win seasons and three especially magical seasons, 2006, 2009, and 2014.[98]

His 2006 team posted 43 victories, the second-best total in KU history. Although seeded sixth in the Big 12 tournament, the Jayhawks won four straight games to capture the conference championship and advance to the NCAA tournament. It was KU's first conference baseball title since winning the Big Seven championship in 1949. The Most Valuable Player in the tournament was Jayhawks centerfielder Matt Baty. After defeating Hawaii, 9–6, in the NCAA regional opener, they were eliminated by losses to Oregon State and Hawaii.[99]

The 2009 season was one of the most memorable in the long tradition of Kansas baseball. The Jayhawks won 39 games, posted a sparkling 25–3 home record, and finished fourth in the Big 12 Conference standings. Sophomore third baseman Tony Thompson had a spectacular season for KU, winning the Big 12 Conference Triple Crown with a .389 batting average, 21 home runs, and 82 runs batted in. He received All-American recognition from four different publications. As in 2006, KU advanced to the NCAA regionals. Following an opening loss to Coastal Carolina, the Jayhawks defeated Dartmouth and Coastal Carolina before being eliminated by North Carolina.[100] In 2014, KU won 35 games, finished a best-ever third in the Big 12 race, and advanced to the NCAA tournament. The Jayhawks opened tournament play with a win over Kentucky before losing to Louisville and Kentucky.[101]

Price has coached 44 players who were drafted or signed by professional organizations and four players who went on to play major league baseball. Two of his players, Thompson and relief pitcher Don Czyz, earned All-American honors. He has also had the unique distinction of mentoring his three sons, Ritchie, Ryne, and Robby, as Kansas baseball players.[102]

KU softball began competition in the late 1960s with Marlene Mawson and Linda Dollar coaching the first teams. Following the passage of Title IX, Sharon Drysdale, a professor in Health, Physical Education, and Recreation, took over the reins of the Jayhawks and guided them through five successful seasons, which all included appearances in the Association for Intercollegiate Athletics for Women (AIAW) World Series. In 1977, Bob Stanclift, from Lawrence, became the KU head coach for the next 11 years. Stanclift's teams won over 68 percent of their games, claimed three Big Eight Conference titles, and advanced to the AIAW World Series twice and the NCAA tournament on two occasions.[103]

Three Jayhawks, Jill Larson, Tracy Bunge, and Sheila Connolly, earned All-American honors in the Stanclift era. Larson, a third baseman and KU's first softball All-American, led the Jayhawks in 1981 with a .341 batting average. Bunge, who later in her career served as the KU coach for 13 years, was a standout pitcher and an All-American in 1986. Sheila Connolly earned All-American honors in 1986 and 1987. An outstanding all-around athlete who played shortstop and centerfield, Connolly batted a blistering .391 in her senior year and also led KU in hits, runs scored, triples, and stolen bases. She also was a star in the classroom, earning first-team Academic All-American recognition. KU retired her number 11 jersey.[104]

In 1988, Kalum Haack was hired to replace Stanclift. Coach Haack's teams won 283 games during his highly successful eight-year stint with the Jayhawks. They were ranked in the national polls for four straight seasons, 1991–1994, won the NCAA Midwest regional title in 1992, and advanced to the College World Series that same year. They also played in the Midwest regionals again in 1993 and 1994. Haack's premier athlete during his tenure as KU coach was Camille Spitaleri, arguably the greatest player in KU softball history. A third baseman, she became KU's only three-time All-American (1990, 1991, and 1992). She was also a two-time All–Big Eight first-team selection, ranks second on the KU career hits list, had her number 10 jersey retired, and is a member of the KU Athletics Hall of Fame. Pitcher Stephani Williams and shortstop Christy Arterburn, both second-team All-Americans, also played vital roles in the success of Haack's great teams of the early 1990s.[105]

Former KU All-American pitcher Tracy Bunge served as the Jayhawks head coach from 1997 to 2009. Her squads won over 53 percent of their games and advanced to the NCAA regionals four times. Bunge's 2006 team had a storybook ending to its season. Despite posting an 8–10 conference record and finishing sixth in the Big 12 Conference, the Jayhawks won the conference tournament and thus qualified for the NCAA tournament. In the NCAA regionals, they defeated Brigham Young twice prior to being eliminated by Washington. Outfielder Christi Musser and pitcher Serena Settlemeier earned All-American and Academic All-American recognition for Bunge's teams. Settlemeier is KU's all-time home run leader.[106]

In June 2009, Megan Smith, an assistant coach at Louisiana State University, was named the coach of the Jayhawks, replacing Bunge. Under Smith's guidance, the softball team showed steady progress, culminating with a 34–23 record in 2014 and KU's first NCAA tournament bid since 2006. In 2013, Kansas defeated the country's top-ranked team, the Oklahoma Sooners, in Lawrence on Senior Day and finished fourth in the Big 12 Conference race. It was the softball program's first-ever win over a number one–ranked team. Smith's standout player was outfielder Maggie Hull, who completed her four years on Mount Oread in 2013 and was named a first-team Academic All-American.[107]

Rowing and Soccer as Varsity Sports

In 1995, KU added rowing and soccer as women's varsity sports. With an average of 75 women participating annually, rowing was a big boost for the university's compliance with Title IX regulations. Its first and only coach has been Kansas graduate Rob Catloth. During his 19-year tenure, Catloth has built a strong foundation for the program and achieved many noteworthy results. KU demonstrated its full commitment to the program in 2009 with the construction of the KU Boathouse in Lawrence's Burcham Park. This $6 million facility was a major enhancement for Catloth's program, permitting the team to work out indoors during the winter months and providing a huge assist in recruiting.[108]

KU rowers participate in both the Big 12 Conference and Conference USA. Some of their accomplishments include an Intercollegiate Rowing Association championship in 1999, winning the Kansas Cup competition over Kansas State for five straight years, and 10 first-place finishes in 2005. In 2012, the Varsity Four won the Conference USA and Big 12 championship. In 2012–2013, KU rowers had 31 first-place finishes against the rugged Big 12 and Conference USA competition.[109]

Catloth's women athletes have excelled not only in the water but in the classroom as well. Lindsey Miles and Kara Boston were named recipients of the prestigious Big 12 Prentice Gautt Postgraduate Scholarship in 2007 and 2008, respectively. And in 2013, Elizabeth Scherer was honored as the Big 12 Scholar-Athlete of the Year.[110]

KU's first soccer coach was Lori Walker, a University of North Carolina graduate and former Tar Heels player. Walker stayed on Mount Oread for two years and was replaced by Dan Magner, who also coached KU for two seasons. In February 1999, KU hired Mark Francis, who has been leading the KU soccer program for 16 years.[111]

During his career at KU, the native of London, England, and three-time All-American at Southern Methodist has brought Kansas the stability necessary for a winning program. His accomplishments include a Big 12 Conference championship, six NCAA postseason appearances, including a Sweet 16, and eleven seasons with ten or more victories. Francis has also coached six All-Americans and four Academic All-Americans.[112]

Francis's 2014 Jayhawk squad, led by first-team All–Big 12 selections Liana Salazar, Caroline Van Slambrock, and Ashley Williams, posted a 15–6 record that included a best-ever 8–0 record to start the season. The Jayhawks finished third in the Big 12 Conference and advanced to the NCAA tournament.[113]

His teams had an outstanding run in the early 2000s, earning spots in the NCAA tournament in 2001, 2003, and 2004. The 2004 edition of the Jayhawks was arguably the finest team in KU soccer history. Led by forward Caroline Smith and goalkeeper Meghan Miller, Kansas won the Big 12 Conference with an 8–2 record and also defeated Creighton in the NCAA tournament before falling to Nebraska. Francis was honored as the Big 12 Conference and Central Region Coach of the Year.[114]

In 2008 and 2011, Kansas again returned to the NCAA tournament. The 2008 Jayhawks picked up 13 wins and defeated Denver in the tournament. Several players received recognition for their efforts during the year. Emily Cressy was selected as a Freshman All-American and the Big 12 Rookie of the Year. Cressy, Monica Dolinsky, and Estelle Johnson made the All–Central Region Team. Dolinsky was also a first-team All–Big 12 selection. In 2011, Kansas's success was sparked by junior Whitney Berry and freshmen Liana Salazar and Ingrid Vidal. All three snagged All–Big 12 Conference and All-Central Region honors. Both Berry and Vidal repeated as All–Big 12 first-team selections in 2012.[115]

As indicated earlier, six of Francis's players have earned All-American honors. Four were members of the 2004 team: defenders Holly Gault and Afton Sauer; goalkeeper Meghan Miller; and forward Caroline Smith. Forward Emily Cressy was honored in 2008. Smith, a three-time All-American, is a KU soccer legend, holding career records in points, goals, shots, shots on goal, and game-winning goals. She starred in the classroom as well, being named an Academic All-American twice.[116] Liana Salazar was an All-American selection in 2014, and Caroline Van Slambrouck earned Academic All-American recognition in the same year.[117]

Volleyball

Like most other women's sports at KU, volleyball had its start in the late 1960s under the direction of Marlene Mawson. During the early 1970s, two women who coached other women's sports on Mount Oread, Linda Dollar and Ann Laptad, helped to mold the volleyball squad. Laptad was the coach of the 1971–1972 Jayhawks, recognized as "the first Kansas Volleyball team."[118] From 1975 until 1998, KU had limited success competing in the rugged Big Eight and Big 12 Conferences. Coach Bob Stanclift's teams posted three winning seasons in the mid-1970s, winning over 60 percent of their matches. Frankie Albitz, who coached the Jayhawks for nine years (1985–1993), had her most noteworthy campaign in 1986 when the Jayhawks finished with a splendid 26–9 mark and broke even in Big Eight play.[119]

In 1998, Ray Bechard, the highly successful coach at Barton Community College, was hired as KU's new head volleyball coach. He replaced Karen Schoenweis, who had been the Jayhawks' coach for four years. Over the next 17 seasons, Bechard became KU's winningest volleyball coach, compiling 295 victories and guiding the Crimson and Blue to six NCAA tournament appearances. At KU and Barton, through the 2014 season, he has logged a noteworthy 1,011–286 (.779) career record.[120]

In 2014, Bechard recorded his 1,000th career victory against Cleveland State, and KU—for the third straight year—earned an NCAA tournament bid. The young

© KonstantinChristian/Shutterstock.com

and highly competitive Jayhawks finished the Big 12 conference season in a second-place tie with Oklahoma and Iowa State.[121]

In 2012 and 2013, Kansas had its best-ever back-to-back seasons. The Jayhawks were 26–7 in 2012 and 25–8 in 2013 and hosted NCAA tournament games in Allen Fieldhouse both years. The 2013 edition of the Jayhawks advanced to the NCAA Sweet 16, defeating Wichita State and Creighton before losing to the University of Washington. Bechard was named Big 12 and American Volleyball Coaches Association (AVCA) Midwest Region Coach of the Year for both years. Following the 2012 season, middle blocker Caroline Jarmoc became KU's first-ever volleyball All-American as a second-team selection, and she became a third-team pick in 2013. The 2013 Jayhawks earned numerous honors. Erin McNorton was the Big 12 Setter of the Year, and Chelsea Albers, Sara McClinton, McNorton, and Jarmoc were named to the All–Big 12 first team. Taylor Soucie was selected the AVCA Midwest Region Freshman of the Year.[122]

Under Bechard, the Horejsi Center opened in 1999 and became one of America's most raucous and intimidating volleyball venues. With its loyal fan base, KU volleyball consistently ranks in the Top 50 attendance leaders.[123]

Bechard had several other outstanding student-athletes take the court for him over the years. A few of those were Josi Lima, an All–Big 12 first-team selection for four years; Jill Dorsey and Brianne Riley, KU's career digs leaders; Katie Martincich, the Big 12 Sportsperson of the Year in 2007–2008; and Taylor Tolefree, the Big 12 Scholar-Athlete of the Year in 2012.[124]

Tennis

Kansas women's tennis began competition as a varsity sport in 1976, with former KU basketball player Tom Kivisto as its first head coach. Over the next 20 years, until Kansas became a member of the Big 12, the Jayhawks won six Big Eight team titles. Included in this number were a remarkable five straight championships from 1992 to 1996, with Chuck Merzbacher as the head coach for the last four.[125]

The Jayhawks had several outstanding individual performances during this period. Most notable among them was Eveline Hamers, who captured three straight Big Eight singles titles from 1989 to 1991 and was a four-time All-American selection for four years. Nora Koves, Tracy Treps, and Kylie Hunt also won Big Eight singles titles, while Christie Sim won the Big 12 championship in 1997. In addition to Hamers, other KU standouts to earn All-American honors in singles were Koves, Hunt, and Mindy Weiner.[126]

A spectacular accomplishment for the women's program came in 1994 when Nora Koves and Rebecca Jensen captured the NCAA doubles championship. It has been the only national title in KU tennis history, men or women. Koves and Jensen were two-time All-Americans in doubles competition, and Christie Sim and Kylie Hunt were also All-Americans in doubles.[127]

Kansas had twelve men's tennis coaches from the mid-1960s until 2001, when the men's sport was discontinued by the Athletics Department for budgetary reasons. The most stable and successful period for the program was from 1983 to 1996 when Scott Perelman and Michael Center were the head coaches. Perelman had a career record of 153–106, while Center logged a spectacular 83–28 record. Under Perelman's leadership, the Jayhawks captured three straight Big Eight titles (1987–1989) and were Region V champions in 1987, 1988, and 1992. John Falbo was the Big Eight singles champion in 1988 and also earned All-American honors in doubles, with Craig Wildey in 1988 and Jim Secrest in 1989.[128]

A young fan prepares to watch the Kansas Tennis team in their new facility, finished in fall 2016.

Source: Jordan R. Bass

Michael Center's Crimson and Blue netters won three consecutive Big Eight championships, as well as Region V championships in 1994, 1995, and 1996. Kansas had several Big Eight champions and All-Americans during the 1980s and 1990s. The Big Eight singles champions were Mike Wolf and Enrique Abaroa (also a Big 12 champion). Doubles champions included Wolf and Wildey, Falbo and Wildey, Paul Garvin and Carlos Fleming, and Abaroa and Xavier Avila. All-Americans in addition to Falbo, Wildey, and Secrest were Avila and Abaroa in singles and Abaroa and Luis Uribe and Chris Walker and Wildey in doubles.[129]

Golf

The Kansas women's golf program had its beginning in 1973 with Nancy Boozer as its first coach. Since its establishment, the program has had several dedicated coaches, as well as many outstanding golfers. Two noteworthy team accomplishments came in 1990 when Coach Brad Demo's Jayhawks captured the Big Eight championship and in 2014 when Coach Erin O'Neil's squad had the best year in the history of the program. Both teams advanced to the NCAA tournament.[130]

Over the years, several Jayhawk golfers have earned individual honors. Holly Reynolds had the best performance by a Jayhawk in an NCAA championship, finishing in a tie for 15th in 1993. Reynolds also leads KU women in Top Ten career finishes with 21. Amanda Costner was another Jayhawk superstar on the course and in the classroom. She finished first in the 2007 Big 12 tournament, earned All–Big 12 first-team honors in 2006 and 2007, as well as Academic All–Big 12 selections for three years, and she won the prestigious Big 12 Sportsperson of the Year in 2007. Emily Powers was also a first-team All–Big 12 selection in 2008 and an Academic first-team Big 12 honoree for two years.[131]

The 2014 Kansas women's golf season was one for the ages. O'Neil's team tied for fourth in the Big 12 tournament, qualified for the NCAA tournament by tying for fifth in Central Region play, finished in the Top Ten in every tournament throughout the year, had ten top-five tournament finishes, and placed 23rd in the NCAA tournament. The team was paced by seniors Thanuttra "Fhong" Boonraksasat and Megan Potee, junior Minami Levonowich, sophomore Yupaporn "Mook" Kawinpakorn, and freshman Pornvipa "Faii" Sakdee.[132]

KU men's golf traces its roots back to the 1930s and has had several notable coaches; however, the face of the men's golf team for almost three decades was legendary coach Ross Randall. He headed the program from 1980 to 2007. His Jayhawks won a conference championship and produced a bevy of outstanding golfers. Kansas captured the Big 12 Conference title in 1999, and Randall was named the Conference Coach of the Year. He also produced four runners-up in the Big Eight and Big 12 Conferences.[133]

Several KU golfers have excelled under Randall's leadership and knowledge of the game. Five of his student-athletes, John Sinovic, Matt Gogel, Chris Thompson, Ryan Vermeer, and Kris Marshall, were honored as All-Americans. Thompson, Vermeer, and Marshall, as well as Travis Hurst, Kevin Ward, and Gary Woodland, were All–Big 12 Conference selections. Gogel and Slade Adams were Big Eight Conference championship medalists. And Gogel, Thompson, and Woodland represented KU at various times on the PGA tour.[134]

Wrestling and Gymnastics

During the 1960s, Bob Lockwood, a 1961 KU physical education graduate, was instrumental in introducing wrestling and gymnastics as varsity sports at KU. They were discontinued, however, due to budgetary concerns.[135]

The Ku Marching Band

Although the fortunes of Kansas football have been mixed over the past 50 years, one area of continued excellence on fall days at Memorial Stadium has been the performance of the Marching Jayhawks. During this period, the band has had outstanding directors, such as Russell Wiley, Kenneth Bloomquist, and Robert Foster. Foster, who led the organization from 1971 until 2001, saw it double in size, from 120 to 250 musicians. In 1972, women were added to its ranks. Since the late 1940s, the KU Marching Band has hosted an annual Band Day in Lawrence for high school bands in Kansas and Missouri, typically in conjunction with a football game in the fall. The excellence of the KU Marching Band was recognized in 1989 when it received the prestigious Louis Sudler National Intercollegiate Marching Band Trophy. The band is currently under the direction of Paul Popiel and has grown to 285 members. Adding to the performance of the band is the Spirit Squad, consisting of cheerleaders and the Rock Chalk Dancers. Pep bands also enliven the atmosphere for games at Allen Fieldhouse and the Horejsi Center.[136]

The period from 1960 to 2014 was a remarkable one for Kansas Athletics. As the foregoing suggests, the array of wonderful athletes and teams over the past five decades has been truly extraordinary. Successes on and off the fields and courts, enhancements to facilities, increases in important revenue streams, commitment to an enriched student-athlete experience, and the stability of the Big 12 Conference are sources of pride that need to be built upon and strengthened for the future. Also, lessons learned from a few unpleasant incidents should be remembered to prevent similar occurrences.

Since 2000, there has been a significant upgrade of athletics facilities at KU. The construction of the Anderson Football Complex, the Burcham Park Rowing Boathouse, the Booth Family Hall of Athletics, and Rock Chalk Park, along with enhancements to venerable Allen Fieldhouse and Hoglund Ballpark, provided Jayhawk student-athletes and fans with some of the finest athletics facilities in the nation. The completion of state-of-the-art Rock Chalk Park signals a major step forward for Kansas. KU is now able to host national and conference track and field events at this premier venue, as well as soccer and softball tournaments. The next facility on the agenda for major renovation is historic Memorial Stadium, which hosted its first game in 1921.

Funding for KU's athletics program remains an ongoing challenge. Fortunately, Kansas has a generous core of committed and loyal Jayhawk donors. As of 2014, the Williams Education Fund was raising about $18 million annually. These funds are vital, because in all likelihood, costs related to support of student-athletes, tuition and fees for scholarships, salaries for coaches, and construction and enhancement of facilities will continue to grow.[137]

The importance of Big 12 Conference revenues will continue to be a vital element for the financial viability of Kansas Athletics. The primary sources of these revenues are television contracts, bowl games, and the NCAA basketball tournament. As Blair Kerkhoff of the *Kansas City Star* noted in the spring of 2014, for the first time in history at KU, conference revenues exceeded revenue from men's basketball and football ticket sales.[138]

Conference realignment issues had a huge impact on KU in the summer and fall of 2011, with four schools leaving the Big 12.[139] However, with former Big Eight commissioner Chuck Neinas serving as interim commissioner, two schools were added, Texas Christian University and West Virginia University, creating a stable ten-member conference. Throughout this unsettling time, Chancellor Bernadette Gray-Little and Athletics Director Dr. Sheahon Zenger were strong and consistent supporters of the Big 12.

Over the past 50 years, there were also troubling episodes for Jayhawk fans and alumni. Two major probations were levied by the NCAA in the 1980s against the football and basketball programs. Then, in the early summer of 2010, the university was rocked by improprieties committed by employees in the athletics ticket office and the Williams Educational Fund.[140]

A commitment to student-athletes remains a high priority for the Athletics Department. The Academic Support Program, which was begun in the late 1980s by Chancellor Gene Budig and Athletics Director Bob Frederick, has had only one director, Paul Buskirk. The operating budget for the program has grown by leaps and bounds over the years. A new program, KU Leads, instituted by Zenger in 2011, focuses on providing student-athletes with the training and resources for a meaningful and fulfilling personal and professional life following their graduation.[141]

The future looks bright for Kansas Athletics. The university is a member of a stable, viable, and highly respected conference, the Big 12. Revenues and donations to support the athletics program are on the rise; its student-athletes are excelling in the classroom and in competition; several KU coaches are regarded among the finest in the nation; facilities are first rate, with plans to make additional improvements; and caring and committed leadership is in place. A sense of optimism, trust, and confidence permeates the Jayhawk faithful as they wave the wheat and chant: "Rock Chalk Jayhawk—KU."

Jayhawks in the Field

Chris Huey

Graduate Assistant for St. John's University Men's Basketball

Hometown
Kansas City, KS

Education
UG 2015 – University of Kansas (Sport Management, Business)
G (Projected) 2018 – St. John's University (Sport Management)

Previous Positions
Philadelphia 76ers Basketball Operations Intern
Santa Clara University Men's Basketball Video Coordinator

1. As a manager at KU you got to suit up for a game. Describe that experience and how it impacted you moving forward.

Growing up a Kansas fan playing in Allen Fieldhouse was something I always dreamed of as a kid. I had practiced with the team for most of the year and Coach Self rewarded my hard work by suiting me up against TCU late in the year. At the time, I really couldn't describe the feeling; I was just in awe of it all. Looking back it's something I'll never forget. I'm just truly grateful to Coach Self and the staff for allowing me the opportunity. The feeling of running out of the tunnel or checking into the game still gives me the chills. There really is no place like Allen Fieldhouse, you appreciate that much more when you're gone. This opportunity was so special to my family and I. A lot of people from home reached out to me about it and I heard from friends from all over. I was also able to build some connections in basketball through it, with coaches knowing who I am because I was a manager who played in a game at Kansas. I hear about it from time to time when applying for jobs or meeting new people, but for the most part the impact has died down.

2. Describe the process you followed to obtain your previous position in California and current one at St. John's.

I obtained both jobs through the help of connections. In basketball, like many jobs in the world of sports, it is all about who you know. My first job after graduation was with the Philadelphia 76ers as a Basketball Operations Intern. I had been in touch with some colleges throughout the year but it was getting later in the summer and after going through a lengthy interview process I was able to land this position on my own. For me, this was rewarding knowing I did not

have to "use" anyone to get a job. I was not in Philly for long before I heard from some of the coaches on the Kansas coaching staff about a video coordinator position opening at Santa Clara University.

The head coach there at the time was Kerry Keating, whose father is an Assistant AD at Kansas and someone who knows most of the Kansas coaches. After discussing with some of the people on staff with the Sixers as well as people at Kansas, I decided to take the job based on the opportunity for a full-time position my first year out of school. The coast-to-coast move was well worth the experience I was able to gain, although only being there one full season. Following that season our staff was let go, another experience I did not expect to go through one year from graduation but something that's frequent in college basketball. Time between jobs is always stressful, constantly in contact with people I know in the business seeing what they're hearing on openings or if they have connections to jobs I have heard are open. Eventually I got in touch with an assistant coach here at St. John's. He and I built a relationship while I was a manager and he was a development coach with the Sacramento Kings.

He spent quite a bit of time in Lawrence in the summer working out Ben McLemore, allowing me to assist in the workouts. Through this, we started going to eat and that sort of thing, kept in touch over the years. When he knew I was out of a job, he reached out to me about the graduate assistant position here in New York. One thing that has been stressed to me that I think is extremely important is doing whatever you can to stay in touch with the contacts you make. Whether this be a handwritten letter from time to time, a text here or there, or even a phone call to catch up. Something as simple as that keeps you fresh in the person's mind and shows that you care. If it wasn't for building connections and staying in touch, I would not have landed these positions.

3. What does a typical day look like for a graduate assistant basketball coach?

As a graduate assistant, every day is different. It is going to vary based on what time of year it is, whether we are in season or out of season, and if the players are around or not. A typical day in season starts with team breakfast around 8:00 am. I try to be one of the first people in the office every day. Early in the morning it is nice and quiet so I typically use this time to do any homework I may have or work ahead on any basketball projects. After breakfast, the players usually lift in 4-5 person groups, during this time the staff is usually showing up and homework opportunity is over. Throughout the morning and early afternoon I am usually working on scouting reports for our upcoming opponents. This is a lot of time watching tape, cutting, and coding games for specific things that stand out to me. I am in charge of putting together a personnel edit for each of our opponents throughout the year. I find clips from each guy in their rotation and put together a film edit that showcases their tendencies and strengths. I also help with the team edit, where we show the team the plays the opponent is going to run and what their style of play is. Typically this takes up most of the time until practice. Prior to practice, we will show the team film on our upcoming opponent in the locker room. For this I am in charge of controlling the computer while Coach Mullin or our assistant talks through the film, stopping and rewinding when necessary.

The great part about being a graduate assistant that differs from full-time support staff roles is the opportunity to be on the floor in practice. As a video coordinator or director of operations you cannot be on the floor at practice. As a GA, you can be on the floor participating in drills and assisting with anything that's asked of you. In my role, Coach Mullin gives me a lot of freedom and responsibility on the court. To start practice, we usually separate into different baskets, where I take the post players and work on player development drills for a few minutes. From there, I assist in other offensive and defensive breakdown drills throughout practice. Usually practice ends with a scout team session, where I play on the scout team mimicking the opposition's plays so that our players can guard them live. The other graduate assistant and myself are two people on staff who watch a lot of the scout games so we fortunate enough to help coach our scout team players through the plays as well. Our scout team is made up of our walk on players, as well as our redshirt kids who transferred to the school and have to sit out.

After practice, I stay after in the gym to help any guys who want to get extra shots or workout. From here, it could go a number of different ways. If I have class, I usually shower after practice and run to class. If there is no class, I will usually do some sort of workout with the staff before showering and getting back to my computer. At night most of my time is spent working on upcoming scouting reports on teams down the line, or watching a lot of games. Like I mentioned, each day is going to be different because something new is asked of me every day. This is just one example of a given day.

4. Who was your favorite player you interacted with at KU and why?

I don't know that there is one specific guy that I would say is my favorite that I interacted with. The Kansas program is such a family and I was able to build relationships and work around some really incredible people. I really can't choose one as my favorite. I have great relationships with the walk on players like Evan Manning and Tyler Self because I spent a lot of time with them on the court with the scout team and off the court in the classroom. Other guys were great to be around as well, guys like Perry Ellis, Andrew White, Wayne

Selden, Frank Mason, Devonte Graham, Tarik Black, Travis Releford, and so on. I was able to build relationships with a lot of these guys and still keep in touch with a lot of them. The environment at Kansas means meeting a lot of former players as well, guys like Nick Collison and Aaron Miles who I grew up watching and now keep in contact with as much as I can. Everyone looks after one another and treats you like family, that's just how it goes at Kansas.

5. What makes someone like Bill Self, John Calipari, or Chris Mullin a good recruiter? Are those skills learned or are they just "born" with them?

Coming from someone who has yet to recruit, I can't tell you for certain. I think what makes these guys so successful is their ability to connect to the recruits and their families. They all do a great job of building relationships with these athletes, showing their families they will be taken care of and given great opportunities on and off the court. Each coach has their own different recruiting tactics, but they're all looking to show a kid that the best chance for him to be successful is at their school. As a coach you have to market yourself and the school, and then be able to back all of that up with productivity with your team. It is much easier to draw a kid to your school when you're winning games. I believe these skills are learned, recruiting comes from putting in the time and learning the ins and outs of it all. Successful head coaches carry many characteristics that they are born with, but I believe recruiting is something that is a learned skill.

6. Describe the favorite parts of your job and give some specific examples if possible.

There are so many great parts of my job, one of the coolest being the opportunity I have every day to be around guys like Chris Mullin and Mitch Richmond. Coach Mullin was a great college player here at St. John's back coaching at his alma mater. He's a three-time Big East Player of the year, played 16 seasons in the NBA, 5 time NBA All Star, and a gold medalist with the 1992 Dream Team. Mitch played a junior college before being one of the best players ever at Kansas State, and yes Jayhawks and Wildcats can get along. Mitch's career in the NBA lasted 14 seasons and included being NBA Rookie of the Year, 6 time NBA All Star, 5 Time All-NBA team, Gold Medalist in 1996, and NBA champion with Kobe and Shaq in '01-'02. Learning the game from guys like these two and hearing stories from their playing days make every day enjoyable. Who can say they've watched part of the documentary on the Dream Team with a member of the Dream team? Or heard about the playing days in the Big 8 when Kansas, Kansas State, Missouri, and Oklahoma were all making deep runs in the NCAA tournament in the late 1980s? It's pretty cool stuff.

Here at St. John's, we play half of our home games on campus at Carnesecca Arena and the other half at Madison Square Garden. On campus, the arena is small which creates a great atmosphere, and named after Coach Mullin's Head Coach Lou Carnesecca who took the school to the only final four appearances in school history. Coach Carnesecca is 92 years old and still around the program today, that makes it even more special. Playing home games in the "World's Most Famous Arena," Madison Square Garden for 7 home games out of the year, you really can't beat that. We go into Manhattan the night before the game and stay across the street from Central Park. The bus ride into the game includes seeing Central Park and driving through Times Square. To me this is one of the coolest things about a career in sports, the places basketball has taken me and the things I have been able to see in a few short years pushes me for the future.

Name: _____   Section: _____   Date _____

HSES 289
Introduction to Sport Management
In-Class Quiz and Activity Sheet

Name (or names if done in a group)

Answer #1

Answer #2

Answer #3

© tsyhun/Shutterstock.com

Chapter 4

Careers in Sport Management

Jordan R. Bass • *University of Kansas*

KEY TERMS

College Athletics

Professional Athletics

Qualifications

Organizational Hierarchy

Icon Sportswire/Getty Images

In Chapter Two, a plethora of University of Kansas alumni detailed the favorite part of their careers in the sport industry. I hope you noticed the wide range of positions and organizations in which they were employed. The term "sport industry" encompasses thousands of organizations across the United States and world. You should be struck by the variety of job titles present in the KU Sport Management Professional Society member list and move past a narrow understanding of sport management as just working in intercollegiate or professional athletics or being an athletics director or sport agent. In the pages that follow, we'll detail positions that exist across various industry segments and the skills and qualifications desired for positions.

Intercollegiate Athletics

Every semester, I ask students their ultimate career goal. The vast majority of students select a position in intercollegiate athletics with most desiring to be an athletics director. While I'm sure a few of you in the room will obtain this goal, there are a limited supply of head athletics director positions. There are, however, a vast amount of employment opportunities in the college athletics space. We'll begin with a quick overview of the organizational structure of the University of Kansas athletics department.

As evident in the Table 4.1 it takes dozens of professionals to perform all the operations within a major intercollegiate athletics departments. From facilities and events to fundraising, numerous opportunities exist for a career in college sport. A quick method to get a perspective on the responsibilities and skills desired for positions in this space is to examine advertisements for open positions. For example, a posting for the General Manager of Ticket Sales at the University of Oklahoma states the employee is responsible for (among 20 other bullet points) "training, mentoring, motivating and coaching the ticket sales staff" and "work(ing) closely with university athletic department marketing staff on ticket sales promotions as it relates to driving ticket sales revenue." The qualifications for the position include a Bachelor's degree in Sport Management or related field, a proven track record in ticket sales, and familiarity with ticketing and other advanced software.

Another posting in a different area is for an Athletics Events Manager at the University of California, Berkeley. The posting states the person hired will, "assist in overall operation of California Memorial Stadium, Haas Pavilion, and all other athletic facilities during home events, facility rentals, and post-season championship events." Additionally, he or she, "assists in coordinating event logistics and ensuring that all events are run efficiently and safely within the rules and regulations of the NCAA, Pac-12 Conference, MPSF Conference, and the University of California." Qualifications required or encouraged range across soft and hard skills (notice a strength requirement).

Required Qualifications

- Bachelor's degree or equivalent training/experience.
- 3–4 years of experience of event management experience.
- Extensive experience in managing small to large crowds and working under stressful situations.

TABLE 4.1 University of Kansas Athletics Organizational Structure

Administration

Example positions include Athletics Director, Deputy Athletics Director, Senior Women's Administrator, Associate Athletics Director for Numerous Areas, Chief Financial Officer, and Corporate Counsel

Coaching/Sport Specific Positions

Example positions include Head Coach, Assistant Coach, Graduate Assistant, Director of Operations, and Director of Technology

Academic Support

Examples positions include Associate Director of Academic and Career Counseling, Tutoring Director, Learning Specialist, and International Student-Athlete Support

Communications

Example positions include Executive Director of External Branding, Director of Football Communications, Assistant Communications Director, Director of Broadcasting, and Strategic Communications Manager

Compliance and Student Services

Example positions include Assistant Athletics Director of Compliance, Director of Eligibility and Compliance Systems, and Assistant Athletics Director of Student Services

Equipment

Examples positions include Assistant Athletics Director of Equipment and Equipment Manager

Facilities and Events

Example positions include Associate Athletics Director of Operations and Capital Projects, Facility Supervisor, Assistant Athletics Director of Facilities and Events, and Grounds Supervisor

Marketing and Fan Experience

Example positions include Senior Director of Marketing, Assistant Athletics Director for Marketing and Fan Experience, and Graduate Assistant of Marketing and Fan Experience

Sales and Service and Ticket Office

Example positions include Director of Ticket Sales and Service, Team Leader of New Business and Development, Database and Analytics Manager, and Group and Event Sales Consultant

Student-Athlete Development

Example positions include Director of Student-Athlete Development, Coordinator of Special Events, Director of Outreach

Williams Education Fund (Fundraising)

Example positions include Director of Development, Gift Processing Specialist, Associate Athletics Director of Major Gifts, and Director of Donor Hospitality and Events

Source: http://www.kuathletics.com/staff.aspx

- Excellent problem-solving skills.
- Excellent people skills.
- Knowledge of NCAA and general sports rules.
- Excellent computer skills – Microsoft Office Suite, Google Aps.
- Must be able to work nights, weekends, and holidays (including Thanksgiving and Christmas).
- Driver's License (US issued).
- Ability to lift 75 lbs.

Preferred Qualifications

- Master's degree in Sport Management/Administration.
- Ability to operate audio/visual equipment, scoreboards.
- First Aid and CPR certification.
- Beginning to intermediate computer graphic skills.

You should also not limit your search to NCAA Division I institutions. Whether it be in NCAA Division II, III, NAIA, or Junior Colleges, valuable and important positions exist across the spectrum. For example, a posting for a Sport Information internship at Lindsey Wilson College (a NAIA member) lists duties such as, "game management, marketing and promotion, developing media guides, collecting statistical data, writing press releases, managing athletics website, working at special events and other duties assigned by the Sports Information Director." Those searching for positions in intercollegiate athletics should visit a number of different aggregate websites (along with individual athletics websites):

- TeamWork Online: www.teamworkonline.com
- NCAA Job Market: ncaamarket.ncaa.org/jobseekers/
- NAIA Career Center: http://www.naia.org/ViewArticle.dbml?ATCLID= 205340837

Before we move to careers in professional athletics, visit tinyurl.com/ JayhawksInSport and have a look at the different positions Jayhawks have in the intercollegiate sports space. Which position is the most attractive to you?

Professional Athletics

A number of similar positions discussed above exist in the professional athletics realm whereas there are also a number of unique avenues. As with intercollegiate athletics, it is imperative to not narrow your job search to Major League Baseball, the National Basketball Association, National Football League, and National Hockey League. Opportunities exist at every level, from the Oklahoma City Dodgers to the Los Angeles Dodgers. As with intercollegiate athletics, the size of the organization will greatly influence the responsibilities and skills needed. Restated, working as one of a dozen ticket sales employees with the Kansas City Royals will be vastly different than working in a similarly named position for their Single-A affiliate Wilmington Blue Rocks.

Speaking of sales, many entry-level positions in the professional sport industry will include a sales aspect. This is especially true in smaller organizations where you may be forced to wear multiple hats in order to maximize revenue generation for your team. For example, at the Wichita Wingnuts (an independent league baseball

FIGURE 4.1 Wichita Wingnuts Organizational Structure (Summer 2017)

Independent League Baseball Team Based in Wichita, Kansas

team; see Table 4.1), the Assistant General Manager also serves as the Director of Corporate Sales and the Game Day Manager also manages merchandise sales. Thus, it is imperative you have the awareness and skills for at least a minimal sales component of your first internship or position in professional sport.

Activity: Other Career Options

There are endless other career opportunities with your sport management degree. Visit tinyurl.com/JayhawksInSport and identify five positions of interest of you that are not in the first two categories of intercollegiate and professional sport. Write two paragraphs for each position describing both the organization and the responsibilities and skills you believe are needed to work in that position and organization.

Jayhawks in the Field

Will Hoven

Events and Operations Coordinator for the Valero Alamo Bowl

Hometown
Chester, NJ

Education
UG 2015 – The University of Kansas (Sport Management, Business)

Past Positions
National Association of Intercollegiate Athletics (NAIA) Championships Intern
Kansas Athletics Football Operations Intern

1. Give us an idea of your monthly schedule working for the Valero Alamo Bowl.

From July through December, we have over 20 events that vary in scale and scope. No two days are ever the same. When you have so many events of different size and scope—some weeks apart, some days apart, some hours apart—you are always trying to budget your time wisely and work efficiently to make sure you're getting the most out of your day. When you are a small staff like us, you have a hand in a little bit of everything: events, operations, marketing, communications, and social media were all things I was involved in. You must be able to identify your most pressing needs/projects and divide out your hours of the day appropriately.

2. How important are volunteers to your operation and what sets apart good volunteers from average ones?

Being a small staff, volunteers are critical to our success; we could not operate most of our events without them. We are fortunate enough to have many volunteers who have been with us since the bowl's inception, so they have a great handle on our events and what roles they need to fill in order to help us succeed. Our best volunteers are timely, have great attitudes, and are willing to fill any role needed to help out. In other words: our best volunteers have a genuine enjoyment in helping out, being involved, and playing a role on our team, even if it is a small one.

3. What strategies do you use to attract casual fans to the event who do not have "their" team playing?

A good match up always helps. San Antonio does not have pro football, and UTSA (University of Texas San Antonio) is still a relatively new program. The Valero Alamo Bowl is unique in that we get to pick which teams play in our game. We are able to pick the #1 Pac-12 and Big 12 teams after the College Football Playoff; which has resulted in a Top-15 team match–up each of the last three years. Getting a big-time name like Oregon or USC from the Pac-12 will always drive a lot of interest from local football fans that never get to see those teams. The chance of having one of the in state Texas schools—Texas, Texas Tech, Baylor, and TCU—tends to attract more local fans who will cheer for the in state school, even if they did not attend one of those schools.

4. What was your absolute favorite KU sporting event while you were an undergraduate student?

My freshman year KU made it to the Final Four. Running to Mass Street after we beat Ohio State for a shot at the title is something I'll never forget.

5. There is a common narrative that there are too many bowl games and it devalues the experience. What are your thoughts on this debate?

I can see both sides of the argument. Bowl games can be a great boost to local economies for the cities they're played in; the past two years, the Valero Alamo Bowl has delivered and economic impact of over $45 million per year to San Antonio, a city where tourism is one of its primary economic drivers. Before the Alamo Bowl's inception in 1993, December was one of the slowest times of year for tourism in San Antonio—the city used to drain the River Walk during the holidays. The benefit of the game has been obvious for San Antonio, especially in recent years with the match-ups the game has gotten, so it's not hard to see why more cities want to establish their own game.

However, you want to make sure you can deliver a quality experience for the visiting teams and fans. This is easier for larger, more established bowl games that benefit from strong local support from both the city and local businesses. For the Alamo Bowl, having a large, local business that sees the benefit of having this bowl game for the city is a big plus; the Alamo Bowl has that in Valero. When Valero became the title sponsor for the Alamo Bowl, it really took our game to a higher tier. Their level of financial commitment allowed for a higher team payout, which makes you a more attractive bowl that conferences want to partner with (this past fall the Big 12 and Pac-12 both extended their agreements through 2025), allowing you to get better teams and match-ups, which makes you more attractive to sponsors. So when you're a smaller bowl game entering a crowded, established market, it can be difficult to grow and compete.

6. Describe the favorite parts of your job and give some specific examples if possible.

First I'd say the people I get to work with. I wanted to get into sports for the chance to work on projects I am passionate about, and for the prestige working in this industry can bring (though I can assure you it is not a glamorous industry when you're starting out). When you get in, however, you meet people with the same enjoyment and passion for what they do. Getting to work with a group that shares your enthusiasm for what you do makes the work so much more enjoyable and rewarding.

I was fortunate enough to work at the Valero Alamo Bowl during a year where they were hosing an additional neutral site game (the Notre Dame "Shamrock Series"). These types of unique opportunities are not uncommon in the bowl industry, and are a nice added benefit that most people don't think about. For instance, the Final Four will be hosted in San Antonio at the Alamodome in 2018; the bowl staff will get to assist with that event in some capacity. Another example would be the college football national championship; depending what city the game is played in, such as Phoenix or Atlanta, the local bowl game (Fiesta and Peach) staffs will more than likely get the opportunity to assist in the production of those games. If you love working in large-scale events this is a great way to get more exposure and experience, even if it is in more of a support role than a lead role.

It's not all about game day and large-scale events. The smaller events (coaches' dinner, team pep rallies, luncheons, sponsor mixers) allow you to make a strong impression on a small group of people that is more immediately felt. For the average fan, they may perceive their experience at the actual bowl game a poor one if the game is a blow out, but say a coaches dinner, where you control the venue, food selection, and entertainment (we had a modern violinist at our most recent coaches' dinner, who was a big hit with our guests), you can tell right away if you hit the mark or not, and it's always a great feeling when you do. That's really why I've come to love working in sport events; it gives you the opportunity to create memorable, lasting experiences for guests and fans via a platform that already brings so many people together.

Name: _____ Section: _____ Date _____

In-Class Quiz and Activity Sheet

Name (or names if done in a group)

Answer #1

Answer #2

Answer #3

© Branislav Nenin/Shutterstock.com

Chapter 5

The Importance of Networking in Professional Career Development

Olzhas Taniyev • *University of Kansas*

CHAPTER OVERVIEW

Launching a career in the sports industry, defined by "it's not what you know, it's who you know" politics, is a daunting task for a young professional. Networking, the art of building relationships in the industry in which one seeks employment and advancement, is an essential tool that opens doors and fast tracks careers. The greatest hurdle for aspiring students is leveraging connections with influential sports industry professionals to gain employment and cultivate a professional network. Self-awareness and political skill are necessary for navigating the job search environment, getting hired, and moving up the ranks in the sports industry. This chapter demonstrates the importance of professional relationship building and presents several methods that can be used to create and maintain professional connections. Additionally, experts provide opinions on how to establish meaningful connections.

KEY TERMS

Career Development

Networking

Political Skill

Communication Skill

Icon Sportswire/Getty Images

"A wise man knows everything. A shrewd one, everybody"

—Chinese proverb

Networking for Career Development

When I worked with the women's tennis team at California University of Pennsylvania as a graduate student, my goal was to use this experience to ultimately find an internship with a sports marketing firm. My internship search process resulted in frustration because I was applying to hundreds of companies with absolutely no response. It felt like my résumés were being submitted to a black hole. Realizing my approach was not working, I reached out for help by calling my friend and former client, David, a tech entrepreneur. After listening to me vent about my lack of prospects, David asked me a simple question, "What do you want to do?" I described my ultimate dream job and realistic entry-level job to which he said, "My startup team is looking for a marketing intern." We discussed the details of the position and he hired me on the spot. That phone call set my career in motion and showed me the power of networking for career development.

When I began this pursuit, I asked myself, "How many people work in sports?" I soon learned that the odds of landing a promising position in the sports industry were slim. Even though the competition for jobs in the sports industry was fierce, networking would be my secret weapon in the job application process. Networking is the process of developing and using contacts for information, advice, and moral support as you pursue your career (Welch, 1980). Start networking as a student by politely inquiring about the professions of relatives, friends, coaches, teachers, professors, and even the person next to you on the plane. By taking a genuine interest in the employment of others and asking meaningful, open-ended questions, you will learn about many different jobs and industries. Eventually, persistence and tact will lead to connections with professionals in your desired industry. Nurture these connections and convert your best contacts into mentors. A mentor who knows an executive at a property where you apply can lead to an interview. While networking comes naturally to some students, it serves to remember that it is a learnable skill that requires practice and dedication to master. Of all the aspects related to a job search in the sports industry, effective networking skills should be the top priority for many young professionals. I prefer to see networking as building one's net worth, the process that requires time, diligent research, and strong communication and political skills.

Political and Communication Skills

Political skill is referred to as "the ability to effectively understand others at work, and to use such knowledge to influence others to act in ways that enhance one's personal and/or organizational objectives" (Ahearn, Ferris, Hochwarter, Douglas, & Ammeter, 2004, p. 311). Politically skilled professionals tend to rely on social astuteness, the ability to accurately decipher social situations and analyze the interaction process and behavior of others (Kimura, 2015). How can political skill help you with networking? Not only will political competencies and the ability to communicate effectively better prepare one for interaction with diverse networks of professionals, it will also enable one to practice self-awareness, a competency critical to understanding people and their perspective in various social situations (Kimura, 2015; Treadway et al., 2014).

© rolkadd/Shutterstock.com]

One's ability to relate to others' feelings and their social settings will result in effective interpersonal interactions that are instrumental in professional relationship building. Describing the importance of political expertise in the networking process, Ferris et al. (2005) suggested:

> Individuals with strong political skill are adept at developing and using diverse networks of people. People in these networks tend to hold assets

seen as valuable and necessary for successful personal and organizational functioning. By the sheer force of their typically subtle style, politically skilled individuals easily develop friendships and build strong, beneficial alliances and coalitions . . . [These individuals] inspire trust and confidence in and from those around them. (p. 129)

Furthermore, one should network regardless of whether searching for a job or having an established career. Regardless, diligence is required.

How to Develop Meaningful Professional Relationships

Many students, for various reasons, struggle with adding people to their network, thereby hindering their careers. Students must start with identifying the right people within their existing circle including family members, past and present faculty, supervisors, colleagues, fellow classmates, and friends. To expand a network of contacts, reflect and respond to the following questions (Puetz, 2007):

- To whom do I turn most often for help with personal problems?
- To whom do I turn most often for assistance with professional problems?
- Who turns to me for help with either personal or professional problems?
- Who are the three people above me in status or position with whom I would want to share a professional success?
- Who are the three people at my level (professional peers) with whom I would want to share my success?
- Who are the three people below me in status or position with whom I would feel comfortable sharing my success?
- Who are those persons with whom I could share a failure, either personal or professional?

Remember, this strategic relationship building should be an ongoing mutually beneficial process that requires a clear networking plan. "How and where do I

© Gualberto Becerra/Shutterstock.com

network?" The following are some networking tips that will help develop a good networking strategy:

- **Past and/or present faculty, colleagues, friends, and family members**. The best new contacts are your present connections. Talking with people you know will increase your odds of expanding your network. All it takes is asking one of your connections the following question: "Do you know someone I could call for advice about my career?" I called David to simply ask for help with my approach to job searching. In casual conversation, he mentioned an idea he had been developing and arranged for me to meet the rest of his team.

- **Class guest speakers**. These are the people who have been in your shoes and are willing to help. A simple "thank you" note following his or her presentation will show your gratitude and appreciation for sharing their experiences and advice. For example, a student in one of my classes followed up with one of the guest speakers to simply say, "thank you." The guest speaker, impressed by the student's initiative, then introduced the student to several top-tier sports industry professionals within a few weeks.

- **Informational interviews (J. Marvel, personal communication, February 6, 2018)**. Informational interviewing is a vital part of the networking process in the sports industry, especially while looking for a job or an internship. Most résumés or online applications go into a black hole. Be proactive and set yourself apart from others. A follow-up call is imperative once a résumé or application has been sent. If there is no job listing for the sport organization you want to work for, call and ask for a brief informational interview to learn more about the company and how that individual got into his or her position (remember, the worst thing they can say is "no"). If that person will not do it, ask if they can recommend somebody else in the organization to meet with you. Be prepared for the informational interview by extensively researching the company and the individual.

- **Professional associations**. The sports industry is replete with professional organizations that offer networking opportunities. Becoming a member is a big step toward growing your network. Students will also benefit from attending major conferences in the sports industry and learning about latest trends in the field of sport management. Create a list of sports industry-related associations and networking events you can attend. Today.

- **Volunteer experience**. Find a way to volunteer for a sport organization or event. Volunteer experience is an excellent opportunity to meet new people, enhance your skill set, and boost your résumé. Furthermore, various volunteer opportunities will allow you to learn about specific sectors in the sports industry and guide you to more rational decisions. When you finally go for that coveted job interview, your volunteer experience will be a huge bonus in the eyes of a prospective employer.

How to Maintain Professional Relationships

Maintain regular communication with people in your network. Remember, do not call people in your network only when you need a favor. Continuing to touch base every few months will demonstrate interest and keep you at the top of the list when a position becomes available. Additionally, networking should be mutually beneficial. Students should always try to reciprocate and find ways to help their contacts: "You can get whatever you want if you help enough people get whatever they want" (Zig Ziglar). Ask for help, learn how to handle rejection, and keep knocking on the door and casting a wide networking net.

© nelzajamal/Shutterstock.com

References

Ahearn, K. K., Ferris, G. R., Hochwarter, W. A., Douglas, C., & Ammeter, A. P. (20i04). Leader political skill and team performance. *Journal of Management, 30*(3), 309–327.

Ferris, G. R., Treadway, D. C., Kolodinsky, R. W., Hochwarter, W. A., Kacmar, C. J., Douglas, C, & Frink, D. D. (2005). Development and validation of the political skill inventory. *Journal of Management, 31*(1), 126–152.

Kimura, T. (2015). A review of political skill: Current research trend and directions for future research. *International Journal of Management Reviews, 17*(3), 312–332.

Puetz, B. E. (2007). Networking. *Public Health Nursing, 24*(6), 577–579.

Treadway, D. C., Adams, G., Hanes, T. J., Perrewe, P. L., Magnusen, M. J., & Ferris, G. R. (2014). The roles of recruiter political skill and performance resource leveraging in NCAA football recruitment effectiveness. *Journal of Management, 40*(6), 1607–1626.

Welch, M. S. (1980). *Networking: The great new way for women to get ahead.* New York, NY: Harcourt Brace Jovanovich.

Jayhawks in the Field

Hunter Lochmann

Senior Vice President of Marketing & Brand Strategy at Monumental Sports & Entertainment (Washington Wizards & Washington Capitals)

Education
University of Kansas & University of Massachusetts

Previous Organizations
NBA league office, New York Knicks, University of Michigan Athletic Department, Phoenix Suns

Andrew Henrotin

Education
University of California, Berkeley & University of Pennsylvania

Previous Organizations
Golden State Warriors

Given the focus of this chapter, I believe it will be beneficial for young professionals to gain insight into the significance and approaches to professional networking shared by distinguished sports industry professionals. The sports industry experts' responses to my questions are as follows:

Taniyev: In general, how would you describe the most rewarding aspects of working in the sports industry?

Lochmann: That answer is probably twofold. One it is sports and two it is marketing—two things I love. It is very cliché, but it is probably the most team-oriented job you could have. You cannot determine what happens on the court or ice, but what you can determine is what happens off of them. The energy in the building after a win is so much different than after a loss and that includes the offices. The fun thing about sports is you win together and you lose together and when you are winning, there is nothing better . . . but when you lose, it bonds you as a team. On the marketing side, we have to come up with these creative ideas and we know what is coming, so it's fun to see how the fans react if they love something . . . to really come up with a good fun marketing idea, to see it be a home run with the fans.

Henrotin: Relationships with fellow workers, not only the people in my department, but people who are a part of the whole production, ushers, ticket takers, security guards, fans, members of the media, players would probably be the last on my list.

Taniyev: What qualities do you think are necessary to be successful in the sports industry?

Lochmann: I would say one of the biggest is you cannot be scared of hard work. Most people work 9 to 5 jobs and we are just getting started because there are games and events. You have to be prepared to work long and hard hours, but at the same time, you are at an event, and watching it unfold and if you are a sports fan, that is fun. I do not think I have ever had a day in my 21 years of working where the day went exactly like I hoped it would. Sports is dynamic and that is the fun part, you could win 10 in a row and that is going to change your plan or you could lose 10 in a row and something you had planned you are going to have to completely scrap. You have to be a sports fan, but you also have to take a step back and not let that sports fandom cloud your work thoughts. You have to be creative, you have to be innovative, you have to see what others are doing, you have to be on top of trends, you have to read, you have to benchmark what other not only sports brands, but brands in general are doing. That is what I look for when I am hiring. You have to be a good teammate and again it is cliché, but you have to work well with others, you have to work well with other departments. Our world is 24/7, so you have to be able to respond quickly.

Henrotin: I would say humility, do not take yourself too seriously and treat the team President and the team superstar and janitor of the arena the same way. Do not get caught up in trying to impress people or trying to be someone you are not, be genuine and do not burn bridges. Treat everyone the same way, be consistent and do whatever is asked of you to do and, if and when there is an issue that just does not sit well, do not be afraid to address it with your supervisor or whoever is in charge of you.

Taniyev: Tell me about the importance of having a mentor in terms of career development.

Lochmann: Mentors are key. It is always great to learn from the folks who have come before you and who have been in your shoes. I think what is important is that they can give you advice on what to do, but maybe more importantly what not to do and learn from some of their mistakes before you make them on your own . . . There are many folks who have come before me in this industry that I think very highly of . . . Mentors are key, they are out there. You just have to be persistent, you have to find the right ones, and one way to do that is through networking.

Henrotin: I think because like in any profession it is so new, finding someone you can trust and confide in who has some experience is invaluable and I think it is one thing to be ambitious, but it is another to be overconfident and try to prove yourself in ways that ultimately are not in your best interest. So it is always good to have someone to run things by to kind of get a gauge and a better feel on what is appropriate.

Taniyev: How important to your career has networking been?

Lochmann: I have been fortunate. As an undergrad at Kansas, I worked for the football team . . . I worked for the defensive coordinator . . . he was tough and he treated me like any of the other players, but when it came time to write that reference for colleges and grad school and internships, he was the first one to raise his hand and wrote me a great reference. All it takes is that one connection to really unlock who knows how many steps in their career. Mine has been Bill Sutton. Whether it is the sports management seminars or groups, with technology these days, the ability for students to network is so easy. And I appreciate the ones who really have done their research and have some specific questions based on my past versus the blank ones who just want to do a report on someone in the sports industry. Research means a lot, so I think when you network, you need to be smart about who you are networking with, why, and have your research done behind that.

Henrotin: Well, I think it goes back to the last question. If you find someone in a mentor or a boss, who is willing to share their networks and their connections with you, that is huge. As a newcomer to the profession, you have a very small network, so identifying the people who are going to share their networks with you and going to put you in touch with people and facilitate relationships with people outside of your immediate work responsibilities is huge. And learning from that mentor how to network, who to contact, how to contact them, what the nature of the contact should be, how to follow up, knowing when to push, and knowing when to pull back. As intelligent as we may think we are, it is always good to have someone who is guiding you in that networking process.

Taniyev: What advice would you give to undergraduate students in terms of networking strategies?

Lochmann: When I have a young person reach out to me, I always ask them two questions: (1) What is your dream job? And (2) What is your more realistic entry-level dream job? [For example] is it working in the marketing department at a Major League Baseball team? That is important, because if that is the case, that is where you need to start your networking. You need to see who is connected to Major League Baseball, who is in the marketing field, and really drill down into there. Depending on where you are, whether you are in Lawrence, Kansas or you grew up in Chicago, look at those teams and properties you are passionate about and follow up that way. Start there, but do not be afraid to open up a

wider scope. You may want to live in Lawrence and Kansas City and work for one of the teams, but unfortunately the only jobs that may be open are in South Dakota and you have to be willing to pack up and go. To summarize, be specific, use technology to your advantage, be prepared, do research. You have to imagine there are multiple folks who are asking the same thing, so what is going to set you apart is you have done your research, you have more questions, more prepared questions, and that is going to come across very favorably on the other side.

Henrotin: Cast a wide net. Put your name out there. Contact as many people as possible. Follow up. Be persistent and be genuine. If you are going to say you are going to do something, do it. And know, anyone, who attaches their name to you, you have an obligation to respect and uphold their name. Do not be self-serving with networking. Make sure that you are doing it in the best interest of the people who are helping you network. It will always get back to them. Do not misrepresent yourself. Put yourself out there, but show gratitude and humility and appreciation for the people who are helping you network.

Taniyev: Talk about the importance of maintaining professional relationships. How would you go about accomplishing this?

Lochmann: With technology, emails and texts are so easy. I think people have differing opinions on, for instance, sending a "thank you" note versus emailing a "thank you" note. Anything is great. A personal note, that just takes it to the next level . . . In my career, I have made a New Year's resolution to write more notes, and I am trying to, at the beginning of every week, I am trying to identify one or two people I just want to reach out to and if someone I do not know in the industry, just to congratulate them or wish them well, maybe it is somebody internally that I just want to say "great job" on something. You need to be genuine. It is ok to congratulate someone about work, but also have some personal questions too and I know people respect and appreciate that.

Henrotin: Treat each connection with respect. It is not rocket science, it is common sense, but it is human nature perhaps once you get a contact and they are able to help you and get you what you want, it is easy to forget the people who helped you identify the contact and what they have done for you. Keep track of who you are talking to, keep track of what they are doing for you, and do your best to not disappoint them. Do your best to let them know how you are doing and how much you appreciate that. It is pretty simple, but you would be amazed at how so many people do not do it. Do not burn bridges; that is the bottom line.

Taniyev: What is your last piece of advice for undergraduate students striving to work in the sports industry?

Lochmann: Keep your eyes open, and by that I mean read and use resources available to you. Educate yourself not just about what you are passionate about, but get outside the box, look at other leagues, look at other sports maybe you do not like, look at other industries that may or may not interest you. Learn because this world changes quickly and as technology becomes more fragmented, you just have to have this worldly look and feel to it. Again, I think the worst thing you can tell a prospective employer in the sports industry is you are a huge fan because that is a red flag. They are going to think all you are worried about is meeting the players or sitting there and watching the game. We are leery of hearing that as it happens in the industry all of the time. Just put your head down and do the job for the right reasons.

Henrotin: Know what you want and ask for it. If someone says "no," do not be afraid to ask again or in a different way and do not be afraid of rejections, do not take it personally. It is your career, so go after it. But again, do not misrepresent yourself, do not be selfish, do not take a lead and throw it off. You are only as good as what you do. There is nothing wrong with being aggressive. There is no job that is too small. If you think you are above stuffing envelopes 20 hours a week, well good luck. But if you get an opportunity to stuff envelopes for 20 hours a week, take it. You are not above anything at this point and people want to see that, they want to see how serious you are, they want to see your work ethic, they want to see your character, so any opportunity for you to show that, take it.

Name: _____ Section: _____ Date _____

Individual Assignment

Select a sports industry professional who has the career you are interested in pursuing. It is recommended that you seek someone outside of your immediate network. Conduct an informational interview in person, over the phone, or via Skype. Sample questions guiding this interview may include: (a) How did you start out in the sports industry? (b) What specific skills are required in your current position? (c) What is the most rewarding aspect of this job? (d) What parts of your current position do you find most challenging? (e) Could you describe your typical week? (f) What advice would you give someone who wants to work in this field? Summarize your interviewee's responses and reflect upon this information to gain a better understanding of your professional career planning.

_____

_____

_____

_____

_____

_____

_____

_____

_____

_____

_____

_____

_____

Name: _____ Section: _____ Date _____

HSES 289
Introduction to Sport Management
In-Class Quiz and Activity Sheet

Name (or names if done in a group)

Answer #1

Answer #2

Answer #3

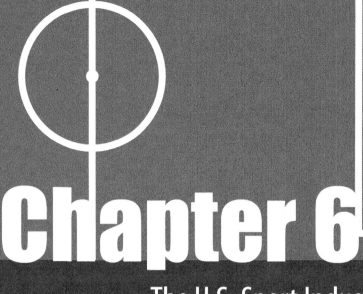
© vectorEps/Shutterstock.com

Chapter 6

The U.S. Sport Industry

Mark S. Nagel • *University of South Carolina*

KEY TERMS

College Football Playoff

Cost of attendance

Football Bowl Subdivision

Football Championship Subdivision

Independent teams

Licensed merchandise

Power 5 Conference

Icon Sportswire/Getty Images

Introduction

The vast majority of entry-level sport-management students will answer the question "What do you want to do in your sport-management career" with one of the following responses:

1. "Become a general manager of a franchise in the National Basketball Association (NBA), National Football League (NFL), National Hockey League (NHL), or Major League Baseball (MLB)."
2. "Become an athletic director at a National Collegiate Athletic Association (NCAA) Division-I athletic department, preferably one that is a member of one of the largest conferences (Big 10, Big 12, ACC, SEC, or PAC-12)."
3. "Become a player agent."

While each of these choices is a potential career option, they are certainly not indicative of the breadth of the sport-management industry. The above-listed positions typically generate extensive media attention, so most students, parents, and non-sport-management faculty tend to think sport-management graduates primarily work in these subsectors of the industry. Though positions in these areas do exist, there are usually few such entry-level positions available and higher-ranking positions are especially scarce. For instance, there are only 32 NFL teams, meaning there are only 32 NFL general managers. Mathematically, students have a higher likelihood of becoming a member of the U.S. Congress than of becoming an NFL, NBA, NHL, or MLB general manager.

In addition to there being few opportunities, general managers, athletic directors, or prominent player agents are often people who were high-level athletes. Though certainly not a requirement, being a well-known former athlete can often provide a springboard to eventual success as a general manager, athletic director, or player agent. It is wonderful if a student desires to someday obtain one of these positions, and, while students should not be discouraged from pursuing a career path with these eventual outcomes as the primary goal, they should understand the reality of the situation. Becoming a NCAA Division-I athletic director, general manager, or prominent sport agent requires intellect, determination, countless hours of learning, and years of preparation. Though it is highly unlikely that obtaining one of those positions will occur, by setting an "ultimate" goal, along with smaller goals that serve as steps along the way, either that final goal will be achieved or other career opportunities will present themselves. While this advice may seem "cliché-like," it is actually true.

This chapter discusses various subsectors of the sport industry that may provide internship opportunities and eventual employment. It is designed to provide students with a broader perspective of the industry than a "traditional" view of sport management that consists of only involving college and professional sport employment or becoming an agent. The categories are certainly not exhaustive as the sport industry is constantly evolving, with new subsectors emerging almost daily. Regardless of your career path (Just a note: By enrolling in a sport-management class your career has already begun!), be prepared to work long hours in order to achieve your career goals. Remember, your career will not develop overnight. The adage, "You learn in your 20s and begin to earn in your 30s" is certainly applicable to the sport-management industry. Maintain your focus while working diligently and good things will eventually happen.

Professional Sport

Professional sport franchises have two distinct sets of employees. The "talent" side of the organization deals with preparing the team to achieve on-field success. The general manager, player-personnel director, coaches, full-time scouts (and certainly the players) usually receive salaries considerably higher than those earned by employees on the organization's "business" side. Players, coaches, and general managers also typically receive extensive media attention and are readily identified by fans and many members of the team's local community. The desire to work on the "talent" side of professional sports is what initially attracts many students to sport-management programs. However, in the vast majority of cases, sport-management students will be hired to work in the business side of the organization. It is certainly possible, but extremely rare, for a sport-management student who is not a former college or professional sport player to be hired by a professional sport franchise to work on the "talent" side of the organization. Most sport-management students who work for a professional sport franchise will be employed in one or more of a variety of sport business areas (marketing, finance, game operations, sales, etc.).

When most students think of working in professional sports, they focus upon the NBA, NHL, NFL, and MLB as likely employers. These leagues tend to attract large fan bases and have games that are often televised. Potential internship or employment openings at these organizations usually attract hundreds of applicants and therefore have extremely low salaries. Much of the "compensation" for working for a franchise in one of these leagues is the ability to say that you work for the team. Sport franchises realize there are often hundreds of potential employees who would "love" to work for their organization, so they often keep salaries low and demand long working hours, particularly for those employees who have been with the team for less than five years.

Professional sport franchises from the "Big 4" leagues tend to have distinct compartmentalized divisions in marketing, sales, game operations, finance, media relations, human resources, and law. Interns or entry-level employees hired to work for these teams may find they work almost exclusively in one area and do not get exposed to many facets of the organization. Working exclusively in the marketing department certainly enables an intern or entry-level employee to learn detailed aspects of marketing, but it may not be conducive to understanding how the other departments interact in order for the franchise to operate effectively.

Though not nearly as popular as teams in the "Big 4" sports leagues, there are many other professional-sport franchises. Sports such as soccer, lacrosse, and volleyball have financially viable professional leagues, and the NBA, NHL, and MLB also have extensive minor-league systems where clubs may be owned and operated by the major-league franchise or owned and operated by an independent owner. In baseball, there are also **independent teams** that operate without the direct support (in the form of players) of a major-league affiliate. Most students do not initially consider a career working with franchises other than those in the "Big 4" leagues, but often there are much greater career advancement opportunities in these situations.

Independent teams
Baseball teams that operate without a direct affiliation with any Major League Baseball franchise.

For instance, though not the norm, it is not uncommon for general managers of minor-league baseball teams to be hired prior to reaching their 35th birthday. It is also not uncommon for talented interns to be promoted quickly after an internship with a "minor league" franchise. There are many prominent sport managers who have achieved great success in (so-called) minor-league sport, who refuse "major-league" job offers because their "minor-league" careers are fulfilling.

Since the team's overall staff is much smaller, minor-league sports franchise employees (including interns) typically have multiple areas of responsibility within the organization. For instance, an NBA team will likely have at least five marketing department staff members. Each employee will likely have a narrowly defined job description. However, an NBA D-League franchise will have a much smaller marketing staff that will, most likely, have daily interaction with members of many different departments. By being thoroughly exposed to the smaller organization's various facets, skills are developed that can be applied to future work activities. Even more prominent minor league sports, such as Triple-A teams in minor-league baseball, will present opportunities for employees to see and understand how the various aspects of the organization function. For instance, it is not uncommon for every member of a minor-league franchise, including the general manager, to help pull the tarp during rain delays.

In addition, the world of professional sports is not limited to "team" sports. There are numerous organizations that operate tournaments for professional athletes in sports such as tennis, golf, fishing, boxing, mixed martial arts, and track and field. Though events such as the U.S. Open Tennis Championship or Professional Golf Association (PGA) Championship garner extensive media attention, there are other internship and employment opportunities in these sports, since tournaments are held most weekends during the year. Sports such as mixed martial arts and lacrosse have only recently launched viable leagues, but they are growing—in both popularity and employment opportunities.

The growth of NASCAR over the past 15 years is an excellent example of an emerging professional sport and the potential for growth. For many years, automobile racing was seen as a niche sport in the United States, with little national interest beyond the Indianapolis 500 each spring. Until the 1990s, NASCAR was perceived primarily as a "southern" sport that did not generate much national media attention. However, as NASCAR racing became more popular, various NASCAR employees were recognized for their expertise in a variety of sport-business areas, particularly sponsorship sales and fulfillment. While NASCAR has recently faced numerous challenges, with a concurrent slowdown in television ratings and revenue, its rise as a "major-league" sport is an indication that "niche" professional sport organizations can provide excellent employment opportunities.

Though working for a team is certainly one of the most popular potential sport-management careers, professional-sport opportunities are not limited to team-sport franchises. Each professional-sport league has a league office. League office employees are charged with creating a fair environment for all league participants, enhancing the league's brand, and developing league revenue sources. Most leagues have a commissioner or league president who oversees the league office. For instance, Major League Baseball has a commissioner who hires a staff that schedules games, hires and supervises umpires, negotiates media contracts, and markets the league. Minor League Baseball (MiLB) has a president responsible for all of the affiliated minor-league baseball teams. In addition, each minor league (Midwest League,

Southern League, etc.) has a president who hires and manages a full-time staff, as well as league interns.

Working for a professional sport league does not offer the emotional highs and lows associated with an individual franchise, because team employees have a vested interest in each game's results. The day-to-day excitement of working for an individual franchise can be intense, especially at the end of the season when a team is in the playoffs. Though "business-office" staff members do not directly influence the outcome on the field, they certainly contribute to franchise success by marketing to fans and providing a positive game-day experience. In recognition of their contributions, most professional sport organizations reward all full-time employees, not just the coaches and players, with rings and other awards if the team wins a championship.

To truly understand the professional-sport environment and to determine if it is a good fit, students should seek volunteer and internship opportunities with individual franchises—as well as league offices. It certainly is appropriate to pursue positions with a "major-league" franchise or league, if that is your primary goal, but do not fail to at least consider a "minor-league" position, since many wonderful career opportunities are available.

College Sport

When most people think of intercollegiate athletics, they tend to focus upon **Football Bowl Subdivision** (FBS) football playoffs and bowls and the NCAA Division-I Men's and Women's Basketball Tournaments. Though these are certainly the most-watched college athletic events, they are a small fraction of the total opportunities in college athletics. The NCAA is divided into three divisions (I, II, III). Currently, there are over 1,100 member schools with 351 in Division I, 320 in Division II, and 450 in Division III. The NCAA organizes championships in 23 different sports with schools offering opportunities for men and women to compete.

To be eligible to be a member of Division I, an institution must offer at least seven sports for men and seven for women (or six for men and eight for women) with at least two team sports for each gender. Division-I members may offer athletic scholarships and most schools recruit potential athletes from various regions of the country. Though nearly every Division-I athletic department is part of a regional conference, most teams schedule some competition with schools outside of their immediate geographic area. Division-II institutions must sponsor at least five sports for men and five for women (or four for men and six for women) with two team sports for each gender. Though Division-II institutions may offer athletic scholarships, their recruitment efforts are usually regionally based. In addition, athletic-competition travel tends to be local or regional. Division-III institutions must offer at least five sports for men and five for women. They are not permitted to offer athletic scholarships ("Divisional difference and . . .," n.d.).

Division I is further separated into three divisions (formerly known as IA, IAA, IAAA). Division-IA institutions that offer "big-time" football compete in the Football Bowl Subdivision (FBS), while D-IAA schools—now **Football Championship Subdivision** (FCS)—do not provide as high a financial commitment to their football programs. Division IAAA members do not field D-I football teams. It is important to remember that all Division-I schools compete for the same championships in

Football Bowl Subdivision
A segment of the National Collegiate Athletic Association that is comprised of schools playing the highest level of football (formerly known as Division IA).

Football Championship Subdivision
A segment of the National Collegiate Athletic Association that is comprised of Division-I schools that are not playing at the highest level of football competition (formerly known as Division IAA).

Division-I football teams usually compete in large stadiums, whereas Division-II or Division-III programs typically have much smaller facilities.

Source: Mark Nagel

all sports besides football. Except for a few rare instances, schools must compete at the same level for all of their sports. Such instances are often in Olympic sports (skiing, hockey, wrestling, etc.).

In 2014, the NCAA Bowl Championship Subdivision further split as a new model permitted **Power 5 Conferences** to create some of their own rules. Leaders of many of the athletic departments in the Power 5 Conferences noted that NCAA rules limiting full scholarships below **the cost of attendance** were inappropriate for most of the top athletic programs as they generated sufficient revenue to compensate their profit athletes with additional monies. The decision to permit greater autonomy to Power 5 Conferences coincided with the first ever College Football Playoff after the 2014 season.

The various NCAA divisions roughly approximate varying philosophical perspectives and financial commitments to intercollegiate athletics. Division-I programs tend to provide coaches with greater financial resources for scholarships, personnel, and equipment; upgraded facilities; large travel budgets; and extensive opportunities to compete against other schools across the nation. Most Division-II institutions offer athletic-related scholarships across a variety of sports, but travel and expenses are typically much lower than in Division I. Division-III members, while still committed to intercollegiate athletic competition, in most instances have deemphasized a highly commercialized approach to college sport. According to the division's mission statement, member institutions prohibit athletic-related scholarships and ". . . place special importance on the impact of athletics on the participants rather than on the spectators. The student-athlete's experience is of paramount concern" ("Divisional differences and. . .," n.d., para. 3).

Most NCAA members have maintained their current affiliation for many years. However, each year a handful of members attempt to move divisions. In most cases, the movement is prompted by a desire to enhance athletic commitment and "upgrade" to a higher division. Most schools rationalize such a move (from Division III to Division II or from Division II to Division I) as a means to enhance the institution's "marketability" and focus on the potentially drastic increases in athletic revenue. Competing at a high level of intercollegiate athletics is perceived by many to be critical to attracting and retaining students, since competing at the Division I-level offers a greater opportunity to be mentioned on ESPN's *SportsCenter* and in other media outlets. Though examining the specifics regarding the costs and benefits of moving up a division is beyond the scope of this chapter and book, a focus on athletic-department expansion and increased use of college sport as a marketing platform has resulted in concern among many faculty, students, alumni, and administrators regarding institutional priorities. These concerns have resulted in a small number of schools "downgrading" their NCAA status. Recently, Birmingham Southern College realized an increase in overall athletic participation and an increase in campus minority enrollment, university giving, and applicant quality after it moved from Division I to Division III.

Though the importance placed upon winning and academic achievement may differ by sport and NCAA division, regardless of division, athletic directors' and athletic department staff roles are similar. Athletic directors are expected to hire coaches and other staff members, manage an athletic department's budget, generate revenues to ensure the department's financial viability, and interact with various on- and off-campus constituencies. Reflecting the enhanced commitment to the business of intercollegiate athletics, the vast majority of coaches and athletic department personnel who work at Division-I institutions tend to not maintain formal roles in other areas of the university. However, at many Division-II and (especially) D-III institutions, coaches and athletic department staff members often teach classes and assume other campus roles.

Students wishing to eventually work in college athletics should develop and fully understand their personal philosophy of the relationship between athletics and academics before pursuing potential college-sport internships. At Division-I institutions, a primary focus (and some would argue the only focus) is winning. Athletes' education and character development, while still ostensibly important, are often secondary, particularly in revenue-generating sports. At the Division-II and Division-III levels facilities typically are not as lavish, and media attention is often nonexistent. As a result, there is often less commercial intrusion, which may allow athletes to maintain more focus on their academic and social development. At most Division-III institutions, coaches and administrators are evaluated primarily on how well their program contributes to students' education.

The Division-I focus on winning, particularly in revenue sports, is not necessarily a "bad" thing, but sport-management students must attempt to ensure that philosophy and expectations match a university's mission and goals. If a student's personal values are incongruent with those of the athletic department in which they work, frustration often occurs. Having a general idea of expectations and the work environment prior to taking a job in college athletics can alleviate potential philosophical disagreements.

Though most students seeking employment in college athletics will gravitate toward a job at an individual school, there are additional administrative positions available at the NCAA as well as other college-sport-governing bodies. Each Division-I conference maintains a league office and employs a full-time staff. Certainly, conferences such as the Southeastern Conference (SEC) and the Big Ten Conference have many more staff members than the West Coast Conference (WCC) or the Western Athletic Conference (WAC), but all conference employees attempt to market the conferences' brand and enhance athletic-related revenue streams. Much like working for a professional sport league, NCAA and conference administrators will not have the emotional highs and lows of individual school employees.

There are also opportunities outside of the NCAA umbrella. The National Association of Intercollegiate Athletics (NAIA) governs sport activities for member NAIA schools. Though not as large as the NCAA, the NAIA currently has over 260 member institutions, and organizes championships in 13 sports. The NAIA maintains a full-time staff that works to organize championships and market NAIA members. In addition, though their athletic departments will likely be small compared to NCAA Division-I institutions, every NAIA school will have athletic employment opportunities.

Intercollegiate athletics opportunities are also offered at many junior colleges. Junior college athletic department administrators are also often members of the physical education faculty. Since junior colleges typically attract students from the local area, rather than from throughout the country, such athletic department budgets are often much more limited. However, many states organize championships for a variety of sports at the junior college level. These championships can attract local media attention and fans. The National Junior College Athletic Association (NJCAA) works to promote the efforts of junior college athletics.

College-Sport License Holders

The development and expansion of the business of intercollegiate athletics has resulted in the proliferation of numerous college-sport marketing companies. Since many athletic departments do not have adequate personnel with the expertise to evaluate and sell sponsorship inventory, negotiate media rights to athletic department content, and seek advertisers, they often partner with third-party license holders. As these license holders have proliferated, they have provided excellent internship and employment opportunities for sport-management students.

There are a variety of college-sport licensees. One of the most important people in the development of this subindustry is Jim Host. In the 1970s, Host established Jim Host & Associates, which provided assistance to college athletic departments looking to outsource some or all of their marketing activities. After initially working with the University of Kentucky, Host's company became more and more successful. As Host expanded his influence throughout the industry, other competitors entered the marketplace. In the early 2000s, prominent college sport-marketing companies included ISP Sports, Learfield Sports Properties, and Nelligan Sports Marketing, Inc.

Licensed merchandise
Granting another entity the right to produce products that bear a trademarked logo.

In 2007, International Management Group (IMG) purchased Host Communications and combined it with the recently acquired Collegiate Licensing Company (CLC), an entity that had initially been established to assist colleges and universities to create and expand their **licensed merchandise** sales, to form IMG College. The merger established IMG College as the nation's largest provider of marketing services to the college-sport industry. In 2014, JMI Sports acquired the rights to the University of Kentucky athletic department with a $210 million deal (Rovell, 2014). Despite the dominance of IMG College, it is likely that other entities will continue to enter the college rights holder industry.

Though the aforementioned companies provide a variety of marketing services to college athletic departments, there continues to be new opportunities for college-sport consulting. In 2009, Georgia Tech hired the Aspire Group to organize its ticket sales for football and men's basketball games. It was believed to be the first time an athletic department outsourced its ticketing operations to a third party (Lombardo & Smith, 2009). Since then, it has expanded its client list to include dozens of colleges and professional sports teams, and some sport leagues. It is likely many future employment opportunities in college athletics will involve working for an outside entity, rather than directly for the athletic department.

Youth Sports

Professional and intercollegiate athletics typically generate significantly higher attendance and greater media attention than organized youth sports; however, over the past 10 years high-school athletics has become dramatically more commercialized. At many high schools, since the athletic director is no longer expected to teach classes, his/her energy can be fully devoted to selling tickets, executing fund-raising initiatives, seeking sponsorship agreements, and raising awareness of the high school's athletic exploits in the media. High-school football and basketball games are increasingly being broadcast on local or regional television and radio stations, or sport networks. In addition, ESPN has recently dramatically increased its coverage of selected games. It is not uncommon for prominent high-school athletic teams to travel via airplane to participate in prestigious tournaments. As many high-school athletic departments have begun to model their structure and activities after prominent colleges, athletic directors with advanced sport-business skills are needed.

Other youth sport activities have also recently seen dramatic changes. Little League Baseball and the Amateur Athletic Union (AAU) have long attracted thousands of participants, but the scheduling and marketing of their athletic contests now mimics commercialized sport properties. Not only are Little League World Series games televised live on ESPN, but most regional championships are also covered extensively by the media. AAU tournaments in a variety of sports no longer merely attract parents and close friends of the participants. With much of the college recruiting for some sports (such as basketball and volleyball) occurring during summer AAU tournaments, fans have begun to attend, and media outlets have begun to cover, some of these events in the hopes of seeing the "next" great college players before they have graduated from high school.

With the growing emphasis on commercialized youth sports, parents now often insist that their children's sporting activities be organized and operated like "professional" sport entities. Some affluent parents have also retained "performance" coaches to work with their child—in some cases before their son or daughter has enrolled in junior high school. The increased emphasis that parents have placed upon organized, elite youth-sport activities is of grave concern to many people. During much of the 20th century young kids participated in athletics without direct parental organization or supervision (Coakley, 2009). Sport was as much about "play" as it was about winning. Participants (children) often amended rules to allow for a more competitive and "fun" environment. While some sociologists lament the current state of youth sports, with today's emphasis on adult-organized and-directed youth sports, there are opportunities for sport-management graduates to establish, organize, and promote youth-sport events.

Olympic Sports

In 1896 the first "modern" Olympic Games took place in Athens, Greece. Though the "first" Olympics attracted "only" 14 nations and 241 athletes, the games slowly expanded during the first half of the 20th century. Since it was impractical to hold competitions for many popular sports, such as skiing and ice-skating, during the summer, in 1924 the first Winter Olympic Games were held in Chamonix, France. As the Olympics continued to attract larger contingents of athletes and greater media attention, they became an outlet for countries' nationalism. During the 1936 Summer Olympics in Berlin, the Nazi Party utilized the Games as the focal point to demonstrate the "rebirth" of Germany after World War I. Despite Adolf Hitler's propaganda campaign about the Aryan "master race," U.S. track star Jesse Owens won four gold medals to become the hero of the 1936 Olympics.

Though the popularity of the Olympics grew following World War II, many Olympic Games have been marred by tragedy, financial problems, and political turmoil. During the 1972 Munich Games, members of the Israeli Olympic team were taken hostage and eventually murdered by Black September, a militant group with ties to the Palestinian Fatah organization. By the end of the ordeal, the death toll stood at 17. The terrorists eventually killed eleven Israeli athletes and coaches and one West German police officer. Five of the eight Black September members were killed during a failed rescue attempt. Though certainly not as tragic as the loss of life in Munich, the 1976 Montreal Games were a financial disaster as millions of dollars of facility investments required decades for the citizens of Montreal and the rest of Canada to repay. At the height of the "Cold War," the United States and many of its allies boycotted the 1980 Moscow Games in protest of the Soviet Union's invasion of Afghanistan. By 1984, there was considerable concern about the financial viability of the Los Angeles Games, especially after the Soviet Union and other "Eastern Bloc" countries boycotted the Games in retaliation for the 1980 boycott. Despite concerns, the financial and marketing success of the 1984 Summer Olympics changed the Olympic movement.

Peter Ueberroth served as the Executive Director of the 1984 Summer Olympics. Where all of the proceeding Olympic Games were primarily financed and operated by government entities, Ueberroth organized the Los Angeles Games as a private entity. Ueberroth managed the Olympics as a separate, stand-alone business and he

solicited extensive sponsorship and licensed merchandise sales to generate revenue. The Los Angeles Olympics was such a financial success that Ueberroth was named *Time Magazine's* Man of the Year. Cities and countries that had viewed hosting the Olympics as a financial risk, changed their opinion of hosting future games. The Los Angeles Olympics caused many worldwide sporting events to become "mega-events" requiring extensive and highly-trained staffs in order to solicit bids, develop financial plans, schedule facilities, organize event employees, and maximize revenue opportunities. Today, sport-management students have the opportunity to pursue an Olympics-based career, whether working for the International Olympic Committee (IOC), U.S. Olympic Committee (USOC), one of the USOC's national sport governing bodies (NGO), or for a potential host city.

The Olympic Games are not the only mega-event to attract competitors and spectators from throughout the world. In 1948 Sir Ludwig Guttman organized the first sport competition for injured soldiers from World War II. Guttman's event would grow and eventually be called the Paralympics. Starting in 1988 with the Seoul Olympics, the Paralympics have been held in the Olympic host city shortly after the Olympic Games have concluded. The Paralympics, as well as other sporting events for the disabled, have grown in popularity. Much like the Olympics, the Paralympics must be organized and managed. With thousands of athletes and spectators attending, there are numerous career opportunities in this area.

Sport Facilities

Regardless of the size or scope of a sporting event, facilities will be needed to ensure the event is successful. Even outdoor events, such as cross-country races, require facilities for spectators, members of the media, and race officials. Certainly, major professional sports facilities and Division-I athletic-department facilities receive considerable media attention, but there are also many potential career opportunities associated with smaller venues. As discussed in Chapter 12, sport facilities may include stadiums (both indoor, outdoor, and retractable roofed) for events such as football and soccer games, arenas for events such as basketball and volleyball games and facilities designed specifically for sports such as tennis, swimming, auto racing, horse racing, and dog racing.

Though high-profile "competitive" sport facilities tend to initially attract sport-management students, there are also numerous opportunities to work in recreation and fitness facilities. Most communities have private and publicly-owned recreation centers that offer general recreation opportunities as well as scheduled events such as tournaments. Over the past 10 years, colleges and universities have come to realize on-campus recreation centers can be utilized to recruit and retain students (as well as faculty and staff). Most campuses have at least one recreation center, and offer extensive intramural programs. Military bases, both in the United States and throughout the world, also offer recreation opportunities. Community recreation centers, like other facilities, require professional, part-time, and volunteer staff members to ensure operational efficiency. Employees at all venue types establish budgets, organize programs, ensure the safety of equipment, and attract and retain customers.

Over the last 15 years, as the importance and complexity of managing sport facilities has increased, numerous private management companies have offered sport facility-management services. Though there are numerous private management companies that offer such full-scale management, three organizations currently dominate the marketplace. SMG World is the leading provider of management for arenas, convention centers, stadiums, and theatres throughout the world. It currently manages 10+ stadiums, 60+ theatres, 60+ convention centers, and 65+ arenas, with more than 1.5 million seats. SMG continues to expand its operations and influence in the sport facility marketplace.

Global Spectrum, a division of the Philadelphia-based sports and entertainment company Comcast-Spectacor, has dramatically increased its presence and influence in the industry over the past 15 years. Global Spectrum presently manages over 100 venues throughout the world; and is expanding its global presence, with offices in the United States, Canada, the United Kingdom, and Singapore.

AEG Live has only recently begun soliciting facility-management contracts as it has a long history of presenting live music and other entertainment events. AEG Live has signed contracts with some of the top-grossing facilities in the world. It currently oversees the development of L.A. Live, a 4-million-square-foot, $2.5 billion sport, residential, and entertainment district. AEG has committed to expanding its presence in the sport facility-management field.

Each of these companies offers extensive internship and entry-level employment opportunities. Since SMG, Global Spectrum, and AEG manage multiple facilities around the world, there are tremendous opportunities to advance your career, if you are able and willing to relocate. It is not uncommon for these companies to "fast-track" exceptional students from internships to full-time employment and from entry-level employment to middle management.

In addition to full-service facility-management companies, there are also potential sport-management employment opportunities in firms that offer specific services in subsectors of facility management. Since selling food and beverages is a critical revenue stream for most sporting events, many facilities have outsourced concession-sales responsibilities to private companies. Though there are many food-service companies, a few dominate the marketplace. Aramark is the largest sport concessionaire and it continues to expand its presence in the United States and international markets. Other prominent concessionaires include Centerplate, Delaware North Sportservice, Levy, and Ovations Food Services (owned and operated by Comcast Spectacor). Much like the large full-scale facility management companies, these concessionaires have multiple accounts across the country, providing employees many opportunities for career advancement.

Though crowd safety has always been an important issue, after the terrorist attacks on 9/11 most facilities and events realized they needed to reassess their crowd-management practices. There are many companies that work directly or indirectly with sporting events to create a safe environment. Contemporary Services Corporation (CSC) is the best known. With multiple offices throughout the United States and accounts with many of the top college and professional sport teams, CSC is a leader in providing staffing for sport-event crowd management.

Most live sport events require patrons to purchase tickets to gain entry to the facility. For many years, tickets were sold primarily at a facility's box office. By the 1970s, tickets could be purchased over the phone with a credit card, but the sales process was still inefficient. In 1976, two Arizona State students founded Ticketmaster—a company that designed software that allowed for "remote" ticket sales. In the 1980s, as Ticketmaster developed and enhanced its technology, it quickly became the industry leader. With the proliferation of the Internet in the 1990s, Ticketmaster captured nearly the entire sport and entertainment ticketing industry. In 2010, it merged with Live Nation. Though many students may not have an interest in working for Ticketmaster, it is important to understand how its operations impact nearly every aspect of live sport and entertainment events.

There are a variety of other employment opportunities in sport facility and event management. Sport events cannot function without office equipment, landscaping, trash removal, and a myriad of other services. There are many lesser-known companies that work intimately within the sport industry. In addition, there are companies that have not even been established that will provide future employment opportunities. For instance, in 1981 Sports Team Analysis and Tracking Systems (STATS, Inc.) was established by John Dewan. In the early 1980s, statistical analysis (particularly in sports) was often seen as a "fringe" activity reserved solely for "nerds." Since 1981 the importance of sport statistical analysis (as well as statistical analysis in all aspects of business) has grown tremendously and companies such as STATS, Inc. (now STATS LLC) play an important role in the industry. Many students reading this book will likely have ideas for aspects of the sport industry that have not yet been contemplated. Do not discount emerging ideas or companies as they may become a critical component of the sport industry in the future!

Licensed Merchandise

In the 1950s, New York Yankee's General Manager George Weiss was asked about having a Yankee Cap Day. He supposedly replied, "Do you think I want kids in New York wearing Yankee hats?" Certainly, the use of team or league logos on hats, shirts, jackets, sweaters, and various other articles of clothing and other products has greatly expanded since the 1950s. Today, any sport executive would welcome the opportunity for logoed merchandise to be worn by fans, especially when the fans pay for the "privilege" of being associated with the sport organization.

Most teams, leagues, and athletic department sell licenses that permit third parties to produce various products that display a sport organization's name and logo. The profit margin on sales of licensed merchandise can be quite high. One only has to look at the price of a plain sweatshirt sold at a department store, and compare it to the price of a sweatshirt bearing a college or university logo, to see the profits generated through licensed merchandise sales. The cost of ink is likely pennies, but the addition of a school logo on a plain piece of clothing can double, triple, or even quadruple the product's price!

Licensed merchandise sales are a critical component of most sport organizations' revenue plans. The tremendous profit margins available through the sale of licensed merchandise have led most sport organizations to devote at least one employee to this area. For extremely popular sport teams, an entire franchise division or functional area may work to investigate potential licensing opportunities, negotiate licensing contracts, and ensure that counterfeit merchandise is not sold. In order to maximize profits, sport leagues typically create league-wide licensing agreements. These league agreements typically disburse revenues to each team, which enables every team (though their individual sales may fluctuate each year due to team performance and other factors) to receive a more consistent revenue stream.

Companies that design and sell apparel have been interested in utilizing sport logos for many years. Recently, various nontraditional products and services have sought associations with sport organizations. Some college athletic departments offer their fans the opportunity to purchase licensed products as varied as seat cushions, plates, silverware, glasses, futons, toilet seat covers, DVDs, photographs, and other new-media products. Some schools and professional sport franchises have even begun offering officially licensed urns and coffins for fans who wish to be buried in "their" school or team colors (Jones, 2008).

Sport Media

Sport events typically attract the attention of fans, and therefore are often covered by various media outlets. Certainly, sport organizations seek to maximize media exposure. Most hire employees to work with the media to generate positive publicity. In addition, media-relations departments must also prepare and handle potential crises that develop. An organization that is not prepared for a crisis will likely experience significant negative feedback from fans and other constituents who view the sport entity as unprepared, uncaring, or unprofessional in their dealings with the media.

The media industry has changed dramatically over the past 100 years. The primary mode of information gathering for most sport consumers has progressed from newspapers to radio to television to the Internet. Changes in media platforms have resulted in employment opportunities and in alterations to some established sport norms. In addition to a proliferation of satellite and cable TV networks and delivery options, many professional and college leagues and conferences now have their own cable sports networks. The NFL, NBA, and MLB all have their own networks. The Mountain West Conference (Mtn) and Big Ten Conference (Big Ten Network) led the way in college sport in the early 2000s, with other conferences creating their own networks, including the SEC starting theirs in 2014. Individual franchises (such as the New York Yankees with the YES Network) as well as individual schools (such as the University of Texas) have developed their own cable networks.

The Internet's "viral" nature (through the sharing of files, video-sharing websites, blogs, digital networks, and "old-fashioned" email) has enabled bloggers to wield significant influence in the sport industry. For many years, many sport franchises did not view Internet writers as "real" journalists. Today, most teams have begun to recognize prominent bloggers are an important part of their media constituencies. As technology continues to evolve, the need for sport organizations to tell their "story" through the media will not change, but the platforms by which that story is conveyed will undoubtedly be much different. Students seeking employment in sport media should understand the unique nature of sport media relations, and prepare for continued rapid changes in the future.

Sports Agents

Though being a "player agent" is probably the number-one career non-sport-management people think of when sport management is mentioned, an infinitesimal fraction of sport-management students will ever work as a player agent. Though multimillion-dollar athlete contracts and movies like *Jerry Maguire* make the layperson think there are numerous player agents and many of them are financially successful, in reality only a few player agents make substantial salaries. For every Scott Boras, Drew Rosenhaus, or David Falk, there are thousands of other agents who have considerably more dreams than clients. In many years, the reported number of agents exceeds the number of players in several sports. Leigh Steinberg was once a prominent agent who fell from grace due to alcoholism and other personal problems. He has written a book describing his own career path and the struggles agents face in a cutthroat industry.

Though the player-agent industry now involves millions of dollars, the first athlete-agent agreement began with little more than a handshake. In 1960, Attorney Mark McCormack noticed that golfer Arnold Palmer had established his career as a successful performer. With television rapidly increasing its coverage of golf tournaments, McCormack approached Palmer about managing his endorsement opportunities. McCormack's success with Palmer's career attracted other golfers such as Jack Nicklaus and Gary Player. McCormack's agency, IMG, would eventually sign numerous other golfers and tennis players. Later, IMG expanded its agency to represent athletes from other sports, as well as entertainers, politicians, and models. IMG also began to manage sport and entertainment events.

The success of McCormack and IMG led other individuals to work in the player-agent business. During the 1970s, numerous attorneys expanded their business to include athlete representation. As the value of player contracts escalated in the 1980s, many individuals became full-time agents rather than attorneys who "also" represented athletes. In the 1990s many prominent agents began to expand their client services. Instead of merely negotiating player contracts, most large agencies began to design marketing and sponsorship campaigns; offer financial advice; retain nutritionists, personal trainers, and sport psychologists; and perform statistical analysis of their clients' athletic performance. Currently, most "successful" agents represent many clients and allow their past successes to supplement their recruiting efforts.

Becoming a prominent player agent is one of the most difficult sport-career paths. Competition within the industry is fierce, with some agents notoriously circumventing established rules, laws, and ethical guidelines (see Chapter 5) to attract clients. The actions of players, coaches, parents, and "advisors" can make the life of an agent difficult—particularly since most agents rely on their commission as a primary source of income and are therefore usually not in a position to say "No" to most requests. Few sport-management students realize an agent's long hours, tough working conditions, and stressful lifestyle. Students wishing to become an agent should seek opportunities to work for an established agency. Though most agents are reluctant to share their secrets regarding recruitment and retention of clients—for fear of training someone to eventually become their competition—there are typically opportunities to work for agents doing a variety of tasks such as coordinating athlete appearances and researching marketing opportunities. Students who desire to become an agent should not abandon that dream, but should realize the incredibly tough environment in which player agents operate.

Athlete Foundations

With the large salaries that some professional athletes earn, there is often a pressure to "give back" to the community. Most prominent athletes have either established charitable foundations or work closely with organizations that attempt to enhance the livelihood of various constituents. Athletes can generate positive publicity through their charitable work with schools, hospitals, and other entities that serve the community. There are potential internship and employment opportunities working for athlete foundations. This has become especially important over the past 10 years as many athletes have been publicly chastised and, in some cases prosecuted, for allowing family members and close friends to improperly operate their charitable foundation. With an increased emphasis on operating athlete foundations as a legitimate non-profit organization, many of these organizations have sought sport-management students for internships and entry-level employment.

Sport Tourism

Though tourism is one of the world's oldest industries, many components of organized sport tourism in the United States have only been developed in the past 30 years. In the United States, the 1904 St. Louis (Missouri) World's Fair was organized in concert with the 1904 Olympic Games. Hosting both events was designed to maximize the number of tourists who would visit St. Louis. Despite the success of the 1904 Olympics, most sport events in the first third of the 20th century were primarily viewed as "local" events. However, during the height of the Great Depression, the 1932 Los Angeles Olympics attracted many spectators who spent money in the Los Angeles area. In 1939, the National Baseball Hall of Fame and Museum was opened in Cooperstown, New York. Despite the ongoing economic depression, the induction of the first class of baseball hall of famers generated substantial onsite attendance and national media attention. Other sports and leagues would later establish their own Halls of Fame to attract tourists.

The San Jose Sports Authority works to bring events such as the Rock 'n' Roll San Jose Half Marathon, with an estimated economic impact of over $16 million annually, to San Jose.

Source: David Eadie

In the United States, the link between sports and tourism has continued to grow. Various companies, particularly those in the restaurant, hotel, and car-rental industries, reap economic benefits when sport events attract tourists from outside the community. Tourists who spend money generate "economic impact," which can spur employment opportunities and enhance tax receipts. Certainly, most cities' convention and visitors bureaus attempt to attract as many sport events, and sport tourists, as possible.

Attracting sport events to a local community is perceived to be important enough for many municipalities that agencies specifically tasked with attracting such events have been established. The San Jose Sports Authority (SJSA) is an excellent example of an agency established to attract sport events to a community, in order to attract tourists and generate economic activity. Long overshadowed by San Francisco and Oakland to the north, the City of San Jose established the SJSA in 1991. Since its creation, the SJSA has worked to bring sport events such as the NCAA Division-I Women's Final Four, NCAA Division-I Men's Basketball Western Regional Finals, Major League Soccer All-Star Game, Siebel Classic (Senior PGA event), and numerous U.S. Olympic trials to San Jose.

There are numerous opportunities to work in sport tourism and new opportunities are continually being developed. Recently, travel companies have developed sport tourism packages that offer organized tours of stadiums and other sport facilities in a variety of cities. It is likely that sport tourism opportunities will continue to expand in the future, making this an important potential outlet for internships and employment opportunities.

Employment Placement

The growth of the sport industry and the proliferation of sport organizations have resulted in the creation of companies that specialize in helping sport-management students find internships and entry-level employment. In addition, many such organizations link established sport management professionals to sport organizations that need specific skills. For instance, TeamWork Online (through its web-based services) assists sport organizations in finding employees and employees finding open sport-management positions. Six Figure Sports is another company that specializes in helping sport organizations seeking employees, but their focus is typically upon executive-level searches. It is likely that as the sport industry continues to develop, additional organizations that provide employment consulting will be established, creating additional sport-management employment opportunities.

Sport Sponsors

The importance of sport sponsorship has grown over the past 20 years—both for sport entities and for local, regional, national, and international companies. With sports becoming a larger component of many individuals' everyday lives, many organizations have realized that they must actively attempt to understand sport sponsorship and its potential costs and benefits. Many Fortune 500 companies have staff members specifically tasked with evaluating sport-sponsorship opportunities. Sport-management graduates often have a unique understanding of what makes a sport athlete, team, league, or event worthwhile for potential sponsorship. Though working in the corporate world may not seem as "exciting" as working for a team or league, there are some potential benefits. Most Fortune 500 companies offer much higher salaries than those in other sport-industry sectors. In addition, though employees are expected to work diligently, especially during sponsored events, there tends to be a more "reasonable" expectation of working hours and better fringe benefits (excluding the opportunity to be a part of a potential championship team). Even if a company does not have a division devoted specifically to sport-sponsorship, most organizations task their marketing staffs with exploring all possible outlets to enhance their brand. There are many sport-management graduates working in "marketing" for non-sport organizations who maintain a close contact to the industry through marketing and sponsorship opportunities.

Conclusion

Opportunities for internships and entry-level employment in the U.S. sport-management industry are extremely diverse. There are myriad avenues for students to pursue. Certainly, developing a knowledge base by studying the industry is important for future success, but understanding the nuances of various subsectors can only be accomplished by working in that industry area. Students should begin to explore potential opportunities immediately, as no employer will ever tell an applicant that they have "too much experience" for a sport-management position.

Learning Activity

Create a list of 25 sport-management professionals who have achieved success in an area you feel you might have interest. Contact each of those professionals and ask to conduct informational interviews so that you can begin to build not only your knowledge base, but also your professional network.

References

Coakley, J. (2009). *Sports in society* (9th ed.). New York: McGraw-Hill.

Divisional differences and the history of multidivisional classification. (n. d.). Retrieved from http://www.ncaa.org/about/who-we-are/membership/divisional-differences -and-history-multidivision-classification

Jones, A. (2008, February 13). Regents board approves logos on coffins. *The Atlanta Journal -Constitution.* Retrieved March 14, 2010 from http://www.ajc.com/metro/content/metro /stories/2008/02/13/coffin_0214.html

Lombardo, J. & Smith, M. (2009, May 25). Ga. Tech hands ticket sales to Aspire Group *SportsBusiness Journal.* Retrieved March 27, 2010 from http://www.sportsbusinessjournal. com/article/62558

Rovell, D. (2014, June 23). UK sells marketing rights to JMI. Retrieved from http://espn.go.com /college-sports/story/_/id/11122483/kentucky-wildcats-sell-marketing-rights-jmi-sports

Jayhawks in the Field

Sean Norris

Elite Account Manager at Hudl

Hometown
Lincoln, NE

Education
UG 2011 – Nebraska Wesleyan University (Sport Management)
G 2014 – University of Kansas (Sport Management)

Previous Positions
Competitive Account Manager at Hudl
Coach Support Specialist at Hudl
Sales Representative at University of Kansas Athletics

1. Hudl has been on the front edge of sport information technology. What about the company was attractive to you and what is "next" in this space?

I have always had an interest in coaching and playing a role in helping teams and athletes improve. With Hudl, I get to work with teams to find and effectively use tools that help them with everything from their pregame preparation, in-game adjustments, and postgame review. Being located in my hometown certainly helped Hudl stand out to me as well.

It's hard to say what exactly is next in this space because it could go so many ways, but we love working with our users to find out what we can do to make their lives easier. This industry is extremely competitive so if we're not continually producing products that add value to our teams, somebody else will.

2. What skills are necessary to work in this unique organization and how would you recommend undergraduate students acquire these skills?

Written and verbal communication skills are the first thing I think of here. Every interaction you have, whether with a client or a colleague, is a representation of yourself and Hudl. Outside of representing yourself, many issues can be simply resolved or avoided by effectively communicating information to the other party. Being an effective communicator will also help you handle the tough conversations better.

The other necessary skill is problem-solving. Most of what I do is figuring out how we can make X work with Y, and vice versa. My best piece of advice with this is to never back away from issues, regardless of the size. Some of my best learning experiences have come from taking on seemingly impossible problems. I would suggest that undergrad students seek and take opportunities to be involved in the sport industry. The more the better. These opportunities—internships, volunteering, part-time jobs, etc.—allow you to interact, connect with, and learn from so many different people. This will help you learn to communicate with many different people. My other piece of advice is to ask questions. It can be difficult to ask questions, but it's the best way to learn. Take the answers you get and apply them to your situation.

3. When you are talking with your current accounts, what are some of their top wants and needs and what products does Hudl use to meet those?

I think the biggest thing we hear is that teams want their different tools to work together so that we can save them time. For instance, I work with a lot of Video Coordinators at the professional and DI level. These guys are working crazy hours during the season adding data to video, picking out the clips to review, and sharing it out with their coaches/team. The last thing they want is tools that aren't going to work together, leading to more work for them. We work to provide them with tools that are effective and efficient—Why do the work twice? It's easy to think, "It'd be great if this all worked together," and not consider the real-life impact it has on these guys. If our tools work together and save them time, it could mean the difference between dinner at home with their family and dinner at the office.

4. What is one day or night during your time at KU you wish you could live again and why?

Any day where I got to work in Allen Fieldhouse! I learned a lot about how athletic departments work in my time working as a Sales Rep at KU. I really miss working the basketball games. Not only is there great energy in the Fieldhouse, but it was also our best way of talking to our clients and learning what they're looking for. Putting a name with a face is always a great way to build a relationship with someone.

5. Describe your typical customer in terms of team size, level, longevity, and use of features. What is the hardest obstacle to overcome when trying to keep an existing or acquire a new account?

I work with what we've defined as the Elite market, the professional and DI teams using our products. Many of these teams have been using Sportscode for quite some time, but the Hudl platform is new to them. Hudl acquired Sportstec in 2015, so one of the main obstacles that I've run into is just explaining to our clients that I'm not somebody spamming them for money! Once we get through that hurdle, it typically comes down to making sure that we're continuing to meet that specific team's needs with the package that they have. Most of this work is done throughout the year. If we wait until it's time for a team to renew to find out that we're not meeting their needs, it's too late. Whether it's renewing an account or acquiring a new one, our products need to be adding value to the team.

6. Describe the favorite parts of your job and give some specific examples if possible.

I really enjoy working with people to solve a problem and building relationships with those people throughout that process. One example is working with a client from the initial discussions about renewing their account to when that account is paid. This process can include everything from reminding them of the value they're getting out of the product, working with them to better utilize the product, and working with their billing department to make sure we receive the money. Often coaches agree to purchase something, then it's out of their hands as they're not the people writing the checks. At this point I've done the work to build a relationship and we're in good light in the coach's mind, it's important to not risk that by making it easy on them from this point forward. The other favorite part of my job is just the people I work with. I have some great coworkers who bring good energy every day and have taught me a ton about a variety of topics. I appreciate emphasis on sharing ideas and challenging each other in the office, I think it helps us reach our potential.

Name: _____   Section: _____   Date _____

HSES 289
Introduction to Sport Management

In-Class Quiz and Activity Sheet

Name (or names if done in a group)

Answer #1

Answer #2

Answer #3

Chapter 7

High School and Youth Sport

Jordan R. Bass • *University of Kansas*

KEY TERMS

Club Sport

Sport Specialization

Socialization

Burnout

Icon Sportswire/Getty Images

© matimix/Shutterstock.com

You'll read statistic after statistic on how many billions of dollars a year are spent in and on the sporting industry. Of these, the one that may shock you most is the youth sport market is a seven-billion-dollar segment . . . in travel alone. A professor at New York University was quoted as saying youth sport was not even considered as a travel and tourism market in 2010 but by 2014 was one of the fastest growing segments. We lead with this anecdote to illustrate that the days of youth sport primarily being neighborhood boys and girls playing pick-up basketball for fun and then playing on their local YMCA team one evening a week are ending.

The mechanics, governance, and desired outcomes of high school and youth sport more closely mirror their collegiate and professional counterparts now more than ever. In this chapter, we will detail the history and trends of high school and youth sport and discuss the consequences of the shift from *sport for fitness/character building/socialization* to *sport for competition*.

Youth Sport

The term "youth sport" is being used here as an umbrella term for physical activity competitions in the pre-high school years. If you research how many young people compete in youth sport, there are a number of varying answers. As one example, in 2016 Project Play estimated close to 40 percent of children ages 6–12 "regularly" played organized team sports, with basketball, baseball, and soccer the most popular team sports. As they noted, this number is actually lower than in 2008; a fact they blame on the increase of money needed to play and compete at ages even as low as six.

As an American society, we largely still view youth sport as a teacher of positive traits that translate into the rest of the player's life. Teamwork, character building, physical fitness, and perseverance are a few of the many reasons parents have for enrolling their children in youth sport programs. Prior to the last decade, the youth sport industry largely operated in the public space where the majority of participation happened in neighborhood, city, or county leagues that were run by municipalities or groups such as the Boys and Girls Club, YMCA, or Parks and Recreation department. This, however, is no longer the case. Entrepreneurs have

fully capitalized on the emphasis we place on sport at the earliest ages and created highly organized, commercialized, and competition heavy youth sport organizations.

Club System

The most common private youth sport structure is the *club system*. In this system, a child joins the club, sometimes as young as three, and progresses within that club as they get older. For example, in Lawrence alone there are multiple swimming clubs. The "Lawrence Aquahawks" start as young as four years old with their *swim academy* where athletes (it sounds weird calling a four-year-old an athlete, I know) progress from the Explorer group as a beginner and can stay with the club all the way to the *Senior Level* when they reach high school (see figure below).

Basketball, baseball, soccer, and most every other sport have similar systems that exist. A quick browse of the Lawrence and Kansas City metro area will turn up a wide variety of youth sport clubs, from MOKAN Basketball to Sporting Kaw Valley (soccer) to the Lawrence Juniors (volleyball). For parents (from the research and my own personal experience as a youth sport parent), the main selling points of these clubs are legitimacy, organization, structure, competition, and improvement. These are all vague and loaded terms, but in essence youth sport clubs provide often year-round training and competition in the same way that a college or professional team does. Basketball is no longer just a winter sport, soccer is played indoors in the winter, and baseball has a fall, spring, and winter season.

While there are some obvious positives to a more structured youth sport system where coaches and organizations that do not provide a quality experience can be held accountable, it also creates quite the conundrum for parents. These clubs are not free, or even affordable at all for many (see the prices on the figure above), and the cost of youth sport is often cited as the main reason for the decline we in overall participation we noted above. Sport is often cited as one of the last true *meritocratic* systems, where the most talented and hardest working person will receive the highest achievements and awards. However, as we move to a youth sport industry that is

BOX 7.1

Lawrence (KS) Aquahawks Swim Club

Club Description: "The Lawrence Aquahawks offer professional technique instruction and training. The program is divided into smaller practice groups based on requirements and expectations. The requirements and expectations are listed below for each group and will take affect starting at the beginning of the 2015 Short Course season. These requirements are not set in stone, and may be altered after the conclusion of the season if the coaching staff sees fit to do so. These requirements are a guide that coaches use to decide which group best fits a swimmer's needs at any given time. The Progression of each swimmer is based on meeting the expectations, time standards, age, and attendance requirements. No child will be moved during a season. All moves will be made at the beginning of the season when needed. Ultimately, all decisions are determined by the Head Coach of the Lawrence Aquahawks and are based on the individual swimmer."

Levels, Price, and Expectations

Explorer Group (Ages 4–8): $100 per month for lessons two times a week

Bronze Level (Ages 6–10): $65 per month, encouraged to attend three practices a week

Silver Level (Ages 7–12): $70 per month, encouraged to attend four practices a week and compete in all meets

Gold Level (Ages 9–13): $85 per month, encouraged to attend 4–5 practices a week and compete in all meets. If they attend less than 70 percent of practices, they may be held back from advancing groups

Platinum Level (Ages 11–15): $115 per month, Attend at least 80 percent of practices and compete in all meets

Senior Level (9th–12th grade): $115 per month, Attend at least 75 percent of practices (along with high school practices) and are encouraged to attend meets

run largely by private, for-profit groups that sell the competition and improvement for why you should join their club this system is likely less about talent and more about the resources each family can afford to spend. Many would argue that your ability to get a college scholarship in baseball is now dependent, if not more, on your parent's income level when you were 5–10 years old when initial skill development happens than your natural ability to hit a fastball.

Sport Specialization

Fitting along with the club system discussed above, another major trend in high school and youth sport is *sport specialization*. If you have been exposed to any news about youth or high school sport, you have likely heard this term. In the simplest term, sport specialization is focusing on one sport year-round. For example, if Mary's parents choose to have her specialize in volleyball as a freshman in high school in the state of Kansas she will begin her fall semester by practicing and playing for her high school team (let's say Lawrence High School) while likely still practicing occasionally with her club team (let's say Lawrence Juniors Under 14). Once her Lawrence High School season ends, she will almost immediately begin multiple times a week practices with the Lawrence Juniors U14 team before a full tournament season takes place from January to May. In the summer, Mary will have summer

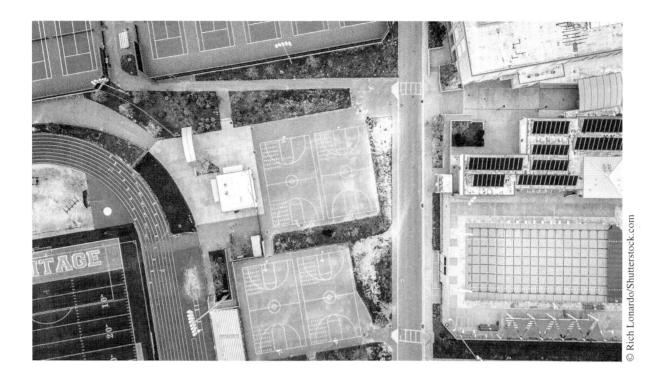

workouts with Lawrence High while also likely playing in more tournaments with her club team. For Mary, there is little to no offseason for volleyball.

For the outside observer, this likely seems obsessive and unnecessary. However, if you're Mary's parents and she loves volleyball and really wants to play in high school and then gets a college scholarship justifying the decision to specialize gets easier. If Mary does not train for volleyball in the winter, and instead plays basketball let's say, there is the potential that all the other girls she will be competing for a spot against will now be better than her and Mary will not make her high school varsity team, lose her starting spot on the club team, and crush her dream of playing in college. See how easy that was to justify a huge time and financial investment in one sport?

As you can guess, there are many negatives to sport specialization. The two most cited are injury and burnout. Overuse injuries are especially common in developing bodies and an athlete who does the same motion 12 months a year is obviously more prone for an overuse injury. The same is true of burnout; studies have shown athletes who specialize in one sport at an early age are far more likely to discontinue playing that sport completely. Further, the research has shown us that many college athletes played multiple sports in high school. Professional athletes like J.J. Watt of the National Football League have begun to speak out against the dangers of sport specialization and encourage parents to enroll their children in a variety of activities. Yet, that instant gratification of seeing your child improve and be the best at his or her age level (or fear if they are not) is still driving up the rate of specialization.

High School Sport

While there is an increased focus on the private, club sport arena high school sport still holds a prominent place in the majority of American communities. The rituals, bonding, and collectiveness that exist around local high school sports are still very prevalent. Further, sport participation has long been associated with higher Grade Point Averages, higher graduation rate, and less deviance. High school sports have different levels of governance, beginning with the National Federation of State High School Associations (NFHS). The NFHS, "publishes playing rules in 16 sports for boys and girls competition and administers fine arts programs in speech, theater, debate and music. It provides a variety of program initiatives that reach the 18,500 high schools and over 11 million students involved in athletic and activity programs."

Within the national structure, rules and regulations also differ state by state. Aspects like eligibility rules, competitive balance measures, sport seasons, and oversight of officials vary by state. All states, however, are adjusting to many of the same trends discussed above. High school sport is no longer "just" used as a character builder or way to stay in good physical shape. Millions of public and fundraising dollars are being poured into the high school sport space. Texas high school football and their college-sized stadiums in places like Allen are the most often-cited evidence for this trend. Other less notable trends include playing showcase games in other states, apparel contracts for certain teams or entire departments, and facility upgrades like indoor practice arenas or dedicated practice gyms.

All of these trends are partially in response to the above discussed increased emphasis on club sports. If we get back to our example of Mary the freshman volleyball player, it is quite easy to see which team she spends the majority of her time with: her club team. For many athletes like her, they may decide to completely eliminate their high school sport participation and only play with their club team. Or, if they do play high school it will still be secondary to their club experience. Thus, high schools are often trying to mirror the look and feel of this club system so they are not losing their best athletes to an outside group with less regulation and restrictions on things like practice time and eligibility.

Conclusion

In conclusion, the youth and high school sport space is fully undergoing a transition from *sport for play* to *sport for competition*. Some would argue that transition is completed, and the altruistic outcomes of this level have been compromised. No matter where you fall on this debate based on your research and experience, it is imperative you understand the dynamics of this landscape before you begin an internship or job in this industry. As you can see by looking at the alumni list at tinyurl.com/JayhawksInSport, a number of our graduates are employed in the youth sport and high school industry. The growth in this space will be tremendous in the next decade as parents continue to believe in the value of sport participation.

References

http://www.cnbc.com/2014/01/13/youth-sports-is-a-7-billion-industry-and-growing.html
https://www.washingtonpost.com/news/local/wp/2016/05/17/youth-sports-participation-is-up-slightly-but-many-kids-are-still-left-behind/?utm_term=.1e33f054b651
https://www.teamunify.com/SubTabGeneric.jsp?team=mvsla&_stabid_=29219

Jayhawks in the Field

Olivia Kinet

Customer Support at CaptainU

Hometown
Winnetka, Il

Education
UG 2013 – The University of Kansas (General Studies)
G 2015 – The University of Kansas (Sport Management)

Past Positions
Graduate Assistant Women's Rowing Coach at University of Kansas

1. CaptainU sounds like a really interesting company. Describe the main idea of the company and the most innovative thing you've been able to work on there.

CaptainU is designed to be a communication platform between college coaches and high school athletes throughout the recruiting process. CaptainU gives athletes the tools to accomplish their mission to make a great college team. We help them find schools that fit academically, athletically, and socially, and enable them to message directly with coaches at any school in the country in a way that's organized and efficient. My team is responsible for working directly with the athletes to guide them through the process and assist them with any questions they may have.

I have constant direct contact with athletes to discuss their individual recruiting journey and help guide them each step of the way. Whether it's talking about creating and organizing their college list, or giving them tips on how to initiate contact with a coach, the athletes are always engaging and excited to be moving forward in the whole process. The best part of the job is when an athlete contacts you to let you know they've signed an NLI and have committed to the school of their dreams!

2. High school athletics has become increasingly commercialized and focused on the outcomes (i.e., a scholarship) instead of the process. Given your experiences, what is your view on this shift and the positives and negatives?

I think it's a little disappointing how commercialized high school athletics has become. When I was in high school, I was involved in many sports for a multitude of reasons, but I can honestly say it wasn't just so that I could get an athletic scholarship for college.

Sports were my competitive outlet and a way to socialize. Not only did my involvement in sports help me develop my athletic ability, but also grew as an individual. There are many lessons that I learned from my experience in athletics that I have found extremely valuable in other areas of my life. Amongst those life lessons, is that strength of character counts. Teamwork counts. Never giving up counts. Hard work counts. I hope I never lose those life lessons.

I worry that the more high school athletics become commercialized the less athletes will learn the necessary lessons/skills that will serve them in later life. It is scary the number of professional athletes that lose their way when their professional careers are over. Bankruptcy, suicides and loss of jobs are all too common.

3. What are some of the biggest cultural sport differences you noticed between the United States and London?

Obviously there are different sports that are more important in the UK than the United States – soccer is all-dominant, rugby is played widely, and cricket is another national sport. There is some basketball but our major sports of hockey, American football and baseball are virtually non-existent except in certain niche areas. Professionalization has firmly taken place there, too, but sportsmanship and teamwork are still widely emphasized.

4. What was your proudest moment being involved with the rowing team at KU?

This is such a hard question to answer because there are so many moments I could list. Honestly, even just being a member of the KU women's rowing team gave me so much pride. I loved wearing the Jayhawk and representing the university.

One of my proudest moments as a member for the KU women's rowing team was at our last regatta my senior year, Conference USA Championships. Our team competed the best we had all season. All of our boats made the grand finals, which was our first goal and we had several top 3 finishes. My boat, the 1V8, beat teams that we had lost to earlier in the season so it felt really good to know that the hard work we put in all year was worth it and we proved to ourselves and everyone watching that we were a strong team. Hard work proved itself and certainly paid off.

Although it was difficult to leave the team at the end of my four years, I felt confident that I and the rest of my class had left a lasting impact on the program physically and mentally. We came together as a team when it mattered and everyone encouraged and pushed each other to be the best we could be.

5. If the idea behind CaptainU existed 15 years ago, what would it look like? Another way, what would you compare the model to that may have existed in the past?

Difficult question. But the answer lies is in what caused Captain U to be founded in the first place. First, brilliant founders who saw an opportunity to connect athletes, coaches, and college sports programs. Second, the availability of risk capital to get it started, firstly a bootstrapped company and later professional venture investors. Third, we have technologies available today in the internet and cell phones and apps that make connecting people that much easier. Fourth and perhaps most importantly, a culture in this country that encourages risk taking, that there is no stigma to trying and failing.

All four of those characteristics were needed for the start-up of Captain U—perhaps only two or three of them existed 15 years ago.

6. Describe the favorite parts of your job and give some specific examples if possible.

My absolute favorite part of my job is when I hear from an athlete or parent that I have been working closely with that they have committed to a university and athletic program of their choice. I love engaging with the athletes and parents throughout their recruiting process and providing them with some insight from my personal experiences as a college student-athlete and coach.

Life is a journey, not always straight up. There are ups and downs. Sports teach many of life's lessons and if I can help an athlete on his or her journey toward personal fulfillment, then it makes it all very worthwhile.

Name: _____   Section: _____   Date _____

HSES 289
Introduction to Sport Management

In-Class Quiz and Activity Sheet

Name (or names if done in a group)

Answer #1

Answer #2

Answer #3

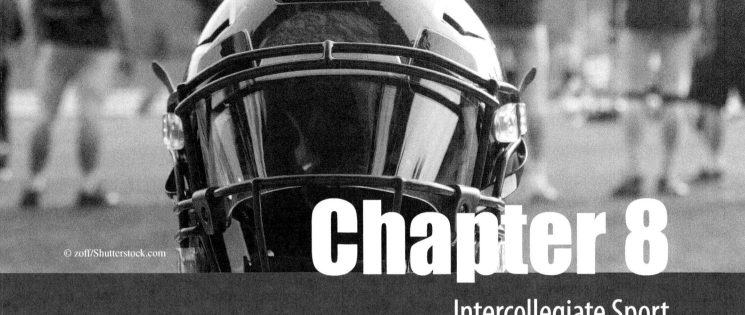

Chapter 8

Intercollegiate Sport

Jordan R. Bass • *University of Kansas*

KEY TERMS

NCAA

NAIA

Revenues and Expenses

Flutie Factor

Over 450,000 student-athletes compete in intercollegiate athletes on an annual basis. While sports such as Division I football and men's basketball get tremendous amounts of media attention, there are hundreds of thousands of athletes who compete across dozens of sports who will never be on ESPN or even their local newspaper. From the very first intercollegiate athletics event, a crew race between Harvard and Yale in 1852, athletic competition has been an integral part of college campuses in the United States. The history and evolution of intercollegiate athletics have been widely documented in texts such as *Big-Time Sports in American Universities, College Sports Inc.,* and *The Front Porch: Examining the Increasing Interconnection of University and Athletic Department Funding.* In this chapter, we'll focus on the current state of intercollegiate athletics and trends that will impact those will desires for a career in this space after graduation.

Intercollegiate Athletics Structure

The most commonly known intercollegiate athletics level is National Collegiate Athletic Association (NCAA) Division I. Your own University of Kansas is a Division I member along with most universities that come to mind quickly when you think about college athletics. However, the majority of college athletes do not compete at the NCAA Division I level. Within the NCAA, there are also Division II and Division III. Outside of the NCAA structure, there are also governing associations such as the National Association of Intercollegiate Athletics (NAIA, based in Kansas City, Missouri), the National Christian College Athletic Association (NCCAA), and National Junior College Athletic Association (NJCAA). Opportunities for athletes (and you as a sport management employee) exist at all of these levels. A brief summation of each level is provided below.

NCAA Division I

For an institution to be a NCAA Division I member, they must sponsor at least 14 sports (7 for men, 7 for women). Division I schools must award athletics scholarships and have specific scheduling and arena size qualifications. Within Division I, there are two football divisions: Football Bowl Subdivision (FBS) and Football Championship Subdivision (FCS). FBS is considered the higher level and schools must average over 15,000 paid attendees per home game to be a FBS member. At the FBS level, the national champion is determined through the Bowl Championship Series. At the FCS level, there is a playoff system to determine the champion. NCAA Division I institutions receive the most media attention, generate the most revenue, and are the most widely known programs in intercollegiate sport. Local examples include the University of Kansas, Kansas State University, and Wichita State University.

NCAA Division II

Division II institutions must sponsor at least 10 sports (5 for men, 5 for women). There are no attendance requirements and there is a maximum on the amount of financial aid that can be awarded based on athletic ability. According to the NCAA website, "Division II teams usually feature a number of local or in-state student-athletes. Many

Division II student-athletes pay for school through a combination of scholarship money, grants, student loans, and employment earnings. Division II athletics programs are financed in the institution's budget like other academic departments on campus. Traditional rivalries with regional institutions dominate schedules of many Division II athletics programs." Local examples include Pittsburgh State University, Emporia State University, and Washburn University.

NCAA Division III

Division III is similar to Division II in the number of sports they much sponsor and the lack of scheduling or attendance minimums. The main difference in Division III is no athletic scholarships can be awarded. Restated, no financial aid may be given to a student for the on-field/court/ice ability. The budget for a Division III school is much, much smaller than their Division I counterparts. Division III is the largest Division in terms of overall participation numbers. Local examples include Washington University and Webster University in St. Louis, Missouri.

NAIA

The NAIA is another governing body from intercollegiate athletics that is separate from the NCAA. The NAIA was founded in 1937 and is based in downtown Kansas City, Missouri. Over 60,000 athletes compete at the NAIA level. The average NAIA school has an enrollment of 1,700 students and over 80 percent of the member schools are private and the average operating budget for the athletics department is just under $3 million. A school is only required to sponsor six sports to be a NAIA member but the Association sponsors 25 national championships. The NAIA is most comparable to the NCAA Division II level. A local example is Baker University in Baldwin City, Kansas.

NJCAA

The National Junior College Athletic Association is a governing body for two-year colleges that offer athletics programs (often called JUCO's). Athletes may compete

© melis/Shutterstock.com

at the JUCO level for two seasons and then may choose to transfer to a NAIA or NCAA institution to complete their final two years of eligibility if they are offered to and choose to attend. Local examples include Butler Community College and Kansas City Kansas Community College.

Finances of Intercollegiate Athletics

In the last decade, the revenues and expenses of intercollegiate athletic departments have received considerable scrutiny. As state and federal funding for higher education has decreased and tuition has increased, the public has seen college coaching salaries skyrocket, multimillion dollar stadiums built, and a general "gold-plating" of the intercollegiate athletics space. This also comes at a time when the common narrative is that only a handful of college athletics departments generate enough revenue to cover their expenses.

This increased scrutiny also comes at a time when a vicious "pay for play" debate is happening. Essentially, extreme pushback has begun against the college sport model where athletes are not "paid" in the traditional sense and cannot profit off their own likeness if they wish to remain an "amateur" (i.e., they cannot be a spokesperson for a local restaurant or other business). A litany of pending litigation is underway against the NCAA and member schools in an attempt to change the financial way college athletics is structured so student-athletes receive greater compensation for competing at the Division I level.

In partial response to this debate, at the NCAA Division I level some conferences now allow their institutions to offer full "cost-of-attendance" scholarships. Thus, in addition to the previous scholarship which covered tuition and room and board, student-athletes can now receive additional funding (around $4,000 at a university like Kansas State) to cover other living expenses. Other landmark cases that have occurred in the last decade include former UCLA basketball star Ed O'Bannon suing the NCAA and EA Sports for using his likeness in a video game and the Northwestern football team attempting to unionize.

BOX 8.1

Main Sources of Revenue for Intercollegiate Athletics Departments
• Ticket Sales
• NCAA and Conference Distributions
• Television and Radio Contracts
• Donations/Fundraising
• Institutional Support and Student Fees
Main Sources of Expenses
• Grants-in-aid
• Salaries
• Facilities
• Team Expenses

© Yevgenia Gorbulsky/Shutterstock.com

Another financial issue on the forefront of athletics administrators' minds is the use of student fees and university subsidies to fund athletics departments. At the vast majority of universities, the general student body pays some form of mandatory fee to help support the athletics department. For example, at the University of Arizona undergraduate students pay a $100 athletics fee. Additionally, many universities provide a subsidy to the athletics department where tuition revenue is used to cover the operating expenses for athletics. In an extreme case, Rutgers subsidized the athletic department to a tune of over $28 million in 2016. Students across the United States, including here at the University of Kansas, have pushed back against these arrangements and voted to lessen or discontinue student fees for athletics when they are allowed to choose. In 2014, the KU Student Senate voted to completely eliminate the athletics fee before it was eventually lessened to $7 a semester.

Athletics Role on Campus

No matter the level, athletics typically play a major role in the campus community. If you asked a random person what the first thing they think of when you say the "University of Kansas" they will more often than not say something related to sport. The same is true of most major universities in the United States. Murray Sperber first highlighted another impact sports can have on the university: increasing awareness of the university and increasing applications to that university. Sperber called this the "Flute Factor" after the famous Boston College quarterback who put that university on the national radar when he completed a "Hail Mary" pass on national television. You can probably think of a number of schools you only know about because of athletics success: places like Wichita State, Boise State, Davidson, and Florida Gulf Coast. It has been shown consistently that athletics success on the national stage leads to an increase in applications to the university along with smaller aspects like visits to the school webpage and applications for financial aid.

At the non-Division I level, athletics often play an even bigger role in the survival of the university. As noted above, schools at these levels are often small, private, liberal arts universities with tuition costs that are higher than their competitors. Many of these schools have relied on their athletics programs to bring students to campus who otherwise would not have considered attending college at that institution. As you will see in your supplemental reading, schools like Hendrix in Arkansas are adding sports with large roster sizes (like football and lacrosse) to increase enrollment at the university. One school administrator even went as far to call the NCAA Division III level the "enrollment division" where roster sizes were more important than wins and losses on the field.

Conclusion

College athletics have arguably never been more popular than they are today. Yet, administrators in this space are facing a number of unique challenges that will shape how the industry is operated and viewed in the next decade. The winds of change are certainly blowing and anyone who desires to work in the college space must be a keen evaluator of the emerging issues. Debates over paying players, student fees and subsidies, and the increased commercialization of college athletics have really just begun and will likely dramatically change the daily operations of college athletics departments. Chapters like these will need to be updated regularly to keep up with a space that is in such flux.

References

http://www.ncaa.org/about/who-we-are/membership/divisional-differences-and-history-multidivision-classification

http://www.naia.org/fls/27900/membership/membership.html?DB_OEM_ID=27900

http://www.njcaa.org/about/mission/Mission_statement

https://www.washingtonpost.com/sports/why-students-foot-the-bill-for-college-sports-and-how-some-are-fighting-back/2015/11/30/7ca47476-8d3e-11e5-ae1f-af46b7df8483_story.html?utm_term=.f78a5f53f3d5

Jayhawks in the Field

Jacob Petty

Athletic Academic Advisor for Men's and Women's Track and Field/
Cross Country at the University of Oklahoma

Hometown
Olathe, KS

Education
UG 2015 – University of Kansas (Sport Management)
G 2017 – University of Oklahoma (Adult and Higher Education)

Previous Position
Football Intern at Ottawa University

1. When you finished your undergraduate degree, what made you want to continue your education and get a Master's degree?

The choice to continue my education was slightly based on the understanding that many career fields in the realm of intercollegiate athletics require a Master's degree. Moreover I felt that I was not finished with my education and personally aspired to learn more about higher education and athletics. Being the first member of my family to apply to graduate school was a difficult process made easier with the help of Dr. Jordan Bass, Dr. Bernie Kish, and the University of Kansas Sport Management faculty. There is no doubt that the lessons I learned in and out of the classroom at the University of Kansas helped me succeed in my pursuit of higher education.

2. You work with student-athletes on a daily basis. What misconceptions does the public have about college athletes that are the most off-base?

A common misconception I hear about my profession, is when I tell people that I am an Academic Advisor in Athletics, they usually respond with "oh, so you write the student-athlete's papers?" This is a frustrating fallacy due to the inaccuracy of that question and the ignorance about my profession. With so many academic misconduct cases being prevalent in the current landscape of the NCAA, it certainly puts a stigma on the profession.

The largest misconception that I hear about student-athletes is the, "dumb jock" stereotype. The student-athletes that I work with at the University of Oklahoma certainly do not fit this stereotype at all and are some of the hardest-working, well-equipped students that I have ever been around.

3. How do you balance helping student-athletes succeed without "crossing the line" or "coddling" them?

Working with student-athletes is a rewarding, yet arduous process. The most important thing when working with others is building trust and respect. Without a solid foundation no relationship can flourish. Understanding the NCAA and conference rules plays a major part in understanding what an advisor can and cannot do in terms of academic assistance. I preach all the time about accountability and responsibility to my student-athletes. I am willing to help any student that is willing to help themselves. In this business, it is important to be able to justify any action you do, because you can be questioned on it at anytime. I make sure that my job security is never at risk because of one student-athlete; you must hold the student-athletes accountable and know the NCAA bylaws.

4. What was your favorite Sport Management class at KU and why?

The KU Sport Management program is so special because it offers students with learning opportunities and hands on experiences in multiple career fields available in athletics. I had so many classes that I truly loved attending in the KU Sport Management program. One course that sticks out to me is Dr. Scott Ward's History and Foundations of Sport. His courses really opened my eyes to the profession of Athletic Academic Advising, plus how can anyone not like Dr. Ward's humor. I also really enjoyed any of Dr. Kish's courses. Dr. Kish sincerely cares for the success of all of his students and always offers his pearls of wisdom.

5. When you first went to the University of Oklahoma you didn't have a position with the athletic department. In the span of two years, you moved into a graduate assistant role and then a full-time position. Describe that journey and strategies you used to be noticed and move up in the organization.

When I first applied for graduate school I was not offered a graduate assistantship, but I did not let that stop me from having an opportunity for higher education. I originally started as an hourly employee in the athletic department as an academic mentor for student-athletes. Through my willingness to tackle any task and good fortune, I was offered a graduate assistantship within two weeks of starting. I made a point from starting as an academic mentor that I would approach every day like I was being on a job interview. I dress professionally, I was always willing to learn new things, I was the first one there and I was the last one to leave. At times I felt as no one noticed but later assured but it wasn't going unnoticed. I was willing to do things that other graduate assistants thought were beneath them or thought was too hard to learn. I spent extra time with full-time members in the athletic department to understand their role and asked for any advice they would give to a young professional. Once an opportunity arose in shape of a full-time position in my final semester at the University of Oklahoma, I was bound and determined to at least get an interview. My reputation spoke where I did not have to. The department knew what kind of employee they were going to get based on all the things I did above and beyond. I was offered and accepted the position of Athletics Academic Advisor for the Men's and Women's Track and Field and Cross Country teams at the University of Oklahoma. The greatest advice for young professionals that I was given and I can pass on is don't be afraid to do the dirty work. Don't be afraid to learn something new; don't be afraid to do anything beneath you, because when you are a young professional nothing is beneath you. If you truly care about working in sports give it your all!

6. Describe the favorite parts of your job and give some specific examples if possible.

My favorite part about my job is that I can wake up every day and go to work impacting the lives of others. Not a day goes by that work feels like work. I'm so fortunate to work in a place like the University of Oklahoma and work with the student-athletes that I work with. Knowing that you maybe played a small role in the educational process of a student is an extremely rewarding experience.

One example in particular, when I was a graduate assistant Academic Mentor with the Football team, I was working with the student all semester that historically struggled in English. Through our weekly sessions and possibly tips and time management skills that I taught him he received a "B" in the class. Once we found out his grade, this 6"4' 250 lbs. football player cried and gave me a hug because he was so happy this was his first "B" in English in his life.

It is instances like that I keep you going. It is instances like that that make what you do all worth it. Knowing that you can make a positive impact on someone else's life and having the ability to reach new heights with them is immeasurable.

I have no doubt that the faculty and staff in the KU sport management program will provide you all with the education, experience, end in sight to excel in the field of sport. Good luck to you all and Rock Chalk!

Name: _____ Section: _____ Date _____

HSES 289
Introduction to Sport Management

In-Class Quiz and Activity Sheet

Name (or names if done in a group)

Answer #1

Answer #2

Answer #3

© Chunni4691/Shutterstock.com

Chapter 9

International Sport

Dominique Kropp • *University of Kansas*

KEY TERMS

Rugby

World Sailing

Cricket

Curling

Judo

Olympic Games

Relegation and Promotion System

Introduction

In sport management classes in the United States, the material presented often focuses on sport within the United States, at the recreational, high school, college, or professional level. It is important to remember, however, that sport is quite popular beyond the borders of the United States. Some professional athletes in other countries compete in sport organizations specific to each country, such as the NFL or NBA within the United States. In addition, certain sporting organizations emphasize competition among people from different countries across the world and hold tournaments globally, such as the Association of Tennis Professionals (ATP) or Professional Golf Association (PGA). Beyond such organizations, there are several notable sporting events that take place on a quadriannual basis which embrace athletic competition in which athletes represent their own country. Most notably, such events include the Summer and Winter Olympic Games and the FIFA World Cup.

As you can begin to understand, the scope of international sport is quite large. In order to provide a comprehensive summary of sport across the world, this chapter will begin with an overview of several popular sports across the world that may not be as recognized or familiar in the United States. Next, a synopsis of the Summer and Winter Olympic Games will be provided. In addition, a discussion of the promotion and relegation systems in European professional sport will enhance your understanding of the differences in professional sport around the globe. Finally, you will read an interview with Dr. Simon Licen, native of Slovenia and Assistant Professor of Sport Management at Washington State University, who has worked in several roles in the global sport industry. My hope is that this chapter enhances your knowledge of sport in a subject that may not be so familiar to you and provides you with a sense of the scope of sport throughout the world.

© Vahe 3D/Shutterstock.com

Popular Sports around the World

Rugby

Often compared to the sport of American football, rugby is a ball sport involving two teams competing against each other to place the oval-like ball in the opposing team's goal area, which leads to an attempt of kicking the ball through an H-shaped goal for a conversion. There are two types of rugby, including rugby union and rugby league. Rugby union is open to amateurs and professionals at this time but in the past, this type of rugby was specifically restricted to solely amateur players. Fifteen players take the field for each team in rugby union. In contrast, rugby league is comprised of 13 players, and is open to amateurs and professionals.

Both types of rugby are popular in both hemispheres of the world. Ireland, England, France, Italy, and even the United States include popular locations for rugby in the Northern Hemisphere while Australia, New Zealand, and South Africa dominate the popularity of the sport in the Southern Hemisphere. The International Rugby Board (IRB) was founded in 1886 and is located in Dublin, Ireland, and recently changed its name to World Rugby. This governing body oversees more than 100 national unions in regard to the sport (Nauright, 2017).

Undoubtedly, the popularity of rugby has continued to grow. In fact, according to World Rugby, more than seven million people are actively playing the game across member unions and the sport is considered one of the quickest-growing team sports in Brazil. In the 2016 Summer Olympic Games, rugby made a return after being removed in 1924 ("Golf and Rugby", 2016). This was only the fifth time the sport has been featured in the Olympics. It is important to note that the format played in the Olympics differs from original rugby. This format is known as rugby sevens, in which the game is divided into two halves of 7 minutes each. In addition, only seven players from each team are on the field at a time ("World Rugby," 2016). The 2016 Olympics featured rugby sevens competition for both men and women.

© wavebreakmedia/Shutterstock.com

Sailing

Another popular international sport is sailing. Governed by World Sailing, this sport is also currently included in the Summer Olympics and the governing body is recognized by the International Olympic Committee (IOC). World Sailing was established in 1907 in Paris, France, and oversees nearly 150 member nations. The goal of the governing body is more participatory than competitive in nature, focusing on ensuring that as many people participate in sailing events as possible ("World Sailing"). The sport of sailing can be described as "the art of moving a boat by harnessing the power of the wind. Mastery over ever-changing conditions requires both great skill and experience" ("Sailing"). Though there are several different types of racing in sailing, the sport is classified under one set of rules which is published by World Sailing. The different racing classifications in the Olympic Games are determined by boat design, reflecting measurements, and weights.

According to the World Sailing organization, fleet racing is most common, involving sail boats taking part in a course race. In contrast, match racing involves two boats of identical design competing against each other in a duel-like race. The sport also features team racing, composed of two teams in three boats racing against each other as well as offshore and oceanic sailing, which incorporates races of over 800 miles. Finally, cruising is considered the most enjoyed form of the sport, usually incorporated in a recreational setting ("World Sailing").

Obviously, sailing events must take place near large bodies of waters, including lakes, seas, and oceans. While this may limit its popularity in some regions, locations such as New Zealand, Australia, and Europe are quite popular in sailing.

Cricket

The sport of cricket, considered England's national summer sport, is not only popular in Britain, but in several countries around the world, particularly India and Pakistan as well as Australia and the West Indies (Alston & Williams, 2017). The sport, somewhat akin to the American pastime of baseball, is believed to have originated in the 13th century, but has evolved with technological developments, as many sports have over the years. The sport is composed of two teams with 11 players in each team. There are typically two innings per game, and each team takes turns batting and bowling (pitching). Similar to baseball, the goal is to score runs while at bat and to dismiss the persons at bat when playing in the field. It is important to mention, however, that unlike baseball, two batsmen are up to bat at one time (Alston & Williams, 2017). In addition, runs are worth more than one point. It is quite typical to have scores reaching the hundreds in the sport (Alston & Williams, 2017).

As with rugby and sailing, there is an international governing body for the cricket, known as the International Cricket Council (ICC). There are 105 member nations, with the largest number of member nations being in Europe (ICC). Nowadays, there are three main formats of cricket. The traditional format of the game, test cricket, spans over 5 days. This form of the game demands "endurance, technique, and temperament in different conditions" ("Cricket", n.d.) because of the nature of the competition. In addition, One Day Internationals are offered, consisting of one-innings matches, consisting of 50 overs, or switching of pitchers per team. This format is utilized for the ICC Cricket World Cup, which takes place every 4 years.

The final format is known as the Twenty20 Internationals, which is the shortest and quickest way to play cricket. This format consists of 20 overs per side and usually takes about 3 hours to complete ("Cricket", n.d.).

Though difficult to measure, some believe cricket may be considered one of the top four most popular sports in the world. SportCal's Global Sports Event Index determined that the cricket World Cup ranked third in popularity of single-sport events between 2009 and 2016, behind football (soccer) and rugby. In terms of social media connectedness, cricket ranks fourth, based on the number of people who follow at least one social media page associated with the sport. Though not necessarily a popular sport in the United States, the sport of cricket must be acknowledged for its global popularity.

© ChrisVanLennepPhoto/Shutterstock.com

Curling

Switching gears to an indoor sport classified as a Winter Olympic sport, curling incorporates two teams of four players each competing on ice. It has been given the nickname, "The Roaring Game" because the 44-lb stones that are utilized in the sport make a rumbling sound as they move across the ice ("Curling", n.d.). Somewhat surprisingly, this sport originated in Scotland in the 16th century. In 1924, men's curling was introduced as an Olympic sport in the first Winter Olympic Games in Chamonix, France. For many years, it was considered a demonstration sport until 1998, when both men's and women's curling were classified as official Olympic sports ("Curling", n.d.).

The World Curling Federation (WCF) is the governing body which oversees the sport. Until 1990, the organization was known as the International Curling Federation. As of 2017, there are 60 member associations within the organization. Afghanistan, Kyrgyzstan, Portugal, and Saudi Arabia are the newest members to join the WCF. As the sport continues to gain popularity in countries around the world, it is important to be familiar with the particular rules of the sport.

Curling consists of 10 ends, which are similar to innings in baseball or softball. The four players of each team take turns throwing the stones, two per end, equaling a total of 16 thrown stones per end. The objective is to get the most stones closest to the curling bullseye on the ice, known as the button. Upon observing curling, one may notice that there are brooms utilized to sweep the ice in front of the stone that is gliding. This is done to warm the ice, which reduces friction. Doing so allows the stone to travel in a certain direction as well as farther than without the broom sweeping (Gregory, 2018).

© Bork/Shutterstock.com

Judo

Judo is a sport that was introduced as an Olympic event in the 1964 Summer Games in Tokyo, Japan. The sport was developed in Japan, and in Japanese, the word judo refers to "the way of suppleness." This actually comes from a Japanese story about a tree branch that bends but does not break under the weight of snow. Men's judo events only last 5 minutes but are considered to be as physically taxing as wrestling and boxing ("Judo", n.d.).

Those competing in a match of judo are known as judokas. Points can be scored in three different ways, including an ippon, a waza-ari, and a yuko, worth 100, 10, and 1 point(s), respectively. There are also two different types of penalties in judo, including a Hansoku-make, or grave infringement, leading to direct disqualification, and shido, or slight infringement, not meriting disqualification. The judoka with the most points at the end of the match is deemed the winner. If there happens to be a tie, a sudden-death overtime takes place. After a winner is determined, both competitors will bow to each other as a sign of respect for competition. Similar to wrestling, a competitor can "tap out" or say "maitta" as a form of surrender when they feel they are in danger of passing out or being choked. Such action leads to the end of the match.

The competitors wear what are known as judogis, or a jacket and trousers, made out of heavy cotton. One judoka will wear white while the other wears blue. The event takes place barefoot. Furthermore, the matches take place on tatamis, or rectangular mats. In the 2016 Summer Games in Rio, the matches took place in an arena holding just under 10,000 spectators.

While the sport has roots in Japan, it has certainly gained popularity across the world since its 1964 Olympic debut. In fact, in the 2016 Summer Games, 289 competitors from 136 different countries participated in judo. According to data from 2014, there are over 28 million judo athletes in the country of Japan alone. Quite coincidentally, Japan will be hosting the judo world championships and the Olympic Games in upcoming years (2019 and 2020), providing an excellent opportunity for the country to showcase their roots in the sport (McGowan & Young, 2017).

© sportpoint/Shutterstock.com]

Olympic Games

As you may notice from reading about the aforementioned sports, the Olympics provides perhaps the most well-known platform for international sport competition. It is important to understand a bit of the history and magnitude of the event(s) when discussing international sport. As many may already know, the Olympic Games originated in Athens, Greece, tracing back to 776 BC. They continued for many centuries, being dedicated to Olympian gods, until in 393 AD, they were banned, being viewed as a type of "pagan cult."

In 1896, the Olympic Games were reborn, being deemed the "Modern Olympic Games." Nearly 250 athletes from 14 different countries participated in the first Modern Olympic Games, which consisted of 43 different sporting events. The decision was made for the games to be held every 4 years in different locations, primarily in Europe and the United States until in 1956, the games were co-hosted by Australia and Sweden. The quarantine laws in Australia would not permit foreign horses to enter the country, so equestrian competition had to be held in Stockholm, Sweden. In 1964, the first Olympic Games in Asia took place in Tokyo. Coincidentally, Tokyo has been selected to host the next Summer Olympic Games in 2020, followed by Paris in 2024 and Los Angeles in 2028 ("Olympic Games", n.d.).

Any discussion regarding the history and structure of the Olympic Games must reference both the Summer Olympic Games and the Winter Olympic Games. In 1924, the first Winter Olympic Games were held in Chamonix, France. Over 10,000 fans attended the week-long event, in which nearly 260 athletes from 16 countries competed in 16 different events, including ice hockey, speed skating, and ski jumping ("Olympic Games", n.d.). The Winter Olympic Games take place on a 4-year basis, just like the Summer Olympic Games; however, the two events always take place 2 years apart from each other. The next Winter Olympic Games will be held in Beijing in 2022 ("Olympic Games", n.d.).

It is also important to note that politics and happenings around the world can play a significant factor in international sporting events such as the Olympic Games. For instance, in 1936, the Summer Olympic Games were held in Berlin, Germany. At the time, Adolf Hitler was at the realm in Germany, and hoped to use the event to prove his theories of the superior Aryan race. Jesse Owens, an African American track athlete, single-handedly proved such theories wrong by being the most popular athlete at the event, winning four gold medals ("Olympic Games", n.d.). However, for the next 12 years, no Olympic Games took place, due to the world chaos attributable to World War II.

Furthermore, in February 2018, the Winter Olympic Games were held in Pyeongchang, South Korea. North Korean and South Korean athletes marched into the opening ceremonies under a unified flag, a happening which developed due to the first open communication between the two countries in years. In fact, the 1988 Olympics held in South Korea were boycotted by North Korea. Thirty years later, a nominal North Korean head of state was sent to South Korea for the first time ever ("North Korea at the Winter Olympics", 2018). Because of the inclusion and interaction among so many countries at the Olympic Games, it is not unusual that tensions between countries become a focal point during the Games, enhancing the scope of the event to include more than just athletic competition.

Relegation and Promotion System in Europe

As we transition from Olympic competition to professional sports beyond the United States, it is necessary to gain an understanding of the relegation and promotion systems often implemented in European and Asian sporting leagues. In essence, the principle of this system is to transfer teams within a league to different levels based on merit of the team. In order for this system to be implemented, teams are evaluated at the end of each season and moved to different divisions of the league. For instance, in England's Premier Football (Soccer) League, the three bottom-ranked teams are demoted (relegated) to the level below the Premier Football League. In contrast, the top teams from the second-tier league are promoted to the Premier League (Steere, 2009).

Across professional soccer in Europe, many leagues utilize this system, but may only have two teams moving up and down between leagues or may include a playoff match to determine the third-place teams that will move up or down. Soccer is not the only sport to utilize the promotion and relegation system in Europe, and the system is quite possible in other regions as well, including Australia and New Zealand. In fact, early baseball leagues in the United States used to utilize the system as well. There are also many international sports tournaments that implement promotion and relegation, including the Davis Cup and Fed Cup in the sport of tennis, the World Cricket League (discussed previously), and the Ice Hockey World Championships. Professional basketball teams in regions outside of the United States also utilize the system in various ways.

The concept of bringing such a system to modern professional sports in the United States has been met with fear. Not only would doing so affect the way in which we support our favorite teams (would Los Angeles Lakers fans still be as passionate about their team if they were not an NBA team?), but the new system could result in grave financial implications for sport in the United States as well. In addition, some have argued the infrastructure of professional leagues in the United States (i.e., number of teams in the league) is not vast enough to support a relegation and promotion system (Steere, 2009).

Conclusion

In conclusion, it is important to realize the breadth of international sport. By gaining an understanding of the numerous sports (not just those mentioned in this chapter) being played outside of the United States, as well as becoming more familiar with the history and structure of the Olympic Games and the relegation and promotion system utilized in professional sport leagues in other countries, it is my hope that you are now more familiar with the scope of international sport. The following section will provide an interview with Dr. Simon Licen, as mentioned in the Introduction, and the chapter will conclude with a list of learning activities to further enhance your knowledge of international sport.

References

Alston, J., & Williams, M. (2017). Cricket. In *Encyclopedia Britannica.* Retrieved from Encyclopedia Britannica online database.

Cricket (n.d.) Retrieved from https://www.icc-cricket.com

Curling (n.d.) Retrieved from https://www.olympic.org/curling

Golf and Rugby-New Kids on the Block. (2016, March 17). Retrieved from https://www
.olympic.org/news/golf-and-rugby-new-kids-on-the-block

Gregory, S. (2018). Everything you need to know about curling for the 2018 Winter Olympics.
Retrieved from http://time.com/5092825/curling-sport-terms-rules-history

McGowan, T., & Young, H. (2017). Tokyo Grand Slam 2017: Inside the world's most spiritual
sport. Retrieved from https://www.cnn.com/2017/12/01/sport/kodokan-institute-noaki-
murata-jigoro-kano-tokyo-2020/index.html

Nauright, J. (2017). Rugby. In *Encyclopedia Britannica.* Retrieved from Encyclopedia
Britannica online database.

North Korea at the Winter Olympics: All you need to know. (2018). Retrieved from http://
www.bbc.com/news/world-asia-42770887

Olympic Games. (n.d.). Retrieved from https://www.olympic.org/olympic-games

Steere, M. (2009). Explainer: How relegation works. Retrieved from http://edition.cnn
.com/2009/SPORT/football/05/18/relegation.explainer/index.html

World Rugby. (2016). Retrieved from https://www.olympic.org/world-rugby

Field Interview

Dr. Simon Licen

Assistant Professor of Sport Management at Washington State University

1. Describe your first role working in International Sport.

My first role in international sport management was as assistant director for a qualifying group of the FIBA Europe Under-20 Championship for Women in Slovenia. I was 18 at the time—younger than the players—and was invited to the "job," a volunteering opportunity with paid room and board, by a friend and fellow basketball referee who worked at the Slovenian basketball federation and was the event director. The tournament was small; it only included five teams, and he was the only federation representative not from the local organizing committee so he needed all-around help interacting with referees and officials, compiling daily bulletins and more. We had refereed games together before and I had designed the very first website of the Slovenian association of basketball referees as a pet project, so he knew he could trust me and rely on my organizational and logistical skills.

Some people working in sport management like to say, "It's not what you know that counts but rather who you know." In this case, knowing the right person was indeed beneficial—but even more important was the skill set and reliability I had displayed before, so what I encourage students to do in addition to networking is to be committed to the tasks they take on and pay attention to details.

2. Have you worked for FIBA in other roles? What is most noteworthy in comparing WNBA/NBA basketball and FIBA basketball?

The U-20 women's tournament in Slovenia allowed me to meet referees and officials from other countries, and I took advantage of these connections for some later projects, including writing several handbooks for aspiring basketball referees.

International or FIBA basketball differs substantially from NBA/WNBA. Most notably, North American professionals—and to some extent event college sports—are much more focused on entertainment. They are traveling shows which cater to large live and media audiences. The athletic centerpiece is accompanied by food, games, and other forms of entertainment for the live audience, and punditry on radio and television. Games are longer, and spectating is an experience.

Most European professional sports, on the other hand, are much more basic, or pure, if you wish: there might be some low-key halftime program or a local cheerleading group, but promotions and Dance Cams are the exception rather than the norm. In turn, soccer in particular is famous for its tradition of organized fan cultures, where supporters groups develop customs and choreographies of their own.

Organizers on all continents have started narrowing the gaps—the Indian Premier League in cricket introduced cheerleader programs very similar to the NFL's while Seattle Sounders' supporters groups are modeled after similar groups in Europe—but differences remain and likely derive from cultural differences that transcend sports.

3. In your opinion, is the relegation and promotion system of sports in Europe something that could be applicable in the United States? Do you find this system more practical than the system in the United States?

Soccer in the United States has periodically discussed the introduction of a system of promotion/relegation. In my opinion, this system is generally not suited to the United States because of the existing business model and the primarily commercial and entertainment nature of professional sports discussed earlier. American sports shows hinge on competitive balance, to the point of team owners (actually, franchisees) introducing rules and procedures aimed at maintaining such balance: think of drafts and salary caps. Grassroots sports and athlete development are completely separate from professional sports and take place in varsity and traveling teams. I cannot imagine profit-driven team owners really having an interest in switching to a broader and much more complex system that requires much more long-term planning and involves reinvesting profits into its grassroots programs and youth academies. Similarly, I cannot envision hundreds of Division-I athletic programs and thousands of league promoters handing over their business to professional sports.

One could point to profitable teams operating in the promotion/relegation model (and uniting tens of thousands of members) such as FC Barcelona or Real Madrid, but they forget these organizations took over a hundred years to build to their current stage.

I don't consider either model better; rather, each is a better fit for the way other societal institutions such as business and education operate on each continent.

4. What was your role with the WTA and what responsibilities did this include?

In 2005, I became communications manager of the newly established Banka Koper Slovenia Open, a WTA Tour (women's professional tennis) event played in Portorož, my hometown. We were a small unit of two people (along with an official photographer and the PA announcer, who would help with some tasks) in a small outfit and my primary responsibilities included preparing materials for reporters covering the tournament, gathering postgame quotes from players, preparing content for the daily newsletter, and sending out score updates, which for a small tournament in 2005 meant emailing recipients every hour during playing time.

In 2008, I was promoted to director of media and communications of the growing tournament. This involved much more work ahead of the tournament, preparing media releases before and during the event, moderating news conferences, facilitating reporters' and broadcasters' work, coordinating interview requests, liaising with the WTA website, and more. The tournament had grown, and so had technology, so we had a much more dynamic online presence with proper live scoring and started using Facebook and YouTube to circulate content. We produced content in three or four languages and I have moderated and interpreted several postfinal news conferences in three languages—Slovenian, Italian, and English.

The tournament eventually closed after the 2010 edition: the stadium capacity did not meet WTA requirements and the Great Recession did not allow the owner to invest into its expansion. The tournament allowed me to work with elite athletes and Grand Slam winners, and inspired later professional and research work.

5. You mentioned you were able to attend the Olympic Games in Rio. Can you provide some thoughts on attending the Olympic Games? Did it meet your expectations? Which events were you able to attend/work with?

Experiencing the Olympic Games firsthand is a pinnacle for a sport management professional and scholar, and I thoroughly enjoyed observing up close every organizational aspect of this mega event. Numerous positive and negative aspects of the Rio Olympics, many of them rather serious, were widely reported by global media. I wonder whether the sheer magnitude of the event, coupled with the increasingly quick pace at which changes in contemporary society occur, is bound to exacerbate flaws, regardless of who hosts the Games. Rio, Brazil, and the entire world were in a different economic, social, and technological situation when the host city was chosen in 2009. Some issues that later emerged were simply impossible to predict then.

My formal duties in Rio were very limited, so I was able to spend most of the time attending athletic events. Highlights certainly included home crowd favorites Larissa and Talita's quarterfinal victory over Joana Heidrich and Nadine Zumkehr in the women's beach volleyball tournament at Copacabana Stadium, Argentina's double-overtime victory over rival and host Brazil in the men's basketball tournament, and the dignified haka by New Zealand's team following their loss to Australia in the final of the women's rugby sevens tournament. Interestingly, all three matches recorded the highest attendance within their tournaments, yet several thousand seats remained unoccupied in all cases.

Name: _____   Section: _____   Date _____

Learning Activities

1. Select a country and conduct a bit of research into the sporting events that take place in that country. What is the most popular sport for spectators and participants? Does the country regularly compete in the Olympic Games and the FIFA World Cup? Which events do athletes from your selected country typically excel at in the Olympics if they are participants? Do the professional teams in your chosen country participate in a promotion and relegation system?

2. Select one of the Olympic Games that has taken place in the modern era and conduct a bit of research to determine how many and which sports were sponsored at the event. Which countries won the most medals and in which sports? How many participants took part in the event? Were there any particular circumstances affecting the event (i.e., location, social issues, etc.)?

3. Examine a professional league or governing body of an international sport. How many teams or member unions are associated with the organization? How is the administration structured? In what year was the organization founded? How does promotion and relegation factor into the organization (if it does at all)?

Name: _____   Section: _____   Date _____

HSES 289
Introduction to Sport Management
In-Class Quiz and Activity Sheet

Name (or names if done in a group)

Answer #1

Answer #2

Answer #3

Chapter 10

Sales in the Sport Organization

David A. Pierce • IUPUI, Nels K. Popp • University of North Carolina,
Chad D. McEvoy • Northern Illinois University

© Gary Glaser/Shutterstock.com

CHAPTER OVERVIEW

Sales is a crucial part of nearly any business organization, including the sport industry. This chapter focuses on the role and importance of sales within a sport organization. Without sales and revenue, funding doesn't exist to field a team, pay administrative salaries, or even play a single game. In Major League Baseball (MLB), a sales staff might be responsible for selling four million game tickets over the 81-game home season. That revenue is essential in order to support a team payroll of $100 million or more annually. Across the industry, it is estimated that approximately $15 billion is spent on sport sponsorships. Salespeople are needed to sell that type of inventory. The chapter will explore the composition of sport organizations and how sales staffs fit into that structure. In addition, the makeup of sales staffs and the different types of sales positions will be examined. Finally, sport sales career opportunities will be discussed.

KEY TERMS

Account Executive (AE)	Inside sales
Analytics	Operations side
Business side	Outbound sales
Corporate sales	Outsourcing
Customer Relationship Management (CRM)	Premium sales
	Retention
Customer service	Season ticket sales
Group sales	Ticket operations
Inbound sales	Ticket Sales Representative (TSR)

Icon Sportswire/Getty Images

Major League Team Sports

Among the most high-profile North American sport organizations are the major leagues in team sports, including MLB, Major League Soccer (MLS), the National Basketball Association (NBA), the National Football League (NFL), and the National Hockey League (NHL), as well as the franchises contained within those leagues. These leagues attract vast media coverage, generate large television ratings, draw strong crowds, and pay athletes millions of dollars in salaries. Unsurprisingly, many aspiring sport industry candidates desire careers with major league sport franchises. They often dream of being the next general manager of a team and one day receiving a championship ring alongside the athletes they admire. While these dreams are attainable (someone must hold those general manager positions after all), probabilities suggest they are extremely difficult to obtain. There are three times as many Fortune 500 CEO positions than there are general manager positions in the five major leagues listed above. Accordingly, let's examine the role of sales within major league sport franchises and where the multitudes of jobs do exist.

Organization Structure

Major league sport franchises typically are structured with two distinct sides of the organization, as shown in Figure 10.1. Like most businesses, a pro sport franchise has an owner or group of owners that serve as the operator and ultimate

FIGURE 10.1 Standard major League Sport Franchise Structure

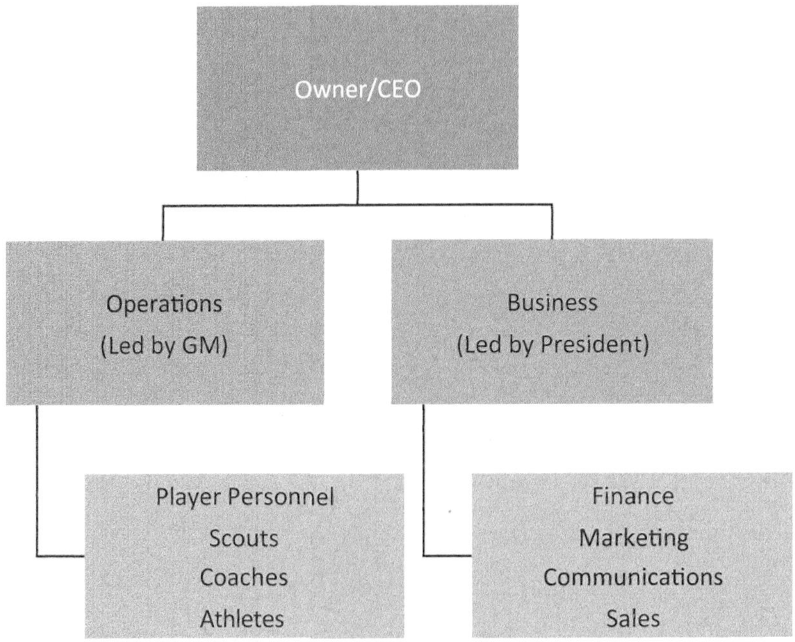

Source: Chad McEvoy

decision-maker for the organization. In many organizations, the leader of the organization may carry the role of chief executive officer or CEO. Beneath the owner/CEO role are the two sides of the franchise: the operations side and the business side. The **operations side** of the professional sport team is the sports aspects of the franchise, including the players, coaches, scouts, and oftentimes the medical staff. The general manager is most commonly the leader of this operations side of the organization. Conversely, the **business side** of the sport franchise is typically led by the team president, although these titles do vary from organization to organization. Similar to a standard corporation or company in other industries, professional sport franchises employ staff across a variety of function areas such as communications, finance, human resources, marketing, and sales. These standard function areas comprise the business side of the professional sport team.

In many of these organizations, the vast majority of employees work on the business side, compared to relatively few in operations. The operations side of the organization is often no more than 10% of the number of staff positions within the franchise. For those with aspirations of becoming the general manager of a team, this presents an extremely difficult challenge. Not only are there thousands of competitors with the same career goals, but operations staffs are quite small, meaning that there are a very limited supply of positions available along the career path that could lead toward a general manager position.

In contrast to the operations side, the business side of the professional sport organization is considerably larger, presenting more employment opportunities for aspiring sport industry employees. In particular, the highest percentage of jobs on the business side of the professional sport franchise is in the sales area. From a probability perspective, you have a much greater chance of securing full-time employment with a professional sport team in sales than you do in operations, marketing, communications, or other functional areas.

Sales Staff Structure

Many major league professional sport franchises employ 50 or more salespeople, with some teams having sales staffs as large as 100. The Philadelphia 76ers possess the largest sales staff in the industry, with 180 sales personnel in 2015.[1] With staffs this large, teams often subdivide their salespeople into smaller groups, or teams, which specialize in specific aspects of sales. Let's examine each of these aspects, or function groups, of the sales operation.

Inside Sales

Inside sales is the most common starting point for new salespeople beginning their careers in sport sales. The traditional definition of the term "inside sales" refers to sales personnel who utilize the telephone and/or online means

Operations side
the sports aspects of the franchise, including the players, coaches, scouts, and oftentimes the medical staff

Business side
typically led by the team president, although these titles do vary from organization to organization

Inside sales
sales personnel who utilize the telephone and/or online means to sell rather than traveling outside the organization's facility to sell face-to-face

---

1 Shelly, J. (2015, June 18). Sixers rely on army of 22-year-olds for marketing. *Philadelphia Magazine*. Retrieved from www.phillymag.com.

to sell rather than traveling outside the organization's facility to sell face-to-face. Note that while telephone and online sales are the most common mediums used by inside sales representatives in professional sports, many teams do utilize inside sales staff in face-to-face sales as at least a small part of their responsibilities.

Major league franchises commonly use their inside sales team as a training and proving ground for potential advancement opportunities into the organization's other sales teams. Inside sales employees, often referred to as **"ticket sales representatives,"** or "TSRs," are full-time employees, although the term of employment is typically for a length of approximately one year. During that time, TSRs receive extensive training about all aspects of the sales process, and then begin to sell under the direction and mentorship of the inside sales director. As their term progresses, TSRs who show promise and initial success as salespeople will have opportunities for promotion to sales functions such as group sales and season ticket sales. Those that are promoted often earn the new title of **"account executive,"** or "AE," and receive an increase in compensation and job security. TSRs who struggle or who don't show the same level of work ethic and future promise will not receive those same opportunities. Quality franchises will help those less successful TSRs find employment elsewhere.

Group Sales

As implied by the term, the **group sales team** is focused on selling tickets to groups of customers. Professional sport teams often define a group as a ticket purchase of 15 to 20 or more tickets to a game. In return for buying this sizeable block of tickets, the group usually receives a price discount, and the tickets may be combined with additional benefits such as hospitality options. Groups traditionally include a variety of community and business organizations, such as a Boy Scout troop, employees from a local insurance company, or a youth sport team. As will be discussed in the next chapter on ticket packaging and pricing, an important aspect of group sales is the cultivation of relationships with group leaders. If the account executive can identify and connect with a key person within an organization, that person can be vitally helpful in convincing peers to buy tickets with the group and even in collecting the ticket money.

Season Ticket Sales

Another area within the sales force that is often a landing spot for new AEs after being promoted from inside sales is the **season ticket sales team**. This team is focused on the sale of season tickets. An indication of the importance of season ticket sales to the success of a pro team is demonstrated by the fact that a specific sales team is charged with focusing solely on season tickets. Consider a team such as the New York Yankees, which plays in the 49,642-seat Yankee Stadium. As Major League Baseball teams play 81 home games, the Yankees sales staff is responsible for trying to sell more than four million total tickets per season. If the Yankees sell 25,000 season tickets, the number of remaining tickets is cut by one half to two million. With demand for individual game tickets subject to factors such as weather, success of the two teams, day of the week, and so on, securing a strong number of season ticket sales prior to the start of the season dramatically reduces the strain

Ticket Sales Representative (TSR)
also known as inside sales employees, these employees are tasked with selling tickets to customers

Account Executive (AE)
TSRs who show promise and initial success as salespeople will have opportunities for promotion to account executives

Group sales
focused on selling tickets to groups of customers

Season ticket sales
focused on the sale of season tickets

on the sales force to sell individual game tickets and other types of ticket inventory during the season.

In line with this same notion, a recent trend in major league professional sports is an increased focus on season ticket sales **retention**—the effort to retain and renew season ticket holders from one year to the next. If a team can successfully renew 80% of its season ticket holders from one year to the next, it has far fewer tickets left to sell that next season. Accordingly, some franchises have relabeled this sales group as "season ticket sales and retention" to signify an increased emphasis on retaining and renewing these key customers, while others have gone even further to create a separate sales team focused solely on servicing and retaining season ticket holders. As examples, the Miami Heat have a sales team called the "season ticket services department," while the Yankees' "season ticket sales and service department" has several staff members carrying the titles of "retention sales specialist."

Retention
retaining existing customers

Premium Sales

One of the most prestigious sales teams is the **premium sales team**. Sales professionals on premium sales teams have generally been promoted multiple times and have established their credentials as strong sellers. This team is tasked with selling the franchise's premium inventory. This includes the luxury suites, club seats, and any other unique, high-priced inventory. A premium sales professional may commonly sit down with a senior executive from a Fortune 500 corporation proposing a five-year contract for a luxury suite valued at well over $100,000 per year. Accordingly, this is not a common starting place for a young, new sales representative still learning the craft. As discussed above with season ticket sales, many franchises have placed an increased emphasis on the retention and renewal aspects of premium sales in recent years.

Premium sales
sales of the franchise's premium inventory

© Ken Durden/Shutterstock.com

Customer Service and Retention

Consistent with the previous discussion, professional sport franchises have learned that it is generally much easier to serve and retain existing customers, particularly key customers like season ticket holders and premium buyers, than it is to replace those customers. As a result, franchises have increased their emphasis on successfully serving and retaining their existing customers and have, correspondingly, hired more staff specifically focused on these key functions.

In two 2013 *Sports Business Journal* columns,[2] expert Bill Sutton discussed the sales staffing hunter/farmer model, and how this model can be utilized by sport organizations. In this model, a "hunter" is a salesperson with strengths in hunting for new customers by actively prospecting for new potential customers and generating sales from those prospects. In contrast, a "farmer" is skilled at building and cultivating relationships with customers, typically existing ones, and can leverage those relationships into retention and renewal success. Organizations utilizing the hunter/farmer model strive to employ a balanced mix of hunters and farmers and to identify which of these roles each sales employee best fits. The organization places its hunters in areas like season ticket sales and premium sales to capitalize on hunters' skills in generating new business, and places its farmers in areas such as customer service/retention to utilize their skills in taking care of existing customers and increasing the likelihood those customers renew the following year.

Corporate Sales

Corporate sales
team focused on the sale and service of corporate sponsorships

While many of the sales teams within a professional sport franchise are focused on the sale and service of tickets, the **corporate sales** team is instead focused on the sale and service of corporate sponsorships. This sponsorship inventory can include a wide variety of opportunities customized to meet the needs of sponsors, such as naming rights, signage, advertising, and hospitality. Similar to premium sales, a salesperson usually must be promoted multiple times in order to reach this function team as it takes experience and skill to meet with a senior executive from a corporation and close a sponsorship sale that may be valued in the millions of dollars.

Ticket Operations

Ticket operations
sometimes called box office management, is a support function to the sales force of a professional sport franchise

In contrast to the sales function areas, **ticket operations**, sometimes called box office management, is a support function to the sales force of a professional sport franchise. The ticket operations area, sometimes referred to as the box office area, is responsible for the processing and fulfillment of ticket purchase orders, the invoicing and charging of payments for those orders, and other issues related to seating and ticketing within the franchise's arena or stadium. The ticket operations managers work closely with the sales staff in performing the functions listed above, and often also work closely with the financial operations of the organization as it relates to the handling of cash and debit/credit card orders, managing the ticket inventory, and financial record keeping. The ticket operations area can be one where farmers instead of hunters are stationed in the organization's staffing strategy.

---

2 Sutton, B. (2013, January 7). On realignment, big screen distractions and sales cultures. *Sports Business Journal*. Sutton, B. (2013, February 11). More on managing hunters and farmers in your organization. *Sports Business Journal*. Retrieved from www.sportsbusinessdaily.com.

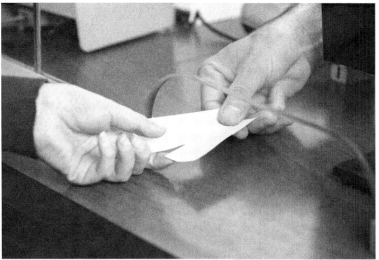

© Tyler Olson/Shutterstock.com

CRM and Analytics

Another sales support area is CRM and analytics. **CRM** stands for customer relationship management. Professional sport franchises have hundreds of thousands of tickets to sell over the course of a season, and those tickets are sold to thousands of separate customers. In previous decades, the extensive record keeping needed for this great number of customers was attempted through paper-based filing systems, but through technological advances, this is now conducted through computerized CRM and ticketing systems. With a few clicks of a computer keyboard or mouse, a sales professional can now instantly identify a specific customer or a desired type of customer profile. In this same vein, professional sports have witnessed a dramatic increase in the use of **analytics** in the business and sales aspects of franchise operations. Ten or more years ago, few if any teams employed specialists in the area of CRM and analytics, but some teams now possess several such staff members. These employees are responsible for using statistical and technological expertise to assist the sales staff in identifying prospects with higher likelihood of purchasing tickets. Consider that if a franchise makes a thousand or more phone

Customer Relationship Management (CRM)
allows employees to merge all information collected from any touchpoint with a customer into a single, easily accessible database, providing a 360-degree picture of that fan or prospect

Analytics
the systematic analysis of data in order to provide information and/ or insight

© Rawpixel.com/Shutterstock.com

calls per day in trying to sell tickets, increasing the closing percentage of those calls by just a couple of percentage points increases the organization's sales revenue by a significant amount. The CRM and analytics teams work to help sales representatives be more efficient in their efforts along these lines.

Minor League Sports

In contrast to their major league counterparts, minor league sport franchises have much smaller staffs, both in sales as well as the entire organizations. Major league franchises may employ hundreds of full-time staff, whereas minor league teams often employ two dozen or fewer on a full-time basis. The level of minor league sport is related to staff size; AAA-level (sometimes called Triple-A level) franchises typically have 30–50 employees on the business side of the organization, but A-level or independent franchises may have just a few full-time staff. At the AAA-level in baseball, or the comparable American Hockey League in hockey, these moderately-sized organizations are sometimes large enough to allow for specialized employee roles. If so, the organizational chart might resemble a smaller version of the major league teams described previously. A Triple-A baseball team might have a group sales function, for example, but it might consist of just one or two full-time staff and interns instead of a group of 8–10 full-time staff as on a major league team. Below this AAA level, organizations are much smaller and this reduced size makes it difficult to have specialized employee roles. In a lower-level minor league team, with perhaps 10 or so full-time employees, those employees often perform several different functions within the organization. An employee might help make outbound sales calls in the morning, prepare the facility for a game in the afternoon, and then work in the box office as game time approaches. That same employee might pitch in to serve hot dogs when the concessions lines get backed up or pull the tarp on the infield during a rain delay when the need arises. The potential downside to this limited staffing is that it becomes difficult to specialize and focus on a single function such as ticket sales, but the trade-off is that the variety of functions performed can keep the job from becoming mundane. Finally, while minor league baseball and hockey are among the best-known minor league team sport organizations, sales opportunities exist in professional sports such as lacrosse, softball, arena football, and other sport leagues as well.

Other Professional Sport Organizations and Innovative Sales Models

Ticket sales opportunities extend beyond just major and minor league team sports. In auto racing, both individual tracks and governing bodies employ sales staff. One of the more interesting sales models has been implemented by the Professional Golfers Association (PGA) Tour in recent years. Most PGA Tour tournaments are operated locally by the individual event organizers, with small full-time staffs and rely heavily on volunteer assistance. The PGA Tour, housed in Ponte Vedra Beach, Florida, has created an inside sales team at its Florida headquarters patterned after the model used in major league team sports. Instead of selling tickets for a single PGA Tour event, this centralized team sells tickets for ten events managed by the

BOX 10.1 Scott Gordon, Inside Sales Manager, PGA Tour

The PGA TOUR Inside Sales Program

The PGA TOUR started an Inside Sales program in January 2014 that focuses on developing sales skills for entry level sales reps for senior level positions and driving new business revenue. With the major focus being on training, the team is provided with three hours per week of sessions involving anything from overcoming objections to appointment training. One way the TOUR's Inside Sales program is unique is how reps are coached on how to drive new business revenue throughout six different markets across the country. Reps are focused on selling corporate hospitality, expo space, advertising and Pro-Am opportunities to businesses who have never spent any money with the TOUR. With each lead that the Inside Sales rep mines, they get the opportunity to co-sell the package with a rep at the tournament. Reps will get the chance to learn from 14 different reps throughout the country and ultimately take what they learn to make it their own. This way, when they are promoted to one of the tournaments in a full-time sales role, they now have learned the fundamentals of what it takes to be successful.

PGA Tour itself. With this bundle of events, the total ticket inventory and corresponding ticket revenues are large enough to support the hiring of 12 full-time salespeople plus 2 executives to lead the team. Tickets are sold primarily over the phone and Internet out of the Tour's Florida headquarters even though the golf events take place across the country. Successful salespeople in the PGA Tour team may have the opportunity to be hired as sales managers for individual Tour events or elsewhere in the sport industry.

Another innovative professional sport sales model is Major League Soccer's National Sales Center (NSC). Somewhat similar to the PGA Tour's inside sales team, the MLS NSC is a centralized model, but the focus of the MLS NSC is on training salespeople more than in generating sales revenue. Located in Blaine, Minnesota, outside of Minneapolis/St. Paul, the MLS NSC selects a group of trainees from its applicant pool and provides approximately four months of hands-on training during

© George Rudy/Shutterstock.com

which trainees learn sales skills, receive feedback from expert trainers including the use of video and audio analysis, and even receive training in interpersonal skills through a partnership with a local improvisational comedy company. Successful trainees through the MLS NSC program are then interviewed and hired by MLS franchises across North America. To date, more than 160 MLS NSC graduates have been hired into full-time sales positions with MLS teams.

College Athletics

Inbound sales

order-takers, waiting for the phone to ring from an inbound call, an order form and check to arrive in the mail, or for someone to show up at the ticket window

While many professional sport teams have possessed extensive ticket sales operations for decades, operations at the college athletics level have been much slower to develop. Historically, college athletic departments have possessed box offices, or ticket offices, that were focused on **inbound sales**, but not outbound sales. In short, these box offices were order-takers, waiting for the phone to ring from an inbound call, an order form and check to arrive in the mail, or for someone to show up at the ticket window. In the 1990s and early 2000s, when professional sport teams were rapidly developing their outbound ticket sales teams, college athletics was slower to adapt and focused predominantly on inbound sales. This is not atypical in the sport industry, as college athletics can sometimes lag behind their professional counterparts in innovation. Other examples of the lag include the growth of sponsorship sales, developments in the public relations/communications area, and in the use of analytics and technology. One potential explanation for this could be that professional sport teams have an owner demanding success both on the playing field and in the financial aspects of the organization, whereas college athletic departments aren't owned but operate as a non-profit organization. Another explanation for slower innovation in college athletics is that athletic departments are a part of a larger university community that typically possesses considerable layers of management and bureaucracy, while professional sport teams are smaller, and thus nimbler business organizations.

Outbound sales

sales personnel who make outbound calls to prospects

Regardless of these reasons for slower development in **outbound sales**, college athletic departments have begun to catch up over the last decade. The early leader in this area was the University of Central Florida (UCF), which hired Matt DiFebo in 2005 from the NBA's Seattle SuperSonics, to help increase its sales revenues. DiFebo's new sales team increased football season ticket sales at UCF by 12,000 tickets and increased annual football ticket revenue by more than $4.5 million in just three years.[3] Other university athletic programs took note and attempted to emulate UCF's ticket sales success. By the early 2010s, most Division I athletic departments had formed their own outbound ticket sales teams, although they typically remain much smaller in scope than their professional sport counterparts. For example, whereas many major league pro teams have 50 or more sales employees, college athletic departments generally have fewer than 10.

Outsourcing

hiring third-party organizations to handle a portion of the business, such as selling tickets

One interesting aspect to this development of ticket sales forces in college athletics has been the use of **outsourcing**. While some athletic departments utilize their own staff to sell tickets, others have outsourced their sales operations to an external third-party company (this is also common with the sale of sponsorships

---

3 DiFebo, S. (2008, September 8). *Season-ticket sales success often starts with staffing, training.* Retrieved from www.sportsbusinessdaily.com

in college sports). External companies may provide an expertise in sales that an athletic department does not possess internally. Furthermore, external companies may compensate their sales employees with commission pay structures, which is often difficult for athletic departments to otherwise do internally because of its rarity in university systems. Two leading outsourcing companies in this area are IMG Learfield Ticket Solutions, originally led by Matt DiFebo after his departure from UCF, and The Aspire Group, which is overseen by longtime NBA executive and sport marketing pioneer Bernie Mullin.

Pursuing a Career in Sport Sales

What does a career path in sport sales look like? The starting place for most new salespeople in sports is inside ticket sales. As mentioned earlier in the chapter, these positions are not intended to be long-term positions but, rather, typically last 9–12 months. Inside sales representatives who show success and promise have opportunities to move up in the organization into more permanent, and higher-paying, sales roles. Those who do not have success do not have such opportunities. For those considering whether to pursue the sales path and inside sales positions, this lack of permanency may be concerning, or perhaps even scary. One way to consider this is not only does the organization have this time period to evaluate the sales representative, but the new sales representative also has the same time period to evaluate both the organization as well as the sales profession, to examine whether this path is right

BOX 10.2

Tips for Interviewing for Your First Sales Position

You have secured an interview for an inside sales position with a professional sport team, or perhaps a college athletic department. You have likely spent years preparing for such an opportunity with hard work in college classrooms and gaining experience through volunteer opportunities and internships. Here is some advice for being successful in that sales interview:

1. Dress conservatively. While relatively casual attire is commonplace in some areas of the sport industry, sales departments typically dress more formally. Unless you have strong evidence that the sales department you are interviewing with has a much more relaxed dress code, wear a suit or comparable type of formal attire. For men, choose subdued, rather than bold, shirts and ties. For women, err on the side of simple and conservative with jewelry and other accessories.

2. Be ready to sell yourself. As you are interviewed for a position as a salesperson, hiring managers will be evaluating your ability to sell. In the interview, you are, first and foremost, selling yourself. Be prepared to confidently describe why you will be successful in this position. Do your homework on the organization and the people you will be interviewing with so that you can show how well prepared you are.

3. Don't be a fan. Your interest in working in sports likely stems from being a sport fan to some degree. That said, sales managers are not looking to hire fans. They are looking to hire employees who can help them reach their sales goals. If you are asked a question like "Why are you interested in this position?" consider discussing your passion for sales and revenue generation more so than your passion for that team or sport. Some hiring managers will go so far as to automatically eliminate any candidate whom answers such a question with a "super-fan" type of answer.

for them. Inside sales representatives who are not successfully promoted often find that this is as a result of effort and/or passion for the sales profession, rather than simply not selling enough tickets.

Inside sales representatives who are successfully promoted often earn positions in group sales, season ticket sales, or **customer service** and retention. Sometimes the path to one of those options is based on how the organization's sales managers believe the representative's skill set fits those options, but the coincidental timing of openings in one area or another can be a factor as well. In terms of fit, the organization learns a lot about the sales representative's strengths and weaknesses as a seller during the inside sales period. Those with a strength as a "hunter" in the hunter/farmer model described earlier in this chapter may be best used in a season ticket sales department as they work hard to drive new business. Those with abilities to develop relationships with potential group leaders from area businesses and community organizations may fit best in a group sales capacity. Finally, those that may not be best suited at making 100 cold calls per day, but who have skills in working with clients, may fit well on a service and retention group.

After a couple of years of success in areas such as group sales, season ticket sales, or customer service/retention, opportunities for further career growth may present themselves. Those with continued success in generating new business may be a fit for the premium sales team, selling luxury seats, club seating, and other premium inventory. Another similarly prestigious area of the sales operation is in corporate sales and sponsorships. Both the premium and corporate areas often involve making single sales worth several hundred thousand dollars, or perhaps even more than a million dollars, so these advancement opportunities are typically reserved for elite sellers. Another path that might emerge is in sales management, such as being the director of the inside sales team, the group sales team, and so on. The skill set needed for success as a sales manager may be quite different than the skills needed to simply sell tickets or other inventory, as the managerial role focuses primarily on leading people rather than selling products. Organizations often struggle to identify and train these managers/leaders given the differences in skills and duties compared to the standard sales role. Sales managers found to have success in leadership capacities may eventually climb to positions like Vice President of Ticket Sales, or even Team President.

Customer service
the interactions a business has with a customer before, during, and after a customer purchases a product

BOX 10.3   Kyle Brant, Director of Group Sales, San Jose Sharks

Succeeding in Sport Sales

So you want to be the next "Wolf of Wall Street"? But you also have a strong passion for the business of sports, knowing full well that you most likely won't be rubbing elbows with the likes of Steph Curry or Aaron Rogers, but rather playing an integral part in the creation of a memory that your soon-to-be clients will recall for the rest of their lives.

Well, everyone has to start somewhere. And when it comes to breaking into the Sport Sales Industry there are ways you can stand out from the pack.

Internship Tips

Having been in the role of Inside Sales Manager for an NBA team and hiring rookie-sellers, I can attest to the important role internships play in standing out. Specifically, when it comes to breaking into sport sales, a general sport team internship where you're doing everything from being an usher to running on-field promotions is great. A more specific sport sales internship where you're cold calling and experiencing the ground floor of selling is better.

As for general sport internships, when you're rolling a tarp on a rainy July morning you probably won't learn much about what it's like to cold-call a single game buyer or how to overcome buyer objections. But you will build character and you will quickly find out during those long hours whether or not you are truly passionate about the *business* of sports. Most hiring managers, like myself, were involved in multiple sport internships before becoming full-time. The hustle does not go unnoticed and gets you one step closer to your dream.

Sport internships in which you are engaged in selling are better for both you and hiring managers. These internships provide you with hands-on, real-life experience of what your future could be like. Many look to sport sales as a way to break into the industry, but when they actually break in, they quickly realize what selling is all about and they typically find themselves out of sports shortly thereafter. This hands-on internship experience provides you the basic building blocks of sport sales: what it's like to cold-call, the importance of relationship-building, and of course, what it's like to be told no 99 times out of 100 . . . not to mention the sweet taste of victory on that 100th call. Experiencing this provides no "surprise" of job expectations on your first day because you know exactly what you're getting into.

For hiring managers, sport sales internships are more attractive for many of the same reasons. As a hiring manager, you want to ensure that there is no surprise of job duties when hiring. The goal is to always have your new employee comfortable with their surroundings and daily expectations before they accept the position. From my experience, very few hiring managers look toward these internships as a way to hire polished ticket sales experts. Being polished is not the expectation from these internships. The expectation is that you've experienced a taste of what sport sales is and that you've found passion in your time spent doing so. My belief has always been that I can teach you how to sell; I can teach you how to build relationships; I can teach you how to overcome objections; I can teach you when to be assertive; I can teach you how to close . . . but I can't teach you to be passionate about what you do; I can't teach "want"; and I can't teach work ethic.

Seeking Employment Tips

As I'm sure you've learned by now, full-time positions within the sport industry don't grow on trees. There are certainly great portals online where you can easily view openings, learn about them, and apply to them online. The downside is that you're relying on just a resume and/or cover letter to get noticed while competing against a mass amount of other applicants with similar background and education as you.

Fortunately, there is another avenue for those seeking employment within the sport sales industry where you not only receive training from some of the best in the industry, but you also have the ability to network and interview with hiring sales managers from both collegiate and professional sport franchises. These are called "Sport Sales Workshops" and they're growing in both popularity and in number; a favorite is the annual "Mount Union Sport Sales Workshop" in Cleveland, Ohio. This is the workshop where I was hired out of, and most teams see it as a must-attend. However, there are other workshops growing in popularity around the country and teams are starting to host their own as a way of attracting local talent.

It is not enough to just attend one of these workshops. Although these workshops provide you a great opportunity to network and build relationships with employers, you still need to stand out amongst the hundreds of other candidates who are attending by taking advantage of that opportunity.

Here are four tips on how to stand out at your next workshop:

1. Come Prepared:

   Have copies of your resume, printed on quality paper, as well as any other applicable documents. Have experience selling? Include your stats!

   Research the teams attending and who is representing each team.

   Create a solid LinkedIn profile with a professional looking headshot.

   Meeting with a team? Do your research on LinkedIn, have a general idea of that person's background. This will create talking points for you as you find common ground, and you will stand out since most attendees will not take the time to do this.

2. Be Professional:

   Business professional—there is no such thing as being overdressed.

   Firm handshake, good eye contact, speak well.

3. Get Comfortable Being Uncomfortable:

   During the training sessions, volunteer when asked.

   If you're nervous or frightened about saying or doing something wrong, then you're on the right track. Just remember, be professional and do your best.

   Don't hide—network, build relationships, be confident.

4. Put Your Passion on Display:

   When it comes to networking and interviewing, tell your story. Everyone has a story, make yours stick out. Many call this an "elevator speech," where you have 30–45 seconds to sell YOU. If you can't sell yourself first, then teams won't trust you to sell for them.

   Sport Sales is an industry that generously rewards those willing to step outside their comfort zones and those willing to go the extra mile. Breaking into Sport Sales requires these same abilities.

© Kendall Hunt Publishing Company

It should be noted that career paths are often not linear. An examination of a professional team's staff directory generally reveals a majority of employees in their 20s and 30s. It is not uncommon for a salesperson in professional or collegiate sport to get hired away by one of their own clients in another line of business, particularly as many other industries pay higher wages or have less demanding hours. Transitioning out of sport is fairly frequent along these lines. Even within sport, sales representatives may move elsewhere within the organization or to another peer organization commonly.

Finally, compensation increases as salespeople move from inside sales to account executive and beyond. Even more encouraging, job and career satisfaction also generally increase as sellers move up the organizational chart.[4] In comparison to non-sport sales positions, Kirk Wakefield notes that "teams are able to attract able-bodied candidates with compensation levels markedly below starting salaries of sales and marketing graduates working in other industries ($51,900). That said, once promoted to an account executive position, prospects begin looking up." Table 10.1 shows the average total compensation, job satisfaction, and career satisfaction for salespeople in various sales positions in professional sports.

---

4 *Baylor S3 Report.* Retrieved from http://baylors3.com/top-5-things-we-learned-about-compensation-salespeople-and-their-managers/.

TABLE 10.1 Compensation and Satisfaction

Title	Average Total Compensation	Job Satisfaction	Career Satisfaction
Vice President	$226,820	93	94
Senior Director	$168,820	80	81
Director	$109,430	91	92
Manager	$ 74,560	77	81
Senior Account Executive	$ 84,360	80	79
Account Executive	$ 48,700	82	84
Inside Sales	$ 26,670	77	73

Note: N = 633*

Baylor S3 Report. Retrieved from http://baylors3.com/top-5-things-we-learned-about-compensation-salespeople-and-their-managers/.

BOX 10.3 Buffy Filippell, Owner, Teamwork Online

How to Make Your Application Stand Out

TeamWork Online is a mobile platform for anyone aspiring to land a career in sports and live events, particularly sales executives. We host a mobile recruiting and networking platform, network events, and career fairs. We also conduct executive searches on behalf of employers in the sports and live event industry. Over 100,000 people have been matched to their dream jobs through TeamWork Online's products and services.

Here are four stories of TeamWork Online hires and how they augmented their applications and landed a position in sales.

Casey Katz, 2015 Mount Union Sport Sales Workshop Attendee, now Account Manager, Miami Heat

One of the more popular events on the calendar for aspiring young ticket sales professionals is the Mount Union Sport Sales Workshop held in February. TeamWork Online is a promoter of this event. Over 50 Inside Sales Managers from the NBA, NFL, MLS, MLB, and other leagues trek to Cleveland, Ohio, to be able to meet up with the next up-and-comers in the sport industry who think they want to start their careers in sales. There have been wonderful connections made and a number of outstanding executives hired.

Casey Katz offered these suggestions on how to interview and land a job after her successful event:

- Don't be afraid to talk to anyone, and have a value proposition—what can you provide the employer?
- When you meet a sales hiring manager, keep the conversation going by asking a lot of questions, about his/her background, how he/she landed the position, what he/she likes most about his/her job, etc.
- Ask for feedback. Sales hiring managers really like "coachable" employees. Show you are willing to learn.
- Line up meetings in advance of events. If you can find out who will be attending an event ahead of time, you will beat out the competition; reach out to the sales hiring managers early. Ask for e-mail addresses from the event organizer, or use the team's home page to figure out someone's e-mail address and write them. Most sport executives use e-mail to communicate.

- Keep introducing yourself to people and remind them of your value proposition.
- After a conference, job fair, or networking event—almost immediately—send an e-mail to each person you met, remind them of your value proposition, and if you can remember anything about your conversation, add that to your e-mail.

Sales is all about how much money have you raised.

Many individuals have raised money for their fraternity or charities of their choice. Whether you've raised $500 or $10,000, any amount is a meaningful and significant accomplishment that can catch the eye of a sales manager in the sport industry.

Matt Ritchie, Manager of Inside Sales, Cincinnati Reds

Matt landed his management position online. How he stood out was through his online 140-character headline, "In my last 4 years of selling I hit my sales goal for selling by over $100,000 in my last 3 out of the 4 years selling." If you can put metrics to what you have to offer, you get attention.

Melanie Seiser, Manager of Major League Soccer's National Sales Center

Melanie was one of the first class of hires for Major League Soccer's National Sales Center. All applicants were asked to send in a video. Melanie's video became one of the most watched elevator pitch videos of all sport and of course landed her in the first class of executives trained to become sales executives. It's pleasing to see she is training the next generation: https://www.youtube.com/embed/hoKztt13WEg

Melanie, a journalism major from Ohio University, is often asked why she chose sales as a profession. She believes that sales is all about relationship building and providing the best possible fan experience. "If you are looking for the opportunity to connect with the fan and create lifelong memories for them, then I would highly recommend getting into ticket sales and particularly the MLS National Sales Center."

Senior executives interested in moving into sales roles need to have a track record of sales as well as good references.

Michael DeMartino, Vice President Corporate Partnerships, Jacksonville Jaguars

Michael DeMartino, was living in New Jersey working for the New Jersey Jets as a suite sales executive and wanted to move from premium seating sales to corporate sponsorship sales. He had sold some sponsorships earlier in his career. His resume said his title was Director of Premium Sales. Michael decided to use a social media platform to tell his story. He crafted an about.me page and made a headline that said: "Sold millions of dollars in corporate sponsorships." He applied for the job online then sent a link to that page to the hiring manager for the Jacksonville Jaguars, who read the headline, called a friend of his in New Jersey, received a good reference, and hired Michael for a sponsorship sales job.

© Kendall Hunt Publishing Company

Chapter Summary

Sales is a vital part of nearly any sport organization. The revenues are the backbone of successful organizations. Professional sport teams and, more recently, intercollegiate athletic departments utilize sales personnel to generate revenue. A career in sport sales can provide an opportunity for employment in the industry and room to grow in this regard.

Chapter activities

Find a current job posting online for one group sales, inside sales, and premium sales position in professional sports. Based on these descriptions, describe the similarities and differences between these three types of sales positions.

1. Create a graphic or image that illustrates the typical career progression in sport sales, beginning at the entry-level and moving toward senior management levels.
2. Explain the hunter/farmer model of sales staffing. What is meant by the terms "hunters" and "farmers"?
3. What function does the CRM personnel serve within a sales team?
4. How does the sales staff differ between a major league professional sport franchise and a minor league franchise?
5. Explain why college athletics programs have been slower to adopt significant sales structures compared to their professional sport team peers.

Jayhawks in the Field

James Kocen

Fan Development Representative for Nashville Predators

Hometown
Milwaukee, WI

Education
2016 – University of Kansas (Sport Management, Business, Leadership)

Previous Positions
Account Coordinator at Cantwe11 Marketing

1. What challenges does working for a team in a market like Nashville present and how do you distinguish the Predators experience from other competitors?

Being located in the south, football is the big sport. Many of our fans are tourists or have another team who they cheer for because they are transplants to the area. That being said, we try our best to tie in the "Music City" theme into our games and make it an experience that goes beyond just the hockey game. Once we get people in the doors and out to watch a hockey game, many of them fall in love with the sport and our team very quickly.

2. What is unique and enjoyable about working for a hockey team that you may not see working for other sports?

Hockey is widely considered one of the "big four" sports, but it is definitely a sport that has less exposure than others. Kids don't grow up playing hockey like they do playing other sports, so when we are able to expose people to a new sport and team and get them to support us it is very rewarding. Hockey is also a sport where watching in person is much more enjoyable and thrilling than watching on TV, whereas other sports such as football are having fans watch from home more and more.

3. You served as the President of the Sport Management Club while you were at KU. Tell us about that experience and the impact it had on your career.

As a young person in college, being in a leadership role was very helpful. Looking back, I always had the help of faculty if I needed

it, but when I was in the role I felt like I needed to handle things on my own and with the help of my peers which forced us to get our hands dirty and figure things out ourselves. Being the main point of contact for the club was also very beneficial from a networking perspective. When I
set up stadium tours or other events, I was able to meet people who have prominent roles in the industry and that is one of the most important aspects of spots.

4. Describe the experience of "walking down the hill" on graduation day at KU.

Best day of my life! Walking down the hill was an amazing experience where I was able to celebrate the end of all of the hard work I put in during my time at KU. What made it even better was getting to share that experience with all of my friends and classmates (many of whom are like family now).

5. If you could go back and give advice to James Kocen when he was sitting in Introduction to Sport Management during his freshman year, what would you tell him?

Work harder. I had a lot of fun during my time at KU and did well in all of my classes, but I definitely could've had just as much fun while doing even better. A lot of the stuff I learned about I thought wasn't important at the time, but being in the real world you find out quickly that some of that stuff was indeed important.

6. Describe the favorite parts of your job and give some specific examples if possible.

Working for a professional team has a lot of benefits. I really enjoy being able to watch games in between my game day duties and your fandom is just different working for a team. Beyond that, I have amazing coworkers and I think a lot of that has to do with the fact that we are all bought into advancing our careers past our current entry level jobs and we all understand what it means to work in sports. Having people like that to share the peaks and valleys with is much needed during a long season. Lastly, I really enjoy being able to talk with people about our team. Whether it is a waiter at lunch or someone I bump into around town, people love talking about sports and having a unique perspective of working in sports, they love talking with me about my job and our team.

Name: _____ Section: _____ Date _____

HSES 289
Introduction to Sport Management
In-Class Quiz and Activity Sheet

Name (or names if done in a group)

Answer #1

Answer #2

Answer #3

Chapter 11

Sponsorship and Endorsement

Kimberly Miloch Texas Woman's University, Heidi Parker University of Southern Maine,
Amanda Glenn Texas Woman's University, Jacquelyn Wilson Texas Woman's University

KEY TERMS

Relationships

Acquisition

Endorsements

Activation

Sponsorship Proposal

Icon Sportswire/Getty Images

It is unlikely that consumers in general, or attendees of an event in particular, will feel any passion toward a product; they do, however, have strong feelings about causes, events, and sports teams with which they are affiliated. Companies that are able to successfully tap into a consumer's psychological connectedness to a property align themselves to something much more meaningful to that individual than a mere product. It would appear that, rather than creating mere awareness, the promise of sponsorship may lie in the opportunity to capture a consumer's 'share of the heart.'

(Madrigal, 2000, 22-23)

Sponsorship

Sport sponsorship has evolved from simple signage at a ballpark to a driver of revenues for sport entities and a key focal point in the marketing strategy of many companies. Even in the midst of an economic recession, companies spent approximately $18 billion on sponsorship in 2011 and are projected to spend close to $18.87 billion in 2012 (IEG, 2012). Of those dollars, roughly 68%, or approximately $11.23 billion, are spent on sport sponsorship (IEG, 2010). For instance, Northeast Delta Dental recently signed a 10-year naming rights deal with the Toronto Blue Jays Double A affiliate team, the New Hampshire Fisher Cats; Safe Auto has signed on as a sponsor of Ultimate Fighting Championship (UFC); Farmers Insurance just agreed to $650 million, 30-year naming rights deal with the yet to be built Farmers Field in downtown Los Angeles; and for the first time in over a decade, the 2011 NHL All-Star game had a presenting sponsor—Discover Card. This chapter will outline the key concepts specific to sport sponsorship and athlete endorsement.

Sponsorship Defined

Sport sponsorship originally represented an uncluttered form of advertising which appealed to companies as a means to differentiate their products and brands from competitors. As sponsorship grew and became more cluttered, the need to strategically

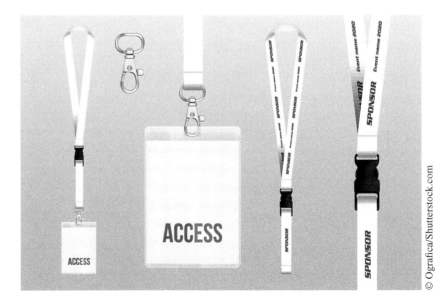

© Ografica/Shutterstock.com

craft and develop unique sponsorships that connected with consumers became a central focus. Sponsorship is defined as "an investment, in cash or in kind, in an activity, in return for access to the exploitable commercial potential associated with that activity" (Meenaghan, 1991, 36). To become a sponsor, a company must purchase **rights** from a sport organization or event, after which, a company can use various marketing strategies to communicate their connection to the sport team or event. Sponsorship is based on the **exchange theory**, the idea that a successful exchange between two or more parties is dependent on both parties feeling what they receive for their services or goods is equal to their offerings (Crompton, 2004). In other words, *both* the sport organization and the sponsor must feel the relationship is beneficial to their respective organizational objectives.

Sponsorships originally started as an altruistic endeavor—organizations looking to support a cause deemed worthy or give back to their communities. However, sponsorship has grown into a complex marketing strategy with emphasis on increasing an organization's bottom line (Meenaghan, 2001). The purchasing and leveraging of sponsorships has become an integral part of the marketing mix and, and for many organizations, is the primary source of communication with consumers (Howard and Crompton, 2005). As a result, the relationship between sport organizations and sponsoring businesses has become more complex with sport organizations dependent on sponsorship dollars and organizations looking to get the most from their investment (Burton and O'Reilly, 2011; Stotlar, 2004).

Sponsorship differs from traditional advertising in a number of ways. Recognizing the need to spend money in leveraging and activating sponsorships is one way in which sponsorship differs from traditional advertising. Additionally, the objectives of an organization are often different when marketing through sponsorship rather than more traditional methods. For instance, with traditional marketing efforts, and advertising in particular, it is somewhat evident a company is trying to promote or sell a product or service. Consumers may be guarded and skeptical and unconsciously block those advertising messages. However, sponsorship works differently as consumers see an organization providing money, goods, and/or services to a sport team or event and a sense of goodwill is created (Meenaghan, 1991). Consumers feel more positively about an organization that supports their favorite team or an event to which they have a personal connection. As Burton and O'Reilly (2011) note, sponsorships are associated with a particular sport entity, and this association may favorably drive consumer perceptions. For instance, consider how seeing a Gatorade commercial makes one feel compared to how knowing Gatorade is the sponsor of your favorite team. It may be that one feels more favorably about Gatorade when connecting to them positively with a favorite team, sport, or athlete.

Perhaps the main difference between traditional advertising and sponsorship involves the development of a relationship between sponsor and consumer. Sponsorship of a sporting event or team allows the sponsor to "establish an intimate and emotionally involved relationship(s) with a target audience" (Crompton, 2004, 270). This ability to connect emotionally with consumers is one of the main benefits of sponsorship. However, the key to this benefit is in understanding the consumer-team-sponsor relationship.

Consumer-Team-Sponsor Relationship

The consumer-team-sponsor relationship is best understood through Heider's (1958) **balance theory**. The balance theory suggests people try to maintain a sense of balance in their lives and their actions and judgments are often influenced by the need to preserve such balance. It is useful to discuss the balance theory using diagrams which represent the consumer-team-sponsor relationship (see Figure 11.1).

In general, the adages "your friends are my friends" and "the enemy of my enemy is my friend" summarize the balance theory. For example, consider the relationship shown between consumer, team, and sponsor in Figure 11.1. The first triangle shows a positive relationship between the consumer and the team as well as the sponsor and the team. The balance theory suggests, given the positive relationships between the team and consumer and the positive relationship between the team and sponsor, that the consumer and sponsor are also likely to have a positive relationship. In other words, the consumer, or fan, will feel better about the sponsor given their mutual relationship with the team, as this results in a balanced relationship. However, as shown in the third triangle of Figure 11.1, if a consumer has a negative relationship with a sponsor of their favorite team, the relationship is unbalanced and perhaps unsettling for the consumer.

For example, research which was conducted on NASCAR fans found that fans felt more favorably toward their favorite driver's sponsor than the sponsors of other drivers (Dalakis and Levin, 2005). Interestingly, the research also showed that fans felt more negatively toward the sponsor of a driver they strongly disliked than other team sponsors. This negative relationship is depicted in the second triangle in Figure 11.1—if the consumer (fan) does not like a team, they are also likely to have more negative feelings toward that team's sponsor.

However, the key to the relationship between the consumer and the sponsor is the *strength* of the relationship between the consumer and the team/event. Consumers that are not highly identified with, or feel strongly connected to, a particular team or sport event do not need to feel more positively about a sponsor in order to maintain a sense of balance. Yet, consumers who are highly identified with a team or sport event feel more favorably about the team/event sponsors and are more likely to purchase their products (Cornwell andCoote, 2005; Gwinner and Swanson, 2003; Madrigal, 2000).

FIGURE 11.1 Consumer-Team-Sponsor Relationships

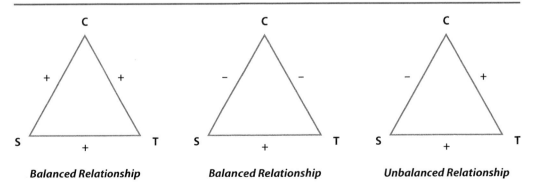

Balanced Relationship   Balanced Relationship   Unbalanced Relationship

Therefore, a sport team or event provides an audience of consumers which sponsors can exploit by capitalizing on the consumer-team-sponsor relationship. If a sport organization or sporting event is a large part of a consumer's self-concept, by attaching a product or brand to the team or event, sponsors become intertwined in part of a "consumer's extended self" (Madrigal, 2000, 22).

Sponsorship Acquisition and Management

Several key steps are central in acquiring sport sponsorships. First, the sport entity must understand the typical goals and objectives of sponsors. Based on that understanding, sport entities must develop and refine their respective **sponsorship inventory**. A sponsorship inventory is a list of items that a sport entity has available to include as elements of a sponsorship. The inventory also includes the number of each item available and the market value of the item. Examples include season tickets, luxury suite, signage, community relations activities, in-arena or on-field promotions, public address announcements, website advertising, and so forth. Within an inventory, categories should be developed. Determining the categories for an inventory depends on the location or property, selecting the different levels of items that can be included in a sponsorship, and how it will be produced when sponsored. After an inventory is developed or refined, sport entities must prospect for potential sponsors. In doing so, sport entities should segment their respective market for potential sponsors just as they would segment for target markets. Depending on the level of sport (i.e., major league, minor league, or interscholastic), the sponsorship inventory and market segmentation may differ. While prospecting, sport entities should identify viable target companies for sponsorship. Sport entities must research target companies and understand their marketing and brand management strategies and goals as well as identify key decision makers within the respective company. Once the key decision makers have been identified, they should be contacted with the goal of scheduling a face-to-face meeting so the sport entity and company can discuss the potential partnership. During this meeting, it is essential that the sport entity determine the objectives of the potential sponsor so that an appropriate sponsorship proposal may be designed and presented. Sponsorship proposals typically include a description of the sport organization or event; the proposed sponsorship, pricing for the sponsorship, important dates and terms, and first right of refusal. A sample sponsorship for a minor league franchise may be viewed in Table 11.1. The sponsorship should also include strategies for leveraging and activation. The paragraphs below outline typical sponsor objectives.

Sponsor Objectives

The growth of sponsorship has certainly changed the sport landscape in recent years. Sport organizations have become dependent on sponsorship dollars and some organizations have consistently utilized sponsorship as an important tool in the marketing mix. However, the growth of sport sponsorship has also led some consumers to feel like sport has become too commercialized and over saturated

TABLE 11.1 Minor League Franchise Sample Sponsorship

Doe's Food Stores
Sponsorship Agreement
XYZ Athletics

This sponsorship agreement expires July 31, 2013.

SIGNAGE
Scoreboard
One (1) 2'x 3' full color advertisement displayed on the bottom of the electronic scoreboard. Since every race concludes with the times being posted on the scoreboard, it will be the area in which the most fans are looking at the scoreboard.

Starting Block
Two (2) full color advertisements on the 1'x 1' area on top of starting blocks.
Four (4) full color advertisements on the 9"x 11" on sides of starting blocks. All races must begin from the starting blocks and this will allow fans and media to view the Doe's logo repeatedly.

Sectional Banner
Two (2) 5'x 7' full color advertisements in the primary viewing area for swimming. Banners will be hung above seating, where spectators on either side of the pool can view the banner across from their designated section.

CONCESSSIONS
Control of the concession stand will be awarded to Doe's upon agreement. This includes the ability to choose the menu or items sold. The concession stand will be staffed by XYZ Athletics Staff, but will be controlled by Doe's Food Stores.

GAME NIGHT SPONSOR
Two (2) event night sponsorships. Doe's will receive the role of title sponsor for two (2) nights of events throughout the season. Doe's will have the ability to distribute items or products consumers as they enter or exit the venue. Since distribution of promotional items and/or product sampling has been proven to increase brand loyalty among consumers, it is favorable for both the fans and the sponsor. Promotional items and/or products will be mutually determined by Doe's and XYZ.

DOE'S FIVE A DAY PROGRAM
Doe's will receive access to assist the Bus Brigade and will receive title sponsorship for local community schools transportation to and from XYZ Swimming Events. The Swimming Bus Brigade program will provide students throughout the community the chance to attend a Division I University campus and swimming events. This will be paired with the Doe's Five A Day program to help promote goal setting, working to achieve them, as well as healthy eating to Dallas youth.

GAME PROGRAM ADVERTISING
One (1) Permanent half page full color advertisement on the back of the official XYZ Swimming Program.
One (1) Full page, full color advertisement on the inside cover of Classic and special event printed materials.

SEASON TICKETS
Eight (8) season ticket passes for all home swimming events, including Classics and Special events. Doe's will also receive two (2) season passes for all XYZ athletic events.

PA ANNOUNCMENTS
Two (2) Public address announcements during each day of home events, Doe's will provide the materials for the public address announcement, however, XYZ announcing staff will perform announcement at appropriate times during the event.

USE OF XYZ LOGO
As a corporate partner for XYZ, Doe's has written permission to use the XYZ Athletics, and XYZ Mustang logo to leverage the sponsorship package. XYZ Athletic Corporate Relations officials will approve any promotional material developed by Doe's which includes the use of the XYZ, XYZ Swimming and Diving, XYZ Athletics, or XYZ Mustangs.

FIRST RIGHT OF REFUSAL

Doe's Food Stores, as a major corporate sponsor, is granted the first right of refusal for the time period of the 2011–2013 seasons.

COST OF PACKAGE: $18,000
$10,000 DUE AT SIGNING
$4,000 DUE APRIL 1, 2011
$4,000 DUE AUGUST 1, 2011

---

with company signage and brand logos. The "clutter," now commonplace in many venues, is ignored by many consumers and has been shown to be ineffective in terms of consumer sponsor brand recall tests. Additionally, some sport fans prefer the traditional feel of a venue, uncluttered with sponsor signage. This has led to some sport organizations, such as the University of Michigan, to forgo venue signage altogether.

Debates have also sprung up over the fit between a sponsor and a sporting event. For example, many American universities will not partner with alcoholic behavior companies. School officials feel that partnering with a company who sells alcohol sends the wrong message to the students of the school, who are predominately under the legal drinking age. Major League Baseball (MLB) and NASCAR have had similar decisions to make regarding the sponsorship of tobacco companies. Ultimately, sport managers must decide what products and brands are an appropriate match to the values of the organization.

Determining what organizations are a good fit to target for sponsorship is not a decision which should be taken lightly. In addition to fit, sport managers should consider company stability, company longevity, and company reputation.

The primary goal of any sponsorship and marketing strategy is to drive sales and revenues. Companies may have many objectives with sponsorship, and all of these objectives serve the ultimate goal of driving sales and revenue. Whether the objective is to increase awareness or to reinforce brand image, ultimately companies desire an increase in revenues and an increased market share. Thus, sponsorships should be designed based on sponsor objectives. In the past, sport entities developed standard sponsorship packages based on level of expenditures. This model is no longer appropriate in today's cluttered and return on

investment driven marketplace. Sport entities should match their sponsorship inventories with sponsor objectives, and be creative in designing sponsorships. Typical sponsor objectives include increasing awareness for a particular product or brand, increasing sales, maintaining a specific brand image, re-branding, increasing business-to-business partnerships, rewarding consumers or employees, gaining an increase in market share, gaining access to a desired target market, establishing a favorable rapport with target consumers, providing hospitality and entertainment opportunities, enhancing community relations, and differentiating from competing products or brands. Regardless of the objective, sport entities must strive to align objectives with the elements of the sponsorship. For example, as part of its desire to align itself with the U.S.G.A. and its consumer base, Polo engaged in a five-year partnership in which it will serve as the organization's official apparel partner. As part of this sponsorship, Polo will provide on-site retail shops at tournaments and promote its association with golf via various advertisements (Smith, 2011a). In efforts

FIGURE 11.2 Steps in Sponsor Acquisition

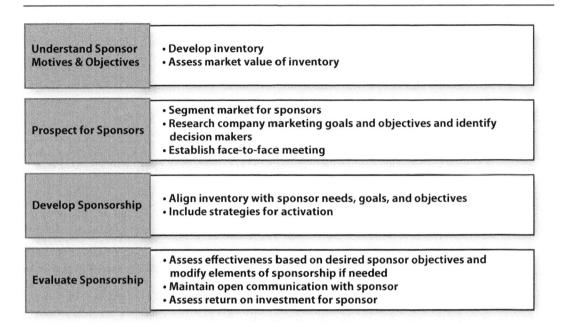

Understand Sponsor Motives & Objectives	• Develop inventory • Assess market value of inventory
Prospect for Sponsors	• Segment market for sponsors • Research company marketing goals and objectives and identify decision makers • Establish face-to-face meeting
Develop Sponsorship	• Align inventory with sponsor needs, goals, and objectives • Include strategies for activation
Evaluate Sponsorship	• Assess effectiveness based on desired sponsor objectives and modify elements of sponsorship if needed • Maintain open communication with sponsor • Assess return on investment for sponsor

Developed from the framework of Irwin, Sutton, and McCarthy (2002), Mullin, Hardy, and Sutton (2007), and Stotlar (2009).

to enhance its fan experience, IndyCar designed the Izod IndyCar Fan Village at races. This piece of inventory not only adds value to the experience for fans, but it also provides a strategic avenue for sponsor activation. As part of the village, Verizon showcases its IndyCar content and phones. Honda is providing player autographs, and Izod is hosting a social media area, the Izod Social Cloud, in which fans are entertained with Twitter feeds, videos, and news (Mickle, 2011).

There are many ways an organization can sponsor a team or an event. For example, an organization may sign on as the title sponsor such as the Tostitos Fiesta Bowl or, in NASCAR, the Chase for the Sprint Cup. As a title sponsor, the sponsor name is incorporated into the name of the event. Likewise, organizations may also buy the naming rights to a building such as Lucas Oil Stadium or FedEx Field. Given the high visibility of the sponsorship, title sponsorships and naming rights are some of the most expensive and are often negotiated for extended periods of time.

Organizations can also become the official sponsor of a particular product category. For instance, Pepsi may sign on as the official beverage sponsor of an event. This type of sponsorship ensures that only Pepsi products are sold and consumed at the event. It is not uncommon for an event to have an official beverage sponsor, such as Coca-Cola or Pepsi, an official beer sponsor, such as Anheuser Busch, as well as official sponsors in a number of other product categories (i.e., apparel, equipment, etc.). For example, at Syracuse University, Pepsi is the official beverage sponsor, Budweiser is the official beer sponsor, and Nike is the official apparel and shoe sponsor.

Sport managers should understand the importance of building relationships with sponsors. This includes working to understand the desire of the sponsor and working together to create a customized sponsorship portfolio which meets the needs and expectations of both parties. For example, at Minute Maid Park, home of

TABLE 11.2 Sport Sponsorships

NBA—American Express	Official title: "All-Star Entertainment Series Presented by American Express."
MLB—Houston Astros and Chick-Fil-A	Chick-Fil-A fowl poles at Minute Maid Park (if a ball hits a fowl pole in the outfield of Minute Maid Park, each spectator receives a coupon for a free Chick-Fil-A sandwich.)
MLB—Houston Astros and Marathon Oil	Marathon Oil Friday night fireworks; largest routine firework display in South Texas, that is designed to highlight downtown and Minute Maid Park on behalf of Marathon Oil.
NCAA—BCS Games	Examples: Tostitos Bowl, Meineke Car Care Bowl; the BCS games are sponsored and marketed on the sponsors packaging or main advertising materials.
2008—Olympics in Beijing and Coca-Cola	Coca-Cola Olympic torch relay; completely sponsored by Coca-Cola and expected to be a majorly watched part of the Olympic Opening Ceremony.
NFL—Coors Brewing and National Football League	Coors placed NFL logos on their cans and bottles during the season to promote the NFL.
NFL—Gatorade and National Football League	Gatorade is the official drink of the NFL on the field and it is routinely marketed during games and especially timeouts.
NASCAR—All Sponsorships	During each NASCAR race, drivers appear in commercials with their sponsors, it is important to both driver and sponsor to keep an open relationship. Often like Dale Earnhardt Jr. and the Budweiser sponsorship; or Clint Bowyer and Cheerios.
MLB—Ranger and Character Race by Ozarka	At the MLB Texas Rangers home games, Ozarka sponsors a race during the baseball game in which performers race across the field and the winner (1 or 3) will determine which card spectators received won the daily prize.
NFL—Snickers and NFL	"Snicker handles the hunger of the NFL"; where the Mars corporation handles the major hunger of the NFL players and fans with the Snickers candy bars.

Source: Choi, J. (2008). "Coca-Cola China's Virtual Olympic Torch Relay program at the 2008 Beijing Olympic Games: adding interactivity to a traditional offline Olympic activation." *International Journal of Sports Marketing & Sponsorship* 9(4), 246-255

the Houston Astros, the sponsorship of the foul poles in the outfield was effective and a humorous play on words for the Chick-fil-a "Eat Mor Chikin®" use of the "Fowl Poles" for the MLB Games. This sponsorship was activated with a giveaway of free sandwiches to 30,000 fans at an Astros home stand during the summer of 2006 (CFA Houston, 2006). Chick-fil-a did not sponsor an entire event, just a small area that was able to be seen both on the field and on screen by at-home spectators.

After potential sponsors have been identified and research has been conducted, contact should be made with potential sponsors. Every encounter with a potential sponsor represents a key opportunity to build a relationship. In building the relationship, it is important to make sure the sponsor does not feel like every other cold call. When

FIGURE 11.3   Sport Sponsor Objectives

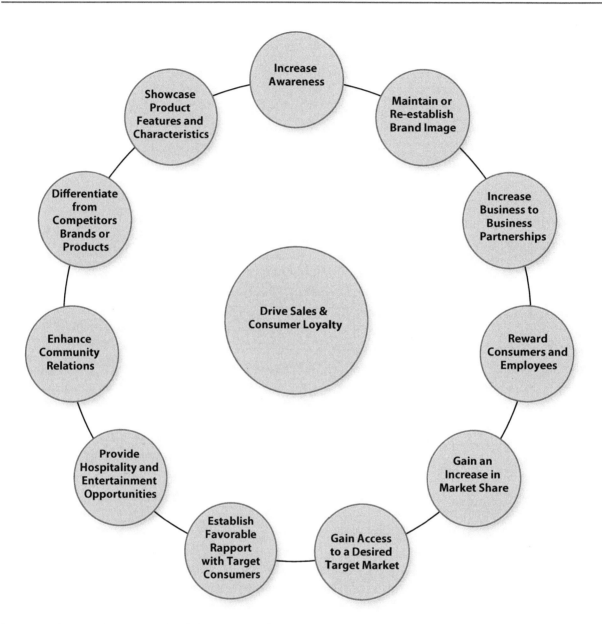

Developed from the framework of IEG (2012); Irwin, Sutton, and McCarthy (2002); Mullin, Hardy, and Sutton (2007); and Stotlar (2009).

speaking to a potential sponsor in person or on the phone, as in sales, it is important to stay personable and understanding. If someone would like to reschedule a time to talk, politely and professionally schedule a time to call back. The more open the communication and the stronger the rapport that a sponsor and an organization can build, the easier it is for both parties to come to agreements and further the benefits of a full sponsorship. It is also common to offer sponsors **first right of refusal**. First right of refusal mandates the sport entity allow the sponsor to first rights to renew the sponsorship. In other words, the sport entity will not offer the sponsorship or any of its components to another potential sponsor unless the current company decides not to renew the sponsorship.

Leveraging and Activation

In meeting the objectives of both parties, **leveraging** and **activation** of the sponsorship are key. Leveraging sponsorship should be a joint effort between the sport organization/event and the sponsor. Sport organizations should work with sponsors to assist them in finding ways to effectively leverage and communicate their relationship. In doing so, sport organizations help ensure sponsors maximize return on investment. If sponsors feel they are getting good return on their investment and view the sponsorship as beneficial, then they are more likely to renew their sponsorships and continue to build the relationship.

Leveraging is the process of communicating and marketing a sponsorship to consumers. In other words, when leveraging a sponsorship, companies desire to create an awareness of their association with the respective sport entity among the target consumer base. For example, Samsung, an official world-wide partner of the Olympic Games, pays for the right to communicate its affiliation with the Olympics through cash, goods, and/or services. Samsung must also find creative ways to leverage sponsorship and let the world know of its relationship with the Olympic Games.

Leveraging is essential for sponsorship effectiveness and the cost of leveraging sponsorship should be factored into the overall budget for sponsoring an event or team. It is common for companies to spend significant additional monies to both leverage and activate the sponsorship, and many often spend as much in leveraging as they spend on purchasing the initial sponsorship rights (Meenaghan, 1994).

Activation of the sponsorship is closely linked to leveraging, but focuses on creating a connection with consumers. While leveraging is intended to create awareness for the sponsorship, activation strategies focus on establishing a connection with consumers and meeting sponsor objectives through the components of the sponsorship. An activation strategy or plan ensures that the components and elements of the sponsorship are being utilized in a manner that meets sponsor objectives. Creating a connection with consumers and appropriately utilizing the elements of the sponsorship may occur through strategic use of media or promotions, social media, mobile technology such as text messaging, websites, and even business-to-business partnerships. Some common tools used for activation include print or television advertising, social media, mobile and web technologies, and public and community relations (IEG, 2005; Miloch and Lambrecht, 2006). Additional avenues for activation include hospitality events, retail outlets, and activities and promotions at the venue (It's all about, 2011).

Sport organizations and companies have recognized the importance of activation as a key driver of return on investment for sponsorships. For example, Major League Soccer sponsors activated their respective sponsorships with the league around its 2011 All-Star Game at Red Bull Arena in New Jersey. Anheuser-Busch designed its brand management campaign with the game as a focal point by using video advertising in Times Square. Pepsi advertised on subway trains. Allstate held a viewing party for fans, and Visa advertised on food trucks during the league's soccer expo. Castrol partnered with AutoZone to offer a sweepstakes in which

BOX 11.1 Samsung as a World-Wide Olympic Partner

Samsung became a World-Wide Olympic Partner in 1997 after a successful relationship as a local sponsor of the 1988 Seoul Olympic Games. Samsung is currently committed to the Olympics through the 2016 Rio De Janeiro games.

As a World-Wide Partner in the wireless communication category, Samsung contributed 7,000 pieces of telecommunication equipment to the 2010 Vancouver Olympics. They also launched a software program, called Wireless Olympics Works (WOW), which allowed mobile phone users to receive real-time Olympic news and updates. Vice President and head of the Worldwide Sports Marketing section of Samsung Electronics, Gyehyun Kwon, had this to say about Samsung's relationship with the Olympics:

> The Olympic Games are much more than sports and competition; they are about community, camaraderie, and individuals challenging themselves to find inspiration and achieve excellence. Samsung seeks to use mobile phone technology ... to unify people around the world and help them discover their own WOW moments during the Olympic Games.

So how exactly did Samsung communicate its relationship with the Olympics? In addition to a series of commercials, advertisements, banners, and signage, Samsung found innovative and creative ways to leverage their Olympic Sponsorship. Among other things—
- Samsung secured prominent athletes, including Wayne Gretzky, Hayley Wickenheiser, Hannah Teeter, and Jarome Iginla, to serve on "Team Samsung" as brand ambassadors for their Samsung products and WOW mobile phone app.
- Samsung sold commemorative Vancouver 2010 Olympic Wrist Straps for cameras and cell phones.
- Samsung held a competition where ten "mobile explorers" were given $2000 of Samsung equipment and challenged to document, via online video blogs, the Vancouver Olympics by visiting venues, talking with spectators, and capturing the Olympic spirit on their Samsung Mythic mobile phones. Winners received $24,000 and were determined through on-line voting.
- Samsung hosted the Olympic Rendezvous @ Samsung Pavilion on site in Vancouver—an exceptional venue designed for hospitality, entertainment, experiential activity, Samsung product interaction, and spectator and athlete relaxation.

the winners would win a trip to the game. MLS was strategic in its sponsorship offerings by holding numerous events in the days leading up to the game. This provided sponsors with numerous avenues to assist in activating their sponsorships (Dreier, 2011). Recognizing that many of its customers had an interest and identification with golf, JPMorgan Chase designed the reward program for its Chase Sapphire Card to include unique golfing experiences including a strategy session with a pro. The company activates its Sapphire Rewards at selected PGA Tour events (Chase delivers, 2011). Understanding its target consumer segment, Taco Bell partnered with ESPN and the BCS to market its $5 Touchdown Box value meal, in which the container converted into a finger football field. The meal was advertised on ESPN mobile applications, and allowed for consumers to easily locate a nearby Taco Bell restaurant or follow the chain's travelling truck. The truck is often utilized at BCS events or MLB games, and is also promoted via its own Twitter feed @tacobelltruck (Taco Bell Goes, 2011).

Sponsorship Pricing

Just as it is with the marketing mix, pricing is often the most difficult element of developing a sponsorship inventory and designing a sponsorship. Essentially, sponsorships should be priced on their respective market value within the respective geographic area of the sport entity and on the type of inventory utilized in the sponsorship. For example, exclusive inventory items such as naming rights or pouring rights mandate significant expenditures. Additionally, the ability of the sponsorship to reach consumers in a local market versus a national market will dramatically impact cost. While an assessment of market value is the primary means of pricing sponsorship, several other methods may prove useful. These are discussed in the following paragraphs.

The **cost-plus method** is determined by calculating the total actual expenses in providing a sponsorship package plus the organizations desired profit. The total expenses listed need to include labor, production, signage, souvenirs, and all other aspects of the event or package. This has been an effective way of determining pricing for several organizations including the USOC (Stotlar, 2009).

With **competitive market** pricing, sport organizations may examine other similar sponsorships either in the respective geographic market or in other similar markets to ascertain appropriate pricing. The *IEG Sponsorship Report,* or *sponsorship.com,* is one of the prominent publications on sponsorship. Published biweekly, the newsletter includes information, interviews, and activities all focused on sponsorship. Other publications like the *SportsBusiness Journal* and *Sport Marketing Quarterly* cover a wide array of industry and academic research focuses on marketing and will likely prove useful in improving sponsorship and assessing price.

Relative value pricing utilizes market research and published data to assess sponsorship value. In comparing pricing for a sponsorship, it is important to understand that a relative value can also be determined using research and a suggested relative value assigned. For example signage at a minor league baseball park could be compared to the cost of a billboard in the same geographic area. Additionally, one could compare the costs per impression of the billboard to that of average attendance at the venue. Similar determinations may be made utilizing public address at the venue and comparing those to radio advertisements (Stotlar, 2009).

Assessment and Evaluation of Sponsorships

Assessment of the sponsorship and the relationship between sponsor and organization must occur regularly. It is important to know if the sponsorship is effective, and that the sponsor is pleased with the results. The most common manner of evaluation for sponsorship is the measurement of return on investment. One particular way to determine the ROI for a sponsor at a major event is to survey spectators after they have left, and ask them about the sponsors' information that they noticed, and how they felt about it. O'Reilly and Madill (2009) highlighted several ways to assess sponsorship effectiveness including measuring sales, public relations efforts, media exposure, and brand perception. However, the researchers also noted a need for greater study and examination of appropriate sponsorship evaluation methods.

In preparing the results of a sponsorship assessment, it is important to provide the sponsor with data that illustrates the effectiveness of the sponsorship and with data that may also assist in enhancing the value of sponsorship. Reports should be customized for each sponsor and relate to the specific sponsor's objectives.

Endorsements

Similar to sponsorship, a well-selected athlete endorser combined with a strategic advertising campaign can resonate with audiences and distinguish products and brands. The use of celebrities and athletes as product endorsers is a well-established advertising technique, which is advantageous in assisting marketers in differentiating their respective products in a crowded and cluttered marketplace. Several theories and factors impact the selection of an athlete as an endorser.

The **associative learning theory** suggests consumers store information in association sets. Typically these association sets contain information that is similar or connected in a particular way. For example, when consumers think of a beach vacation, they may think of products such as sunscreen, swimsuits, and beach towels. These thoughts are part of consumers' "beach" association set. In matching athletes with product endorsements, the intent of the marketer is to connect a specific athlete with a product or brand so that over time the two become part of the same association set. For instance, the pairing of Michael Jordan and Tiger Woods with Nike was and often still is synonymous in the minds of consumers.

Based on the associative learning theory, the **match-up hypothesis** illustrates the importance of "fit" between the endorser and product. The more natural the fit between the endorser and the product (i.e., the more the relationship between the two makes intuitive sense to consumers) the more effective the endorsement is likely to be. For example, athletes who endorse athletic products such as energy drinks, energy bars, or athletic apparel and equipment are more effective than non-athletes who endorse similar products. Likewise, athletes are perceived as more effective when they endorse athletic products than when endorsing non-athletic related products (i.e., cologne, watches, cars, etc.). It is imperative when selecting a celebrity endorser to consider carefully the fit of the celebrity and the brand. The stronger the perceived fit between the brand and the endorser, the more effective the endorsement.

© Digital Storm/Shutterstock.com

However, it is not uncommon for products or brands not typically associated with sport to hire an athlete as spokesperson. For instance, Eli Manning is an endorser for Citizen Watches, Tiger Woods and Roger Federer were endorsers for Gillette, and Maria Sharapova is an endorser for Canon. In each of these cases, marketers strategically connected the attributes of the product to attributes of the athlete. Eli Manning and Citizen Watches were marketed as "unstoppable." The tag line for Woods and Federer with Gillette was "the best a man can get." The intent here was to associate success to the current number one player in golf and tennis to the Gillette products. Sharapova endorsed Canon's Power Shot camera with a tagline of "Make every shot a power shot." While the fit between these athletes and brands was not as intuitive, marketers strategically capitalized on the personal or professional attributes of the player in order to link the two in the minds of consumers.

Fit is not the only requirement for achieving an effective endorsement. Source credibility is also important. If consumers perceive an endorser is credible, they are more likely to have favorable perceptions of the product; thus making the endorsement more effective. Several characteristics impact endorser credibility. **Trustworthiness, expertise,** and **attractiveness** are considered to be the three most important characteristics in positively impacting endorser effectiveness (Amos, Holmes, and Strutton, 2008). Expertise was defined by Hovland, Janis, and Kelley (1953), as the extent to which an endorser is perceived to be a source of valid statements. For example, Nike did not need to prove it had great basketball shoes in the 1990's because Michael Jordan did it every time he played; furthermore he was viewed as an expert of the game of basketball. Trustworthiness is defined by, Hovland, Janis, and Kelley (1953), as the degree of confidence in the endorser's aim to communicate the statements he/she considers most valid. Trustworthiness can be demonstrated in the level of acceptance and the degree of confidence in the endorser and product. Kahle and Homer (1985) concluded that physical attractiveness is an essential signal in an individual's original judgment of a person. In other words, athletes who are viewed by consumers as trustworthy, as an expert at their sport, and as attractive make the most effective endorsers. In the examples above, Woods, Federer, Manning, and Sharapova are all considered as somewhat attractive, as experts in their respective sports, and as trustworthy brand ambassadors.

Endorsements and Controversies

Negative publicity involving a celebrity or an athlete can harshly impact an organization especially if it is a new organization where the endorser was used to establish a first impression to consumers. However, if the organization is more established, then the brand may not suffer; only the endorser's image and credibility will suffer. Hughes and Shank (2005) argue that if a well-liked athlete has a one-time violation it will carry less impact with the consumer than if the athlete has a history of repeated illegal or unethical events. Stock prices decline when there is negative publicity about the celebrity who endorses a company's brand (Louie, Kulik, and Jacobson, 2001). The amount of information known about the athlete and brand, timing of the negative information, and the strength of the link between the brand and athlete are factors that can predict the effect of negative information on the organizational brand (Till and Shimp, 1998).

Numerous athletes have been at the center of controversy. Pittsburgh Steeler quarterback Ben Roethlisberger, Olympian Michael Phelps, retired NFL quarterback Brett Favre, Tour de France champion Lance Armstrong, Tiger Woods, and Michael Vick are just a few of the athletes who have endured controversies and created uncertainty surrounding their respective endorsements. Tiger Woods was one of most recognizable faces in the sports world, especially in professional golf. Before his sex scandal allegations, Tiger Woods had been the perfect example and the gold standard of a great endorser. He was marketable, people loved him, and he was trusted as an expert in his sport. As soon as news broke about his sex scandal, his endorsements with Accenture and AT&T were dropped. Shortly thereafter, Gatorade followed suit and dropped the entire Tiger Woods drink line and his endorsements with the company. Swiss watch maker Tag Heuer and Gillette razor products stopped running his ad campaigns. Nike, NetJets, Upper Deck, TLC Vision, and Electronic Arts remained using Woods as an endorser despite his scandal. As an IMG client, Woods generated approximately $28 million for IMG golf prior to the scandal. This figure dropped to $15 million after the scandal (Smith, 2011b). Woods who earned $105,000,000 in endorsement money in 2008, saw his image tarnished by the multiple accounts of infidelity, which shed light onto a less than perfect personal life and shattered his carefully crafted "family man" image. In light of the accounts and fearing negative consequences, several of Woods' sponsors cut ties with the golfer and Woods lost an estimated $35 million dollars in endorsement revenue between 2008 and 2010.

Michael Vick had become known as the face of the NFL throughout his career. He was the star quarterback of the Atlanta Falcons, and the entire team's image was built around him. In 2007, he was convicted of dog fighting charges. Vick endorsed brands such as EA Sports, Kraft, Nike, and Coco-Cola (Lefton, 2010). After his conviction, a little more than 165,000 messages were sent to Nike convincing them to suspend Vick and two days after his indictment, Nike suspended him and vowed not to release his Air Zoom Vick V shoes. Needless to say Nike suspended Vick without pay, Reebok pulled his jerseys from retail shelves, and Upper Deck removed his autographed memorabilia from the online store.

Negative spillover effects can impact brand alliances. Since the image of the brand is composed of an accumulation of meanings, each time a brand associates with another brand, the experience impacts and contributes to its overall image (Rodrigue and Biswas, 2004). Once a celebrity's image is tainted, it is extremely difficult to restore their image to the public. Most companies will back out of an endorsement if the endorser is involved in negativity. Fear of negative consumer perceptions, and the impact of the controversy on revenue generation cause many companies to drop endorsers, as was the case with Vick and Woods. However, some companies will stand by the athlete during controversy. For example, to date Nike tried to repair its golf department after the Tiger Woods scandal by creating an ad featuring his late father in preparation for Woods' return to golf. The ad served to show the public that Woods continued to be focused and enthusiastic for the sport.

Discussion Questions

1. Discuss the role of sport sponsorship in marketing both the sport enterprise and a traditional company.
2. What, in your opinion, has contributed to the growth of sport sponsorship in the last decade?

3. What factors do you perceive are most important to potential sponsors when engaging in sponsorship?
4. How do athlete endorsers assist companies in connecting with consumers?
5. Who do you perceive as effective athlete endorsers? Why do you perceive these athletes are effective?

Critical Thinking Exercises

1. Consider you have been hired as the new Marketing Director for a minor league franchise in the Southwest. Outline how you will segment your market to target potential sponsors. What companies will you target and why? How might you develop a sponsorship to meet the needs of the company you have identified?
2. Working individually or as part of a group, select a sport team or event. Develop a sponsorship inventory for that organization. Include categories, items, and pricing.
3. You have recently accepted a position as the sport marketing director of a large company in the Northwest. The company desires to target young males. Detail how you will segment the market, and what athlete endorsers might you select to assist you in reaching that consumer segment.

References

Amato, C. H., C. Peters, and A. T. Shao. "An Exploratory Investigation into NASCAR Fan Culture." *Sport Marketing Quarterly,* 14(2) (2005): 71–83.

Burton, R. and N. O'Reilly. "Understanding why spnsorship continues to grow". *SportsBusiness Journal,* January 20, 2011.

CFA Houston. "CFA Houston", July 24, 2006, CHICK-FIL-A "FOWL POLES" TO MAKE DEBUT. http://www.cfahouston.com/pdfs/press_release.pdf

Chase delivers. "Chase delivers the rewards". *SportsBusiness Journal,* June 27, 2011: 14.

Choi, J., D. K. Stotlar, and S. Park. "Visual Ethnography of On-site Sport Sponsorship Activation: LG Action Sports Championship". *Sport Marketing Quarterly,* 15(2) (2006): 71–79.

Cornwell, T. B. and L. V. Coote. "Corporate sponsorship of a cause: the role of identification in purchase intent". *Journal of Business Research,* 58(3) (2005): 268–276.

Crompton, J. L. "Conceptualization and alternate operationalizations of the measurement of sponsorship effectiveness in sport". *Leisure Studies,* 23(3) (2004): 267–281.

Dalakas, V. and A. M. Levin. "The balance theory domino: How sponsorships may elicit negative consumer attitudes". *Advances in Consumer Research,* 32 (2005): 91–97.

Dreier, F. "MLS All-Star sees activation gain". *SportsBusiness Journal,* July 25, 2011: 10.

Gwinner, K., and S. Swanson. "A model of fan identification antecedents and sponsorship outcomes". *Journal of Services Marketing,* 17(3) (2003): 275–294.

Heider, F. *The psychology of interpersonal relations.* New York, NY: John Wiley & Sons, 1958.

Hovland, C. I., I. K. Janis, and H. H. Kelley. *Communication and persuasion.* New Haven, CT: Yale University Press, 1953.

Howard, D. R. & J. L. Crompton. *Financing sport.* Morgantown, WV: Fit Information Technologies, 2005.

Hughes, S., and M. Shank. "Defining scandal in sports: Media and corporate sponsor perspectives". *Sport Marketing Quarterly,* 14 (2005): 207–216.

IEG. "Performance research. Sponsors say return on investment is up and they are doing more to prove it". *IEG Sponsorship Report,* 24(4) (2005).

IEG. "Sponsorship spending", August 5, 2010, http://www.sponsorship.com

It's all about. "It's all about the activation". *SportsBusiness Journal,* 13, June 27, 2011.

Lefton, T. "Neither Vick's agent nor sponsors are in a rush to sign deals". *SportsBusiness Journal,* October 4, 2010.

Louie, T. A., R. L. Kulik, and R. Jacobson. "When bad things happen to the endorsers of good products". *Marketing Letters,* 12(1) (2001): 13–23.

Madrigal, R. "The influence of social alliances with sports teams on intentions to purchase corporate sponsors' products". *Journal of Advertising,* XXIX(4) (2000): 13–24.

Meenaghan, T. "Point of view: Ambush marketing: immoral or imaginative practice?" *Journal of Advertising Research,* September/October, 1994: 77–88.

Meenaghan, T. "Sponsorship—Legitimizing the medium". *European Journal of Marketing,* 25(11) (1991): 5–10.

Meenaghan, T. "Understanding sponsorship effects". *Psychology & Marketing,* 18(2) (2001): 95–122.

Mickle, T. "It takes a village, and IndyCar is planning one". *SportsBusiness Journal,* March 7, 2011: 6.

Miloch, K., and K. Lambrecht. "Consumer Awareness of Sponsorship at Grassroots Sport Events". *Sport Marketing Quarterly,* 15(3) (2006): 147–154.

O'Relly, N. and J. Madill. "Methods and metrics in sponsorship evaluation". *Journal of Sponsorship,* 2(3) (2009): 215–230.

Rodrigue, C. S., and A. Biswas. "Brand alliance dependency and exclusivity: An empirical investigation". *Journal of Product and Brand Management,* 13 (2004): 477–488.

Smith, M. "Drop in Woods' endorsement income made Steinberg too expensive to keep". *SportsBusiness Journal,* May 30, 2011b: 3.

Smith, M. "Polo dresses up U.S. Open merchandise sales". *SportsBusiness Journal,* June 13, 2011a: 6.

Stotlar, D. K. *Developing Successful Sport Sponsorship Plans.* 3rd ed., Morgantown, W.V.: Fitness Information Technology, 2009.

Stotlar, D. K. "Endorsements". *Berkshire Encyclopedia of World Sport,* 2 (2005): 506–510.

Stotlar, D.K. "Sponsorship evaluation: Moving from theory to practice". *Sport Marketing Quarterly,* 13 (2004): 61–64.

Taco Bell Goes. "Taco Bell goes mobile with truck, activation". *SportsBusiness Journal,* 19 (2011).

Till, B. D., and T. A. Shimp. "Endorsers in advertising: The case of negative celebrity information". *Journal of Advertising,* 27(1) (1998): 67–82.

Jayhawks in the Field

Connor Terry

Manager of Business Development for Billikens Sports Properties/ Learfield at Saint Louis University Athletics

Hometown
Overland Park, KS

Education
UG 2014 – University of Kansas (Sport Management, Business)

Previous Positions
Account Executive at Kansas City T-Bones Baseball Club
Corporate Sales Intern at Kansas City T-Bones Baseball Club
(Corporate Sales Intern at V-8 Supercars

1. St. Louis is an incredibly crowded sports market. What initiatives have you developed to attract attention to the university athletics programs?

When I meet with potential sponsors of Billiken Athletics for the first time I explain to them that we can't compare our product to professional sports. We have something different to offer them: an affluent, educated, and passionate fan base that has strong brand loyalty to their favorite college team. College sports fans tend to be more career focused than they are job focused, which in many cases mean they typically have a higher income and more discretionary income to spend on sponsor products and services. In regard to SLU, an added benefit is that we are the largest NCAA Division 1 sports program in St. Louis, and furthermore, there is no NBA franchise in town that we need to share the basketball limelight with. In 2018 SLU will be approaching its 200-year anniversary—we are an instrumental educational institution and staple of the St. Louis community; we are committed to the area and will never pick up and leave town like the Rams did.

2. Even though sport managers largely can't control the product on the field, how much does team success impact attendance and how do you try to mitigate the risk on relying on wins?

After making the NCAA tournament three years in a row, our Men's Basketball team has been very bad on the court the past few seasons. There are two ways I offset this when meeting with potential sponsors. First, I explain to the them the steadfast loyalty alumni have with

their college programs—more often than not they support their teams (and studies show their sponsors as well) through thick and thin. Second, specifically at SLU we have just hired Coach Travis Ford who was previously at Oklahoma State. He has already brought in a plethora of talent for the future and I enjoy speaking to that as well.

3. You worked in minor league baseball before college athletics. What about that model did you bring with you to your new position?

Work ethic was the biggest aspect. That made me successful on the minor league baseball level in selling sponsorships. At SLU, I've combined that, along with other sales skills Learfield has taught me to become more polished at my craft.

4. Has living in Missouri enhanced or lessened the natural dislike every Jayhawk has for the University of Missouri athletics?

I'm torn on this question because my company, Learfield, also handles the multi-media rights for Mizzou and there are some great people over at that property that I've gotten to know real well. Nevertheless, there are so many Mizzou fans in St. Louis it makes me sick to my stomach. I can't stand the black and gold and proudly wear my crimson and blue here.

5. Describe the favorite parts of your job and give some specific examples if possible.

I love meeting with people in person and building relationships. In addition, because all sorts of companies sponsor sports organizations, I enjoy learning more about different industries I don't work in: Banking, telecommunications, home improvement, insurance, law, etc. At the end of the day, it's most rewarding to see how I can help these individuals drive their business through a partnership in college sports.

Name: _____   Section: _____   Date _____

HSES 289
Introduction to Sport Management
In-Class Quiz and Activity Sheet

Name (or names if done in a group)

Answer #1

Answer #2

Answer #3

© razorbeam/Shutterstock.com

Chapter 12

Sport Communication

Brad Schultz • *University of Mississippi*

KEY TERMS

Access

Agenda-setting

Distribution

Fragmentation

Image

Interactivity

Public relations

Icon Sportswire/Getty Images

"You folks (the networks) are paying us a lot of money to put this game on television. If you want us to tee it up at two in the morning, then that's when we'll tee it up."

—Paul "Bear" Bryant, former Alabama football coach.

As cited in Schultz, B. (2001). *Sports broadcasting* (Woburn, MA: Focal Press), 18.

"This is a time when consumers want whatever they want wherever they want it on the device they want. It's no longer about just sitting in front of the TV."

—John Skipper, ESPN President

Introduction

On February 2, 2014, the Seattle Seahawks beat the Denver Broncos, 43-8 in Super Bowl XLVIII. At one point, Seattle led, 36-0, leading many to call the one-sided blowout the worst game in Super Bowl history (Folck, 2014). Yet, the game still attracted the largest audience to ever watch a television show in U.S. history—112.2 million viewers.[1] The live Internet stream of the game attracted an average audience of 528,000 viewers per minute to set another record as the most-viewed live stream of a single event in U.S. history. That so many people would tune into such a bad game tells us a lot about sports media, audiences, and technologies. "Sports makes compelling TV and provides great storytelling for producers in the non-scripted side of the business," said Bob Horowitz, president of Juma Entertainment. "When you have authentic, real competition like the Olympics, it can result in unbelievable numbers. Best of all, sports is TiVo-proof—you can't DVR sports" (Pursell, 2008).

This chapter seeks to more clearly define this relationship from a communications perspective. Sport, media, and audiences have changed drastically in the past hundred years, and will likely continue to change in the future. The changes have affected the nature and methods of the communication process. As technologies continue to be developed, the relationships and methods of communication will likely move in new directions. Certainly students aspiring to eventually work in the sport industry should not only remain abreast of changes in communication, but they should also anticipate future changes and prepare for those eventualities.

Figure 12.1 displays a good way to conceptualize the communications relationship between sports, media, and audiences. In a broad sense, sport athletes and events provide *content* for the media outlets that cover them. Large-scale events, such as the Super Bowl and World Series, as well as small-scale events, such as a city golf tournament or 5K run, give the sports media content to fill newspaper and magazine pages, and television and radio rundowns. In turn, the media serve as the means of content and information **distribution**; getting those events and the news related to them disseminated to sports audiences. While the means of distribution have greatly changed over the years, with newspapers and other print sources now augmented by various broadcast and Internet outlets, the distribution of sports events

---

1 By comparison, the Chinese New Year celebration event, broadcast the same weekend by China Central Television, reached a staggering 704 million viewers on television and another 110 million online.

FIGURE 12.1 The Relationship between Sport, Media, and Audiences

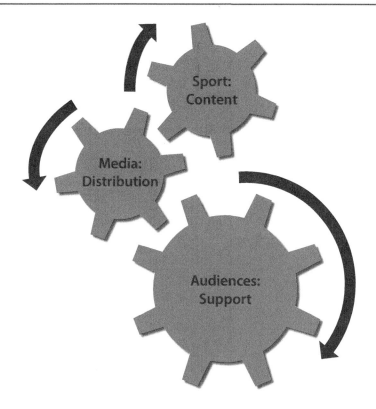

to consumers continues to directly *support* sports organizations, teams, and athletes. This support is primarily economic through such things as the purchases of event tickets, merchandise, and ancillary items.

The meshing of gears is a good way to think of sport representation, because sport, media, and audiences are all interrelated and the effect is not simply in one direction. For example, in addition to sports, audiences also support the media through subscriptions, pay-per-view plans, and advertising. In addition to distribution, the media also directly support the sport by paying rights fees to broadcast events. These interrelationships can be examined on a much closer level.

MEDIA

Media and Audience

Media's primary role is to serve as the conduit through which sport content and information passes to the consuming public (Figure 12.2). This has been the media's main function since sports first gained popularity with mass audiences in the late 19th century. The industrialization and urbanization of that time period created audiences large enough to support both sporting organizations and the mass media. The media quickly realized their financial interests were tied to supplying information to a growing sport audience. Fueled by information supplied mainly through newspapers and magazines, interest in sports grew tremendously during

FIGURE 12.2 Information and Image: How Media Affect Audiences

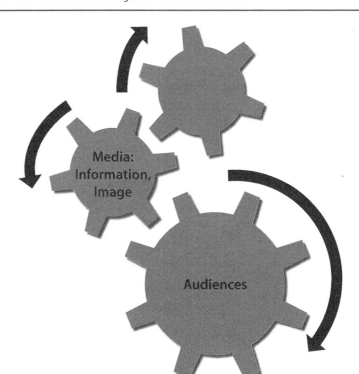

this time period. Long-time baseball manager Connie Mack (1950) who was involved in baseball as either a player or manager from 1886 to 1953, saw how much the media meant to the growth of the game. "How did baseball develop from the sandlots to the huge stadiums?" he asked. "From a few hundred spectators to the millions in attendance today? My answer is: through the gigantic force of publicity. The professional sporting world was created and is being kept alive by the services extended the press."

The media role of sports information provider has not changed through the years, although dramatic changes regarding the means of distribution have occurred. Author Mike Sowell (2008) suggested that national sports coverage became possible in 1849 when the telegraph was first used to cover a championship boxing match. Distribution technology has evolved from 19th-century telegraph to 20th-century broadcast (television and radio) and now to more sophisticated 21st-century new media (Internet and digital forms). New distribution methods have created three major changes to the media's information role: (1) There is much more potential information, (2) the information is available instantaneously or nearly instantaneously in most cases, and (3) the information is now accessible almost anywhere. With the advent of the Internet and other broadband technologies, the amount of sport information available to consumers has increased exponentially. The sheer volume of information is almost incalculable, but a look at some of today's most popular sports websites suggests both the size and amount of today's sports audience are growing (Table 12.1).

TABLE 12.1 Growth in Most Popular Sports Media Websites, 2008–2014

Site	2008 Ranking	2014 Ranking	2008 Audience (unique audience in millions)	2014 Audience (unique audience in millions
Yahoo! Sports	1	1	26.0	125.2
ESPN	2	2	22.8	75.5
Fox Sports	3	8*	16	18
CBS Sports	4	5	13.3	28

*BleacherReport moved up to third on the 2014 rankings with 38 million unique visitors.
Sources: Nielsen Online, NetView (September 1, 2008 - September 30, 2008); Alexa Web Traffic Rankings, December 2008; ebizmba, February 2014.

As new media technologies such as mobile television and Google glass continue to grow, so will the amount of sports information available to audiences. Watching a game on mobile television or through live streaming is called second-screen possibilities, and they are becoming much more common. "The standard sports fan move on mobile is, if they're at a child's baseball game or running errands on a weekend, to go their mobile device and check a score," said Clark Pierce of Fox Sports. "What I'm seeing with streaming is that people are doing the same thing, but checking the live game" (Burg, 2014).

These new media technologies have also shrunk the sports-information *news cycle*; that is, the information that is now available to sports audiences is getting to them much more quickly. For the print media the news cycle had typically been about 24 hours, which is how long it took for information to permeate through to most audiences via this distribution channel. The cycle shortened to minutes with the coming of radio and television, and now is only a few seconds due to the availability of the Internet.

This change has had significant consequences for the print media as they have struggled to adapt to the new Internet environment. In the spring of 2013, *Pro Football Weekly*, a magazine that had covered the NFL for 46 years, had assets of $143,000 and liabilities of $8.5 million, and publishers made the difficult decision to cease publication. "We built some truly great stuff that you all seemed to love, but try as we might, we couldn't get enough of you to pay what it cost us to deliver it," said editor Hub Arkush (2013). "There comes a time when there is just no more money to lose, and now we are forced to close the doors." NFL writer Mike Florio (2013) observed, "News and analysis must be delivered in real-time via electronic means, not once per week in a publication that looked and felt more like a newspaper than a magazine."

The sports print media have been quick to transition to the Internet, which given its ability to store large amounts of information and offer consumers the ability to interact with one another is ideally suited for sports coverage. Magazines such as *Sports Illustrated, The Sporting News,* and *ESPN The Magazine* all have an extensive web presence. In 2008, *The Sporting News* debuted a daily digital sports newspaper, what the magazine called "the first step in a reinvention of a title continuously published for 120 years; perhaps the ultimate test of how to take part in the transition to online beyond a website" (Kramer, 2008). As digital subscriptions eventually climbed over 200,000 *TSN* made the difficult decision to go exclusively digital and end its print edition after 126 years. "Having spoken with many of our longtime subscribers, we recognize this is not a popular decision among our most loyal fans," wrote *TSN* President Jeff Price. "Unfortunately, neither our subscriber base nor the current advertising market for print would allow us to operate a profitable print business going forward" (Price & Howard, 2012).

Much of the content is the same as the magazine offers in print, but is provided free on the web. That has raised some concerns about revenue, but the web versions make money from advertising and also offer additional content that requires a subscription. *The Sporting News* originally distributed its digital edition for free, but then began charging a $2.99 subscription price. That's known as building a paywall, and it has met resistance and criticism from audience members accustomed to getting content for free. In some cases, the backlash involves concern for any content being only available for subscription and in other cases, the resistance is to the paywall prices being seen as exorbitant ("Globe and Mail paywall . . .," 2012).

Though an increase in speed is certainly valuable and appreciated by consumers, it also increases the dangers of publishing rumor, speculation or information that is simply untrue, and in many cases the media has lost credibility. As the news cycle gets shorter there is a tremendous pressure to be "first," and the time to consider whether or not to publish gets shorter. "We're losing the vetting process and a degree of journalistic integrity," said former NFL player and now broadcaster Reggie Rivers. "There's no time to consider or edit anything. A good example is someone who shoots an interview in a locker room. The person behind them may be naked or say something profane, but in the rush to get it posted it may go unnoticed" ("Ahead of the Curve," 2010).

While information is an essential part of the media business, it would be wrong to say that members of the media serve merely as impassive channels of communication. Information does not simply come from the media like water from a faucet; rather, the media also shape the context, form, and tone of that information. Media scholars Maxwell McCombs and Donald Shaw (1972) call this **agenda-setting**—how the media exert a significant influence on public perception through their ability to filter and shape media content. According to McCombs (2002, p. 1), "Not only do people acquire factual information from the news media, readers and viewers also learn how much importance to attach to a topic on the basis of the emphasis placed on it in the news."

In a sports sense, the media present a particular **image** of sporting events and athletes. This image can depend on several factors, including the economic and cultural conditions that exist at the time. For example, the 1920s were a time of great excess and achievement, and athletic heroes such as Babe Ruth, Red Grange, and Jack Dempsey were lauded as heroic figures in the mainstream media. Ruth received perhaps more adulation from the media than any other sports figure, before or since. He was not only the "Babe," but "the Bambino," "the Sultan of Swat," and "the Colossus of Clout." Former teammate Harry Hooper observed of Ruth, "I saw it all from beginning to end, and sometimes I can't believe what I saw: this kid, crude, poorly educated … gradually transformed into the idol of American youth and a symbol of baseball the world over. I saw a man transformed from a human being into something pretty close to a god" (Connor, 1982, p. 66).

Sportswriters like Grantland Rice, Damon Runyan, and Heywood Broun played key roles in creating the athlete's heroic mystique. "When a sportswriter stops making heroes out of athletes, it's time to get out of the business," Rice once said (Inabinett, 1994, p. ix), and he created plenty of heroes in his 54-year career. He's most often remembered for naming Notre Dame's famous "Four Horsemen" in an article he wrote after the 1924 Notre Dame–Army football game. The story's opening—"Outlined against a blue-gray October sky the Four Horsemen rode again . . ."—is one of the most famous lines in sportswriting history.

By contrast, the 1960s was a time of protest and anger that saw the emergence of the "anti-hero"; athletes celebrated for their flaws rather than their heroism. A younger generation of athletes like Joe Namath and Muhammad Ali rejected many of the traditional notions associated with sport, such as morality, clean living, and humility. Author Marty Ralbovsky (1971) noted, "Why, said Ali, can't a black athlete be proud of his blackness and be called what he wishes? Why, said Namath, can't an athlete admit publicly to drinking, smoking (and) making love to beautiful women? Traditionalists answered them by removing them from the mainstream and clouding their accomplishments in controversy" (p. 74).

Sports became a television staple during the 1960s and 1970s, a growth that was further fueled by technological developments. Cable and satellite television dramatically increased the amount of sports content, and also the competition for sports audiences. This ended the dominance of the three major television networks (ABC, NBC, and CBS) in terms of televised sports programming and opened the field to a host of new competitors. Media mogul Ted Turner began broadcasting many of his Atlanta Braves' games on Turner Broadcasting System, which was available to any cable subscriber across the country. Entertainment and Sports Programming Network (ESPN) emerged in the late 1970s and made following sports a 24-hour a day, seven-days-a-week enterprise.

It could be argued that the recent growth of media and competition in the 1990s and 2000s has led to a "celebrity" portrayal of athletes and sports. "This is a tabloid-crazy society," noted longtime CBS sportscaster Jim Nantz. "We love nothing more than a good scandal" (as cited in Schultz, 2005, p. 15). Nowhere was that more evident than the January 2013 story involving Notre Dame football star Manti Te'o. Te'o's story was compelling—he finished second for the Heisman Trophy and led Notre Dame to the national title game, all despite suffering the loss of his grandmother and a girlfriend during the fall. He was portrayed as the shining star of college football on the cover of *Sports Illustrated*.

But shortly after Notre Dame lost in the national championship game in January 2013, the sports website Deadspin published a story claiming that Te'o's deceased girlfriend never existed and the entire story about her was a hoax. The story was further complicated by rumors that Te'o himself may have perpetrated the fraud. Ultimately, a friend of Te'o's named Ronaiah Tuiasosopo admitted to the hoax, but it was Te'o who saw his reputation and his life unravel. Almost overnight he went from football hero to the punch line of a national joke. "I mean, I can't wait till the day I can turn on the TV again or read the sports page without seeing this story about me," Te'o said. "When I went out and around, I could tell people were looking at me. I could hear them whispering and talking about me. And that's when I really started to know how bad this was" (Zeman, 2013). Instead of portraying him as the shining knight of college football, the national media now took a much different view.

TABLE 12.2 Athletes with the Most Twitter Followers, 2014

Athlete	Sport	Number of Twitter followers (in millions)	Comment
Cristiano Ronaldo	Soccer	24.3	One of the most recognizable figures in sports, Cristiano Ronaldo, or his PR team, tweets on his page nearly every day, primarily about soccer. Sometimes the Portuguese star announces contests and sweepstakes to win signed memorabilia.
Kaka'	Soccer	17.9	Kaka tweets in Portuguese, English, and Spanish, tweets photos of himself and other soccer stars, and even responds to fans and followers who tweet him.
LeBron James	Basketball	11.6	James has been known to be honest, and at times reckless with his Twitter. His tweets have made news, but recently, James has shown a softer side, posting pictures of his children, whom he is quite proud of.
Ronaldinho Gaucho	Soccer	8.4	If you speak Portuguese, then you should probably follow Ronaldinho on Twitter. If you don't speak the language, you should probably still follow him simply because he is one of the greatest players of his generation.
Shaquille O'Neal	Basketball Announcer	8.0	Now a TNT broadcaster, O'Neal is one of the funniest figures in sports, and even in retirement is capable of saying something hilarious. After all, his bio does read "Very quotatious. I perform random acts of Shaqness."

Source: "Top 10 Twitter Athletes," (2014, February 5). Tweeting-athletes.com.
From:http://www.tweeting-athletes.com/TopAthletes.cfm; Comments from: Martin, 2012.

The growth of social media demonstrates how the traditional media's ability to exclusively shape and control the nature of sports content has weakened. When long-time Yankees' shortstop Derek Jeter announced his retirement in 2014, he did not take the message through the traditional media. Instead, Jeter announced the news on his personal Facebook page in a 15-paragraph statement that he crafted and controlled. Other media outlets had to report on the announcement secondhand.

Technological developments like personal websites, Twitter accounts, Facebook pages, and blogs have created content outlets for sports athletes, organizations, and even fans. Twitter, while limited in terms of depth, allows athletes and fans to carry on a real-time conversation that bypasses traditional outlets. As can be seen from Table 12.2, both groups are taking advantage of this opportunity.

Media and Sports

The media primarily support the sports industry by distributing events and games to large audiences (Figure 12.3). In the early 20th century, sports events and organizations

FIGURE 12.3 Rights and Fees: How the Media Affect Sports

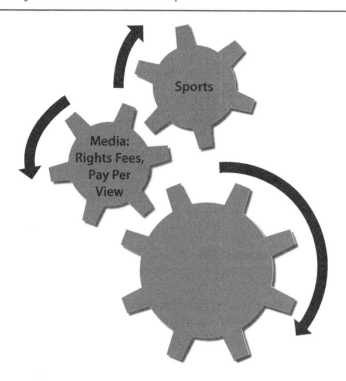

depended mainly on ticket sales for revenue. During that time, newspaper coverage helped increase audience interest, spurring higher ticket sales. When radios became common in the late 1920s and 1930s, baseball owners were worried that broadcasting games live would decrease live attendance by giving away the product for free. Thus, the three Major League Baseball teams in New York agreed to a ban on radio broadcasts until 1938. Later, Major League Baseball, horse racing, and boxing would later make similar ill-fated decisions regarding television in the 1950s.

However, baseball and other sports eventually realized that radio and television broadcasts actually increased interest, ticket sales, and profits as the excitement of the ballpark and arena could quickly be relayed to a large audience. More people became exposed to sports through the mass media and in turn the interest resulted in great attendance. As sports became more popular and more in demand by audiences, sports organizations began charging fees to television and radio stations for the rights to broadcast events. An important legal development was passage of the Sports Broadcasting Act (SBA) of 1961. Until that time, teams were required by antitrust law to individually negotiate their own television rights deals. The act removed the antitrust restriction and allowed leagues to negotiate as a whole on behalf of their member teams (and distribute the money equally in a revenue-sharing plan). The NFL was the driving force behind passage of the SBA and it immediately saw dramatic increases in television rights fees. Today the NFL has one of the richest rights-fees packages among all sports leagues ($3.7 billion per year). Rights fees for the Olympic Games have also increased dramatically since the 1960s (see Table 12.3).

TABLE 12.3 U.S. Olympic Rights Fees

Games	Site	Network	Rights Fees
1960 Summer	Rome	CBS	$394,000
1984 Summer	Los Angeles	ABC	$225 million
2008 Summer	Beijing	NBC	$894 million
2012 Summer	London	NBC	$1.18 billion
2016 Summer	Rio de Janeiro	NBC	$1.23 billion
2020 Summer	Tokyo	NBC	$1.42 billion
Summer and Winter Games through 2032	TBA	NBC	$7.75 billion

Source: "NBC Retains," 2011; Martzke, 2003.

The media recoup the payment of rights fees via advertising contracts. Larger audiences generate greater interest—and therefore higher payments—from potential advertisers. For example, the Super Bowl typically draws an audience of more than a hundred million viewers (in fact, the five most-watched programs in U.S. television history in terms of total audience are all Super Bowls). The cost of a 30-second Super Bowl commercial has increased from $42,000 in 1967 (Super Bowl I) to around $4 million for the Seattle-Denver Super Bowl in 2014.

But in general, Super Bowls are the exception rather than the rule. Television ratings for sports events have declined sharply in the past 10 years, even for such signature events as the World Series (Sandomir, 2003). Such declines reflect the fact that while televised sports still draws big audiences, television audiences in general have splintered into smaller niche audiences. This **fragmentation** is due largely to new media technologies which give audiences more channels and more consuming options. Thus, the last decade or so has seen the rise of specialized sports channels such as the Golf Channel, Speed TV, and the Tennis Channel (not to mention channels created by the NFL, NBA, NHL, and Major League Baseball), which cater to devoted, but smaller groups of viewers.

The media still pay rights fees to distribute games, but are reluctant to pay enormous sums except for events like the Olympics that can draw massive, diverse audiences. Increasingly, the media are turning to a *pay-per-view* system in which smaller audiences pay directly for the rights to access content. Technologies like digital television, mobile TV, and the Internet make this possible, and the amount of pay-per-view material has increased significantly. NBC's "Triple Cast" Olympic coverage in 1992 was a precursor of today's pay-per-view model. The network offered its usual free coverage of the Barcelona Olympics during prime-time hours, but also gave audiences a chance to purchase additional programming on one of its three sister networks. The plan was largely ridiculed at the time, but today almost all networks and sports leagues offer a similar plan (Payne, 2006). In addition to their free programming offered on television and radio, the NFL ("Sunday Ticket"), NBA ("Full Court), NHL ("Center Ice"), and Major League Baseball ("Extra Innings") all offer pay-per-view content on television and radio. NFL "Sunday Ticket," a program that allows subscribers access to every televised game each Sunday, is probably the most popular of the pay-per-view plans. DirecTV pays the NFL about a billion dollars per year to offer the package, which attracts around 2 million subscribers.

The money DirecTV pays to the NFL is an example of how teams and leagues are creating new revenue opportunities. Several leagues and individual teams are also increasing revenue through the creation of their own networks and Internet sites. When the Big Ten Network began in 2007, many critics wondered how it would fill its ambitious 24/7 programming schedule having to televise only those games the major networks didn't want. Several years later BTN is thriving with a dozen prime-time football games and more than a hundred basketball games scheduled each season. "You can see that the network has become ingrained in the sports television landscape," said Northwestern University's Senior Associate Athletic Director John Mack (Matter, 2010). And other conferences and schools have taken notice. In 2011, the University of Texas, with the largest athletic budget of any school in the country, debuted the Longhorn Network, a joint venture with ESPN that will give Texas $300 million over the course of the 20-year contract. And in 2013, the Southeastern Conference, considered the king of college sports, announced a 20-year partnership with ESPN for creation of an SEC Network that began in August 2014.

SPORTS

Sports and Media

In some instances, the goals of sports organizations and athletes are compatible. Sports and the media are dependent on audiences for revenue; sports provide the content, which the media then distribute. Audiences financially support both the media and sports entities. But there are times in which the goals of the media clash with the goals of athletes and sports organizations. As noted earlier, today's media often emphasize scandal, investigation, and full disclosure. This is often in direct conflict with athletes and sports organizations, who always want to be portrayed positively. Thus, there is a constant information tug-of-war between sports and the media as both fight to capture the attention of audiences.

Athletes and sports organizations have a major advantage in this struggle: They control the content that the media need. So just as the media try to shape the style and tone of sports content, athletes, teams, and organizations do the same. One of the ways this is accomplished is through **access**, which is the degree to which the sports content providers make themselves available to the media in terms of reporting and coverage (Figure 12.4). Sports figures can usually control and shape the nature of information that gets to the public by determining how much and how often that information is released. Access to practices, games, and interview opportunities is typically controlled by the individual content provider. On the professional level, athletes usually determine for themselves how much access to allow. In some cases, teams or leagues will require access, such as in the case of a Super Bowl or All-Star Game media day. Athletes have been punished for failing to make themselves available for league-mandated media events. But on the whole, athletes determine how much media access they will allow, and some have decided to rarely speak to the media. Duane Thomas, Steve Carlton, and Albert Belle were athletes who refused *all* media access at one point in their careers.

FIGURE 12.4 Control and Access: How Sports Affect the Media

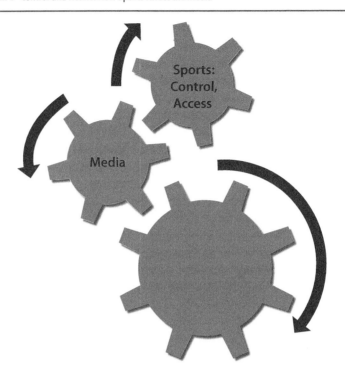

Limited access can create potential problems for the media, which needs content for its audiences. By nature, athletes and coaches are usually suspicious of the media and reluctant to provide any information that might prove to be misinterpreted, damaging, or simply embarrassing. At Super Bowl XLVIII Media Day, Seahawks' running back Marshawn Lynch did not refuse to talk, but his answers were so short as to be almost unusable. For several questions, Lynch simply stared into space and did not respond at all. "I'm just about action," he did say in one of his rare statements. "You say 'hut' and there's action. All the unnecessary talk, it don't do nothing for me" (Myers, 2014). But because the media need content, they keep trying to get coaches and athletes to talk. During Lynch's media appearance, he spoke briefly and then spent the next 50 minutes in bored silence. "Here's the embarrassing part," said one of the reporters covering the event. "The media were lined up five deep in front of Lynch waiting him out" (Myers, 2014).

While Lynch reacted with boredom, other athletes and coaches can react with hostility, as tension can sometimes escalate into open hostility. "Who wouldn't like to yell at a reporter sometimes?" said former NFL quarterback Ryan Leaf (Halverson, 2011). In the course of breaking a story for *Sports Illustrated* in 2009, reporter Selena Roberts flew to Miami to try to get an interview with baseball star Alex Rodriguez about his alleged use of performance-enhancing drugs. After the article was released Rodriguez called Roberts a "stalker" who had tried to break into his home (Koster, 2009). Although Rodriguez later backed off his comments when challenged by Roberts, there have been numerous cases where athletes and the media have clashed, sometimes physically (see Box 12.1). Veteran newspaper and television reporter Bill Plaschke (2000, p. 44) observed, "Athletes are at their most vulnerable when dealing with the media. We're everywhere; and we're not looking

BOX 12.1

Major Meltdowns: Notable Athlete-Media Confrontations		
Date	**Incident**	**Result**
November 19, 1977	Enraged after his Buckeyes fumbled against arch-rival Michigan, Ohio State coach Woody Hayes punched an ABC sideline cameraman.	The Big 10 put Hayes on probation for this incident, but he was ultimately done in when he physically attacked a Clemson player near the end of the 1978 Gator Bowl. Ohio State fired the volatile coach immediately after the game.
April 26, 1993	Kansas City Royals manager Hal McRae trashed his entire office, throwing things off of his desk including a phone, which cut a reporter, and yelling profanities at reporters. McRae was angry at the questions reporters asked him after a 5-3 loss to Detroit.	McRae was not officially punished, but managed the Royals only one more season.
March 17, 1995	Indiana University basketball coach Bob Knight launched into a lengthy diatribe against an NCAA media liaison at a post-game news conference. The liaison had earlier suggested to the media that Knight would not be attending the session.	It is hard to pick just one incident from Knight's long career of media intimidation. For this one, the NCAA reprimanded Knight and fined the university $30,000.
September 21, 1998	After a particularly bad game against the Chiefs, Chargers' rookie quarterback Ryan Leaf yelled at a photographer for standing too close to his locker. When Jay Posner of the *San Diego Union-Tribune* wrote about the incident, Leaf at first denied it, and then confronted Posner in the locker room the following day, shouting obscenities and threatening a physical confrontation.	If only this were the worst thing to happen to Leaf in his career. The former first-round draft pick spent four undistinguished years with four different teams before leaving the NFL in 2001. He is currently serving a seven-year prison term for a variety of charges, including burglary, theft, and drug possession.
June 30, 2005	As he walked on the field for a practice, Texas Rangers pitcher Kenny Rogers pushed KTVT photographer Larry Rodriguez, threw his camera to the ground and kicked it. Rodriguez was taken to a hospital.	Major League Baseball fined Rogers $50,000 and suspended him for 20 games.
September 22, 2007	Oklahoma State football coach Mike Gundy went on a tirade at a post-game press conference. He verbally attacked news-paper columnist Jenni Carlson for a story she had written about one of Gundy's players.	Gundy was not officially censured, but his comments—including "I'm a man! I'm 40!"—became an instant Internet classic. The YouTube version of the incident has now received more than 3 million views.
March 24, 2010	University of Florida football coach Urban Meyer accosted *Orlando Sentinel* reporter Jeremy Fowler on the practice field, poking a finger at Fowler and threatening to deny him and the newspaper access. Meyer was upset about a quote Fowler printed that was mildly critical of quarterback Tim Tebow. "If that was my son," Meyer lectured Fowler, "we'd be going at it right now."	Meyer personally apologized to Fowler in a 20-minute meeting the two had. The lesson?—don't criticize Tim Tebow, at least among Florida coaches and fans.

Sources: *Sports Illustrated*, NBC, ESPN.

to make friends, but front pages. With the proliferation of TV, radio and Internet reporters, pro athletes often need to be rude and pushy just to catch their breaths."

Most sports organizations, and even some athletes, have a system in place to prevent such incidents from happening. On the professional sports level, teams and organizations have a full-time **public relations** staff, which has several responsibilities.

Members of the media need adequate space and good sightlines to report the results of sporting events.
Source: Harrelson Photography

Sufficient space outside the locker room is often needed for post-game interviews.
Source: Mark Nagel

One is the production and distribution of information related to the organization and its athletes. This could take the form of a news release (timely or factual information), fact sheet (statistics and related information), quote sheet (direct comments from players, coaches or support personnel), or media guide (a lengthy and detailed compilation of facts, quotes, pictures and historical information). For some staff members their sole responsibility is creating and distributing this information to the media. The other main responsibility of the public relations staff concerns media access and activity. This mainly includes credentialing media members to cover games and scheduling interview access with players and coaches. Although public relations staff members try to accommodate the media as much as possible, access is ultimately decided by the individual athlete.

On the college sports level the public relations functions are usually handled by a sports information department, headed by a *sports information director* (SID). The SID is responsible for all communication with the media and the public, and access is usually much more controlled than at the professional level. Because college athletes have class and outside responsibilities and do not get paid to play, SIDs work with coaches to limit their media access. Most schools have a system in place where access to players and coaches is allowed only through the SID or someone else in the sports information department. In some cases, coaches and SIDs completely prohibit access to certain athletes, most typically for younger players. These restrictions can be frustrating for media members when the story has the potential to put a player or coach in a negative light and in such instances, the media often try to circumvent official channels to get the information they need. A famous example occurred in 2006 and 2007 during coverage of an alleged rape involving members of the Duke University lacrosse team. Duke naturally shut down access to the players and coaches involved, leaving the media to fend for themselves. "We were hampered early on by the unwillingness of the players … to speak with our reporters," said Melanie Sill, at the time the executive editor at the *Raleigh* (NC) *News & Observer*. Responding to charges that media coverage of the case was biased against the players, Sill noted, "Our overall reporting was solid and on point, however . . . it intensified as we ran into obstacles. Nonetheless, we should have stated more emphatically that we had not been able to get their side of things" (Ham, 2007, ¶5-7).

The sports information department is organized much like a professional public relations department, with different staff members in charge of different aspects of media relations. For example, in 2008 the University of Texas in Austin listed 25 full-time members in its Communications/Media Relations department. The size of the sports information department depends on the size of the school. A large school like the University of Texas has dozens of staff members, while a smaller Division-II or Division-III school might have only one or two full-time people (Table 12.4).

The size and scope of the sports information department depends on the sizeof the school and its athletic budget. When the first edition of this book came out, it profiled the sizes of the communications specialists at three different schools—the University of Texas, Vanderbilt, and Ohio Northern. We wanted to show you how those schools compare today. Notice how the bigger schools keep adding staff to handle the increasing communications duties. This includes someone to oversee social media, particularly as it regards student-athlete use.

Regardless of size, much of the emphasis in today's sports information departments is shifting from printed to digital material. Traditionally, these departments would send out reams of printed press released each week, and also produce a bulky printed media guide. Now, much of this information is sent by electronic mail or incorporated into the school's athletic web site.

For athletes who are high-school age and younger, there is really no one that controls access other than a coach or parent. Few high schools have anything like a public relations staff or a sports information director, and as a result, media access is often arbitrary. Traditionally, coaches and parents have kept a fairly tight rein on teenage athletes, but technology is changing this dynamic. On the athlete side, many high-school stars now promote themselves through websites, blogs, and social media. They find these tools helpful for self-promotion and as a way of attracting the attention of interested college coaches.

Media members, fans, and college recruiters also use these methods to bypass the high-school coach and administrators and talk directly with the athletes. The most obvious example is the recruiting process, especially for football. "National signing day," the first date at which high-school athletes can officially sign letters of intent to play college football, falls each year on the first Wednesday of February, and it has become a fierce competition not only to sign recruits, but for media members seeking to get the best and latest information. Reporters will monitor the social media of athletes, especially Twitter, for any breaking news about a college decision. College coaches use Twitter as a recruiting tool and send messages right to the athlete, although the NCAA has set a limit on how much social media contact a coach may have. The successful coaches, like Les Miles at LSU, use social media as a fundamental part of the recruiting process. "Coach Miles understands that social media gives him the forum to promote his program to tens of thousands of people at any given time," LSU athletic department spokesman Michael Bonnette said. "He's careful and mindful of the rules when it comes to using social media as a recruiting tool, but he's savvy enough to understand the impact that it can have" (Megargee, 2014).

At any level—high school, college, or professional—access becomes extremely limited and almost nonexistent during a crisis situation. A crisis situation is any type of bad news that could damage the reputation of the athlete, team, or organization.

TABLE 12.4 University and College Sports Information Departments

School	Enrollment	Full-time Communications Employees—2008	Full-time Communications Employees—2014
University of Texas (Austin)	52,076	22	28
			Senior Associate Athletics Director for Communications
			Publications Supervisor
			Communications Coordinator
			Senior Associate Athletics Director for Communications
			Associate Athletics Director for Media Relations (Football)
			Assistant Athletics Director for Media Relations (Men's Basketball)
			Special Assistant to Football Coach for Communications
			Associate Media Relations Director (Football)
			Associate Media Relations Director (Volleyball, Men's/Women's Golf)
			Associate Media Relations Director (Web Video Coordinator)
			Assistant Media Relations Director (Rowing, Men's/Women's Swimming and Diving, Women's Tennis)
			Assistant Media Relations Director
			Assistant Media Relations Director (Women's Basketball, Men's Tennis)
			Assistant Media Relations Director (Soccer)
			Assistant Media Relations Director (Baseball, Football)
			Assistant Media Relations Director (Football/Clyde Littlefield Texas Relays, Track and Field/Cross Country)
			Assistant Media Relations Director (Director of Creative Services/ Football)
			Assistant Media Relations Director (Videographer/Editor)
			Assistant Media Relations Director (Web Video Supervisor)
			Assistant Media Relations Director (Videographer/Editor)
			Assistant Communications Manager
			Senior Administrative Associate
			Assistant Athletics Director for New Media
			Senior Web Manager
			Web Manager
			Web Manager
			Photographer
			Photographer

Vanderbilt University	12,795	8	10
			Director of Communications Associate Director (Internal Operations) Associate Director (Digital Strategies) Assistant Director (Football) Assistant Director (Men's Basketball, Golf) Assistant Director (Baseball, Football) Assistant Director (Women's Basketball, Cross Country, Track & Field) Interim Editor, Commodore Nation Social Media Coordinator Administrative Assistant
Ohio Northern University	3,619	2	2
			Sports Information Director Assistant Sports Information Director

Sources: University of Texas; Vanderbilt University; Ohio Northern University.

Typically, crisis situations occur away from the playing field. Examples might include a baseball player being accused of using steroids or a football player being arrested for drunk driving. During a crisis situation, media access to the involved athlete, coach, or administration is likely to be next to zero. In many cases, information will be limited to an official statement released by the player or organization or perhaps to a statement from a representative such as a lawyer. Former sports broadcaster and now college educator Charlie Lambert observed, "Journalists who cover top-level sport are facing a real challenge. Teams and organizations are so powerful and so wealthy that they want to control everything that is said or written about them" ("Journalism leaders," 2008, ¶5).

Resistance during a crisis will not mean that the media will give up trying to get access to pertinent involved officials. Certainly, media members will continue to look for access and sources who will adequately help them find and report the needed information. In their attempt to report on the Bay Area Lab Cooperative (BALCO) steroids scandal, newspaper reporters Mark Fainaru-Wada and Lance Williams were stonewalled through official sources. "Going in, we were completely blind," said Fainaru-Wada. "No one had heard of BALCO. It was a matter of chasing as much as you could" ("Mark Fainaru-Wada," 2004, ¶ 4). In their three-year investigation, the reporters eventually turned to anonymous sources to uncover the story. They defied a U.S. district court judge by refusing to identify their sources, and although they were sentenced in September 2006 to 18 months in prison, they never served a day in prison. In his statement before the court, Fainaru-Wada said, "Throughout

BOX 12.2

The Bay Area Lab Cooperative (BALCO), under the direction of founder and owner Victor Conte, marketed performance-enhancing drugs to several prominent athletes, most notably in baseball and track and field. Conte eventually pleaded guilty to providing steroids and laundering money in 2005. The work of investigative reporters Mark Fainaru-Wada and Lance Williams was instrumental in developing the BALCO investigation.

BALCO Investigation Timeline

September 3, 2003:   Local and federal authorities raid BALCO offices.

Dec. 2-3, 2004:   The *San Francisco Chronicle* publishes stories containing grand jury testimony given by Jason Giambi and Barry Bonds as part of the BALCO investigation. In it, Giambi admits to steroid use while Bonds says he may have unknowingly taken steroids.

March 23, 2006:   Fainaru-Wada and Williams publish *Game of Shadows*, a best-selling book that highlighted details of their BALCO investigation.

May 5, 2006:   Fainaru-Wada and Williams are subpoenaed to testify before a federal grand jury about how they obtained the testimony of Bonds, Giambi, and other athletes.

Sept. 21, 2006:   Judge Jeffrey White tells *San Francisco Chronicle* reporters Fainaru-Wada and Williams he will order them jailed for up to 18 months if they do not comply with his order to reveal their sources.

February 14, 2007:   The identity of the source of the illegally leaked grand jury testimony is revealed as Troy Ellerman, one of the BALCO defense attorneys. Federal authorities agree to drop their efforts to send Fainaru-Wada and Williams to prison.

Source: Balco investigation timeline, 2007.

the BALCO affair, critics have questioned the motives of our reporting, suggesting that it has been little more than a witch hunt or an effort to profit off the big names who have been drawn into the scandal. Supporters have portrayed us as champions in the global fight against performance-enhancing drugs. For us, however, BALCO has always been an earnest and sincere effort to present the truth" ("Fainaru-Wada's statement" 2006, p. A14). In 2004, Fainaru-Wada and Williams won an Investigative Reporters and Editors award and the George Polk Award (Box 12.2).

Given the inherent tension between reporters trying to discover information and athletes and organizations trying to control it, some communications strategies have evolved. The oldest and most traditional strategy is to *stonewall*, or simply refuse to give the media any comment or information. When a scandal erupted at the University of North Carolina in 2013—that its athletes were funneled to bogus classes in order to keep them academically eligible—the school's original reaction was along three lines: "1) There's nothing to see here. Everybody move along. 2) This situation was confined to two bad apples in the African and Afro-American Studies Department who have since departed and 3) Everybody does it. Why are you picking on us?" (Barnett, 2014).

However, it is becoming increasing difficult to control information in the age of digital communication and Internet access. Information can leak from a variety of sources, including blogs, tweets, and Internet bulletin boards. Stonewalling allows others to manipulate and shape public perception since there is no comment from the involved parties. It further suggests that those involved have "something to hide" by not talking to the media. In the North Carolina case, other media picked up the story and made it front page news. The faculty member who originally reported the problem kept the story in the public discussion, even in the face of severe rebuke from her own administration.

That finally convinced UNC officials to change direction and take up the strategy of *full disclosure*. Many believe that freely giving information to the media can prevent the problems associated with stonewalling and bad publicity. In addition, an athlete or coach who is cooperative usually enjoys better media treatment and has a better public image. New UNC chancellor Carol Folt addressed university trustees and said that the school needed to "fully acknowledge and accept lessons of our past" ("Chancellor Folt," 2014). It was a small step that many thought needed to go further. "While it's fine for Folt to want the university to put a multi-year crisis of its own making behind it," editorialized one Carolina newspaper, "that will not happen without candor and full disclosure of pertinent facts, no matter how embarrassing" ("Chancellor Folt," 2014).

Most athletes, coaches, and organizations use a strategy somewhere in between stonewalling and full disclosure. The strategy depends on several factors, including the severity of the incident and the nature of athlete or organization involved. But all those involved are working with one goal in mind—to protect the image and public reputation of those at the center of the controversy.

A more recent communications strategy that has emerged is used by athletes and organizations in both crisis and non-crisis situations. New developments in media technology have given athletes and organizations much more power and control over the messages they send to audiences. Primarily, the ease and **interactivity** of the Internet makes it possible for them to bypass the mainstream media and take their messages directly to sports audiences. While several athletes create their own blogs, many more have turned to Twitter, perhaps because of its ease, compatibility with cell phones, and mobility.

Social media allow the athlete to deliver his or her message without media interference, and thus take much greater control in attempting to shape public opinion. European soccer player Stuart Holden, with more than 400,000 Twitter followers, "uses his Twitter page to present entertaining thoughts on everything from soccer, bros, and even underpants. Of course, he also poses deep philosophical questions to his followers like he did in this June 16 tweet: is it humanly possible to eat a single grape and be done?" (Martin, 2012).

There are obvious drawbacks to teams and athletes getting involved in social media. With so much material available, there is a danger that the message will simply get lost in cyberspace. Studies suggest that most people who use social media do it for personal reasons and create material that is personal and subjective, but not necessarily truthful. As a result, most audiences take blogging and Tweeting for what they are: opinions published to push a certain agenda. To be done well, social media require a lot of time and constant updating, especially for Twitter

The biggest problem may be the unfiltered nature of the medium, and several athletes have run into trouble. Former NBA player Charlie Villanueva was fined for tweeting during halftime of a game. Other athletes have learned that instantly posting material—especially when it's controversial or critical—can force them to apologize and/or delete the offending material. New England Patriots' player Rob Gronkowski found this out in 2011 when he tweeted pictures of himself shirtless with porn star BiBi Jones. He soon apologized, but the pictures are still out there in cyberspace. "If Gronkowski is guilty of anything it's trying to increase his Twitter profile," opined CBS Sports. "And we're pretty sure he did that" (Wilson, 2011).

Sports and Audiences

The relationship between sport and audiences is fairly straightforward and does not require a great deal of elaboration. Across any media platform, the primary benefit sport provides to audiences is attractive and highly popular content (Figure 12.5). One could make it a chicken-and-egg argument: Is there so much sport content in the media because it is popular with audiences or is it popular with audiences because there is so much of it in the media? The likely answer is that sport has a primary place in U.S. culture and its significance is reflected in the high demand for sport content across various media outlets. Author James Michener (1976, p. 355) observed that "one of the happiest relationships in American society is between sports and the media."

Historically, the demand for sports content has been met through a combination of newspapers, magazines, radio, and television. Television is ideally suited because of its ability to present the live drama of sports to large audiences. In fact, the top five television shows in U.S. history, at least in terms of total audience, are now all Super Bowls.[2]

New developments in media technology are creating new distribution systems and dramatically increasing both the total amount of mediated sport content and the demand for it. Broadband technology now allows audiences to access sport content, including video and live game action, directly through a computer via Internet access. The two biggest areas of growth seem to be mobile phones and live streaming. A study conducted at the time of the London Olympics in 2012 suggested that online viewing of sports was as popular as traditional television, especially among younger viewers. More than half of consumers (58%) said they planned to watch part of the Olympics online, while another 46% of the 18-26 age group said that "smartphones and tablets have transformed their sport viewing" ("The revolution," 2012).

Sports teams and leagues are taking advantage of these new opportunities by creating their own websites, networks, and pay-per-view packages, all of which potentially increase their revenues. The NFL's Sunday Ticket package enables satellite subscribers to access every televised game each Sunday, and similar services exist

---

2 In terms of television share, which measures how a show does in competition with what's also airing at that time, some shows, including the final episode of *M*A*S*H*, do rank higher.

FIGURE 12.5 Popularity: How Sports Affect Audiences

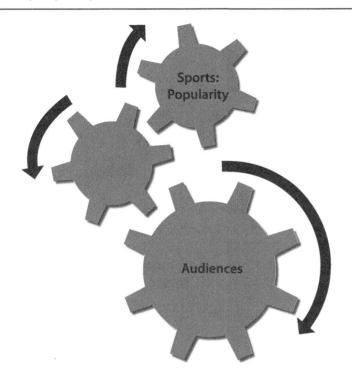

for professional baseball, basketball, and hockey. Content providers have learned that audiences are willing to pay hefty subscription fees (in the case of Sunday Ticket, around $250 for the full season of games) for the rights to access this material. "[All of this] builds stronger fan bases among more people who will watch more," says Tennis Channel CEO Ken Solomon. "The more you see, the more you want to see — which is why sports will continue to get stronger and stronger" (Miller, 2008, ¶4).

AUDIENCE

Audience and Media

Traditionally, the audience has been a passive consumer of sport's content. Athletes and sport organizations created the content, the media distributed it, and finally audiences watched, read, or listened to it. Other than niches like sports talk radio, most sport communication was a one-way communication process in which the audience had little or no input other than the decision to consume. This relationship has changed drastically in the past 20 years, due mainly to advances in media technology. This new technology has significantly empowered audiences who now have more consumption options, and have greater input into how the content is presented (Figure 12.6).

Much of this new power comes from developments in broadband technologies, such as the Internet, digital television and radio, and satellite delivery. Sports fans

FIGURE 12.6 Empowerment: How the Media Affect Audiences

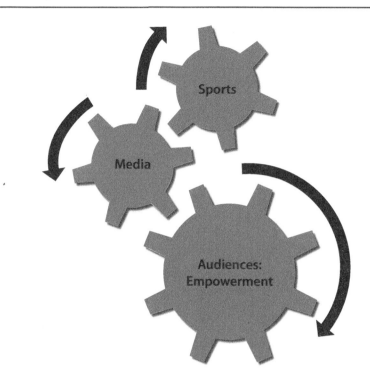

now have access to much more information and can get it almost instantaneously, which puts pressure on the content providers to have more content choices. The number of channel options has increased tremendously and much of that space has been used to meet the increasing demand for sports content. Audiences can now customize their consumption habits by picking and choosing from a variety of sports content offerings.

Perhaps the greatest advances are occurring on the Internet, where audiences not only have greater access, but now also have the opportunity to create and distribute their own sports content. Message boards, community fan forums, and blogs allow audiences much greater control over what content they choose to consume and how they consume it. In 2007, four anonymous fans decided they weren't getting the kind of sports coverage they wanted on the Internet, so they decided to start their own company to write and distribute content. Thus, Bleacher Report began as:

- An amplified outlet for writers whose unique voices were routinely drowned out by cookie-cutter analysts and celebrity "experts."
- A localized network for readers whose favorite teams were routinely undercovered by national wire services and mainstream news corporations.
- A civilized community for commenters whose intelligent debates were routinely overrun by message-board blowhards and mean-spirited trolls ("Company overview," 2014).

By reaching out to similar disaffected fans, writers and contributors, Bleacher Report became one of the most popular sports sites on the Internet, and in 2012 was acquired by Turner Broadcasting for a reported $200 million.

It's sometimes tempting to dismiss such efforts as the opinions or ravings of a few rabid fans, but increasingly such audience-generated content is directly competing with and impacting the traditional sports content providers. The website Deadspin has pushed several stories into the mainstream sports discussion, including Brett Favre's alleged sexual misconduct with a journalist, and most famously, the hoax surrounding Notre Dame linebacker Manti Te'o. The story "was further proof that a website, once derided as little more than a repository for juvenile jokes and throwing spitballs at the mainstream press, had become a permanent presence in the sports mediasphere" (Freedlander, 2013).

The Manti Te'o episode and other similar situations have direct consequences on the traditional sports-media-audience relationship, particularly in terms of how the media must now adjust to new competition. "I would watch ESPN and it didn't appeal to me," said Jack Dickey, who wrote the Te'o story as a senior at Columbia Univeristy, "and I didn't understand to whom it would appeal" (Freedlander, 2013). ESPN is still the undisputed leader in providing sports content and commentary, but a new breed of Internet journalists—young, hip, and unafraid—are certainly challenging that authority.

Traditional sports journalists have reacted with a combination of disgust, anger, and derision, but there's no doubt this new breed has changed the landscape. "I go on [the Internet] every day," says Steve Irvine of the *Birmingham News*, "but mainly for the humor. They're clowns, basically, but you get a pulse on what the fans think. Everyone on this beat is looking at them, though" ("Internet allegation," 2003, ¶8). Adds Mike Fish, a senior writer for *Sports Illustrated*'s website, "They make our jobs harder because there's so much stuff out there [and] we have to do a massive amount of screening. There's a lot of vicious, ugly stuff" ("Internet allegation," 2003, ¶6).

More media and more attention also mean that sports athletes, teams and organizations lose some ability to control their content and image. It is extremely difficult for athletes to escape the spotlight; the camera is always on, mainly because since most cell phones now have cameras, aspiring investigative sport reporters can not only blog about their breaking news but also can easily provide digital photos. Just as Manti Te'o was caught in a difficult and unintended situation, other athletes and coaches must now be aware that anything they say or do can be caught on camera and put into the public domain. In 2014, NBA superstar Kevin Durant was embarrassed when a photo of him smoking hookah showed up on his Twitter page. Durant quickly deleted the image and issued a statement saying that his cell phone had been hacked. Exactly who took the photo and how it got to Durant's account remained a mystery, but Durant's clean-cut image took a bit of a blow.

There is a big debate in journalism today about this audience-generated content and whether is qualifies as "real" journalism. In some cases, the people who write and distribute this content ignore many of the traditional journalistic values such as checking facts and citing sources, and do not even consider themselves journalists. However, there is no debate about its impact on today's sports media. Sites like Deadspin and Bleacher Report are both extremely popular and financially successful. Even mom-and-pop sites can carve out their own unique space in sports cyberspace, if they have enough time and dedication. Many of them, especially at the youth and high-school levels, serve niche audiences that otherwise would not get covered by traditional media.

Conclusion

The basic framework that athletes, teams, and organizations provide content and related information for the media to distribute to interested audiences, who financially support both entities, certainly still exists. However, there are important changes taking place within that basic framework that will have consequences for the future of the interrelationship. These changes raise several questions, the answers to which might significantly alter the accepted communication model involving sports, media, and audiences.

What role will technology play in the future? Emerging technologies have already influenced the sports-media-audience relationship. As technology gets more sophisticated how will it affect communication? With a few exceptions, the mass audience of yesterday has evolved into the smaller, niche audiences of today. Communication is more targeted and more specific, meaning that audience *demographics* are now just as important as sheer audience size. Will future technological advances make audiences even smaller? In other words, will we soon be seeing such things as an ESPN channel dedicated specifically to 18- to 24-year-old male outdoorsmen who like to hunt deer with a crossbow? The sports information of the future might be tailored to a specific individual and delivered to that person via cell phone or other similar device. Technology also promises to continue increasing the amount of information available and the speed at which it is delivered. Sports organizations and the media will have to make sure they are technologically up to date and able to satisfy the growing demand for sports information.

Where will audience-created content lead? The hot trend now is social media message and anything else that lets the audience participate in the sports communication process. Athletes, teams, leagues, and the media have been quick to pick up on the trend and incorporate it into their communication strategies. In fact, it is almost impossible today to find an outlet that does not let the audience participate through such methods as fan contests, message boards, trivia games, and the like. What will be the next new developments in this area? Now that audiences have both the means of creating and distributing content, will that seriously threaten the traditional distribution function of the media? Will the media respond by incorporating more audience content?

How will economics affect all this? Obviously, all sports communication takes place within a larger economic context that makes all such communication possible. The media are able to distribute and shape sports content and information only to the extent that they can do so profitably. In a media era where there is increasing emphasis on the bottom line, some sports content and communication could be altered, reduced, or simply eliminated. Several local television stations, including those in Wichita, Pittsburgh, and Albany, have made major changes to the sports segments within their newscasts. WTEN in Albany, New York, did away with the sports anchor and its traditional sports content. "The traditional sportscast features highlights and scoreboards from national teams that most viewers just don't care about, and those who do already know if their team won," said news director Rob Puglisi. "In the days before the Internet, before ESPN, people had to rely on their local TV sportscast for these national scores and highlights. It's just not the case anymore" (McGuire, 2005, ¶13). This might be another reason that tweeting, websites, and audience-generated content are becoming increasingly popular. Such content is relatively inexpensive to produce and distribute, which makes it attractive for media outlets.

The basic economic model of the sport communication system is also changing. Advertising to mass audiences through print and broadcast sources has been the main economic engine for decades, but with the breakup of the mass audience into niche audiences there are questions as to whether advertising can continue to sustain the established system. Increasingly, media outlets and content providers are turning to subscriptions (such as with the NFL's Sunday Ticket) and pay-per-use plans. Advertising on the Internet is also growing and may one day exceed advertisement levels for television and newspapers, especially as technology opens up more opportunities like mobile television. If the economic system of the future changes drastically it will have a corresponding effect on the sports communication process.

Will the delicate balance of the sport communication process tip in a certain direction? This is the big question—will technology, economics, or some other factor cause one group to dominate the other among sports, the media, and audiences? Technology has empowered audience members and taken away a certain degree of power from the media. However, it is highly unlikely that consumer-driven content could one day ever completely replace the distribution function of the traditional media. Although much of today's online content is produced by volunteers, numerous analysts doubt they could fill the information gap that would occur if traditional media organizations disappeared.

It is more likely that the basic communication relationship between sports, media, and audiences will stay intact, but undergo some retooling. After all, athletes, teams, and organizations still own what drives the entire process—content and information. That fact is inescapable, no matter what the media and audiences do. Despite trends toward audience participation, the media are still the most efficient system of distributing that content and the communication related to it. The media and sports are still dependent on audiences for feedback and support. As long as those pillars remain in place, one group or another may become more powerful for a time, but the traditional relationship between sports, media and audiences will continue long into the 21st century.

Study Questions

1. Looking at some of the new communications technologies coming out on the market, which are the ones most likely to impact the sports-media-audience communication process? How do you think these might make an impact and what part of the process would they be most likely to affect?

2. If you could remove one part of the sports-media-audience communication process without harming the overall system, which part would it be and why? Is it even possible to remove one of the parts without rendering the entire system dysfunctional?

3. There has been a recent movement toward more pay-per-use and subscription models in sports content and communication. Assuming all the material currently on the Internet became pay-per-use, which of the following do you think audiences would be most willing to pay for and why?
   a. Live game action of a favorite team or player(s)
   b. Statistics and/or other factual information
   c. Interviews with athletes, players, coaches, and other sports figures

    d. Commentary or stories contributed by sportswriters

    e. Interactive sports material such as fan forums and message boards

Learning Activities

1. Peruse some of the Internet sports sites dedicated to audience-created content (such as Bleacher Report). Why do you think people would want to spend the time and money creating and distributing such content? Is such content merely a fad or perhaps the future of sport communication? Explain your reasoning.

2. Consider the well-publicized steroid scandal in major league baseball (and all of sports, for that matter). How did baseball handle the situation in terms of protecting its image and controlling its message? What, if anything, should baseball executives have done differently?

3. You are the beat reporter for the local college football team. A star player for the team is arrested on drug charges and the school has refused all media access beyond an official statement. What are some ways you could go about getting the information you need to report the story?

References

Ahead of the curve. (2010, August 5). Panel presentation at the national convention for the Association of Education in Journalism and Mass Communication, Denver, CO.

Arkush, H. (2013, May 31). Pro Football Weekly says goodbye. *Pro Football Weekly*. Retrieved June 7, 2013 from: http://www.profootballweekly.com/2013/05/31/pro-football-weekly-says-goodbye

BALCO investigation timeline. (2007, November 27). *USA Today*. From: http://www.usatoday.com/sports/balco-timeline.htm

Barnett, N. (2014, January 11). Time to come clean at UNC-CH. *Charlotte News-Observer*. Retrieved February 6, 2014 from:http://www.newsobserver.com/2014/01/11/3522217/ time-to-come-clean-at-unc-ch.html

Breech, J. (2014, January 9). Colts punter fined for tweeting naked photo of Andrew Luck. *CBS Sports*. Retrieved February 5, 2014 from: http://www.cbssports.com/nfl/eye-on-football/24403939/colts-punter-fined-for-tweeting-naked-photo-of-andrew-luck

Burg, N. (2014, January 31). What is the future of mobile streaming for major sports events? *Adweek*. Retrieved February 5, 2014 from: http://www.adweek.com/brandshare/should-marketers-care-who-live-streaming-big-game-155289

Chancellor Folt must face UNC scandal with candor. (January 23, 2014). *Charlotte News-Observer*. Retrieved February 6, 2014 from: http://www.newsobserver.com/2014/01/23/3558726/chancellor-folt-must-face-unc.html Company overview. (2014). *Bleacher Report*. Retrieved February 6, 2014 from: http://bleacherreport.com/about

Connor, A. (1982). *Voices from Cooperstown: Baseball's Hall of Famers tell it like it was*. New York: Collier Books.

Fainaru-Wada's statement to the court. (2006, September 22). *San Francisco Chronicle*, A14. Florio, M. (2013, May 31). 46-year run ends for Pro Football Weekly. Pro Football Talk. Retrieved June 7, 2013 from: http://profootballtalk.nbcsports.com/2013/05/31/46-year-run-ends-for-pro-football-weekly/

Folck, J. (2014, February 4). Super bowl: Was Denver Broncos-Seattle Seahawks game the worst one in history? *Lehigh Valley (PA) Express-Times*, 4 February 2014. Retrieved

February 5, 2014 from: http://www.lehighvalleylive.com/sports/index.ssf/2014/02 / super_bowl_was_denver_broncos-.html

Freedlander, D. (2013, February 5). Deadspin rides Manti Te'o hoax story to renown—and keeps heat on ESPN. *The Daily Beast.* Retrieved February 6, 2014 from: http://www /thedailybeast.com/articles/2013/02/05/deadspin-rides-manti-te-o-hoax-story-to-renown-and-keeps-heat-on-espn.html

Globe and Mail Paywall upsets readers unwilling to shell out $20 a month for news site. (2012, October 15). *The Huffington Post.* Retrieved from http://www.huffingtonpost. ca/2012/10/15/globe-and-mail-paywall-up_n_1967807.html

Halversen, M. (2011, September 21). The redemption of Ryan Leaf will be televised. *Seattle Met.* Retrieved February 5, 2014 from: http://www.seattlemet.com/news-and-profiles /people-and-profiles/articles/redemption-of-ryan-leaf-october-2011/2

Ham, J. (2007, April 16). Media rehab and the Duke lacrosse case. *Carolina Journal Online.* From: http://www.carolinajournal.com/mediamangle/display_story.html?id=4011

Inabinett, M. (1994). *Grantland Rice and his heroes: The sportswriter as mythmaker in the 1920s.* Knoxville, TN: University of Tennessee Press.

Internet allegation comes true for Alabama coach. (2003, May 6). *USC Online Journalism Review.* From: http://www.ojr.org/ojr/glaser/1052193609.php

Journalism leaders forum. (2008, January 16). 8th forum asks to explore the impact of digital on sports journalism. From: http://journalismleadersforum.blogspot.com/2008_01_01 _archive.html

Koster, K. (2009, February 9). Alex Rodriguez takes shot at Sports Illustrated writer Selena Roberts. *Chicago Sun-Times.* From: http://blogs.suntimes.com/sportsprose/ 2009/02/alex_rodriguez_takes_shots_at.html

Kramer, S. (2008, July 29). 'Sporting News Today' Publisher: New Digital Daily Has 75,000 Subs, Aims For 200,000 Before Ad Push. *paidContent.* Retrieved May 14, 2013 from: http://paidcontent.org/2008/07/29/419-first-look-sporting-news-today/

Mack, C. (1950). *My 66 years in the big leagues.* Philadelphia: John C. Winston. Mark Fainaru-Wada on the sports doping probe and protecting sources. (2004, December 17). *Columbia Journalism Review.* From: http://www.ergogenics.org/blc28.html

Martin, P. (2012, June 23). The 50 best athletes to follow on Twitter. *International Business Times.* Retrieved February 6, 2014 from: http://www.ibtimes.com/50-best-athletes-follow-twitter-704050

Martzke, R. (2003, June 6). NBC keeps rights for Olympic broadcasts through 2012. *USA Today.* From: http://www.usatoday.com/sports/olympics2003-06-06-nbc_x.htm

Matter, D. (2010, January 22). Big Ten's behemoth. *Columbia Daily Tribune.* Retrieved May 9, 2013 from: http://www.columbiatribune.com/sports/big-ten-s-behemoth /article_a6b4a2d5-c3df-5588-bce1-e3d1232c7785.html

McCombs, M. (2002). Agenda-setting role of the mass media in the shaping of public opinion. *Suntory and Toyota International Centres for Economics and Related Disciplines.* From: http://sticerd.lse.ac.uk/dps/extra/McCombs.pdf

McCombs, M., & Shaw, D. (1972). The agenda-setting Function of Mass Media. *Public Opinion Quarterly, 36*(Summer), 176–187.

McGuire, M. (2005, March 23). WTEN to alter nightly sports. *Albany Times-Union.* From: http://timesunion.com/aspstories/storyprint.asp?StoryID=344447

Megargee, S. (2014, February 5). College staffs turn to Twitter for recruiting edge. *Highschoolot.com.* Retrieved February 6, 2014 from: http://www.highschoolot.com/ college-staffs-turn-to-twitter-for-recruiting-edge/13360720/

Michener, J. (1976). *Sports in America.* New York: Random House.

Miller, S. (2008, November 24). Playing the online field. *Multichannel.* From: http://www.multichannel.com/article/CA6617210.html

Myers, G. (2014, January 28). Seahawks' Marshawn Lynch not doing himself any favors with Super Bowl Media Day silence. *New York Daily News.*

Retrieved February 5, 2014 from: http://www.nydailynews.com/sports/football /myers-super-bowl-confidential-silence-golden-lynch-article-1.1594861

NBC retains Olympic TV rights. (2011, June 7). *ESPN*. Retrieved February 5, 2014 from: http://sports.espn.go.com/oly/news/story?id=6634886

Payne, M. (2006). *Olympic turnaround.* New York: Praeger.

Plaschke, B. (2000, January-February). 'That's twice you get me. I'm gonna hit you, right now, right now!' *Columbia Journalism Review*, 42–44.

Price, J., & Howard, G. (2012, December 11). An update on Sporting News for 2013. The *Sporting News*. Retrieved May 14, 2013 from: http://aol.sportingnews.com/sport /story/2012-12-11/sporting-news-magazine-ipad-yearbook-2013-ios-android

Pursell, C. (2008, August 24). Sports: TV's power play. *TV Week*. Retrieved from http:// www.tvweek.com/news/2008/08/sports_tvs_power_play.php

Ralbovsky, M. (1971). *Super bowl.* New York: Hawthorn. Sandomir, Richard. (2003, September 10). The decline and fall of sports ratings. *New York Times*. http://www .nytimes.com/2003/09/10/sports/10ratings.html

Schultz, B. (2005). *Sports media: Reporting, planning and producing.* Burlington, MA: Focal Press.

Sowell, M. (2008). The birth of national sports coverage: An examination of the *New York Herald*'s use of the telegraph to report America's first "championship" boxing match in 1849. *Journal of Sports Media 3*(1), 53–75.

The revolution in sport viewing. (2012). *Level 3 Communications*. Retrieved February 6, 2014 from: http://www.iptv-news.com/wp-content/uploads/iptv-news/2012/08/Level3 -Sport-Report.pdf

Wilson, R. (2011, October 26). Rob Gronkowski apologizes for pics with porn star. *CBS Sports*. Retrieved February 6, 2014 from: http://www.cbssports.com/mcc/blogs /entry/22475988/32953549

Zeman, N. (2013, June). The boy who cried dead girlfriend. *Vanity Fair*. Retrieved May 10, 2013 from: http://www.vanityfair.com/culture/2013/06/manti-teo-girlfriend-nfl-draft

Jayhawks in the Field

Matt Gardner

Senior Director, Promotions and Digital Strategy for St. Louis Blues

Hometown
Emporia, KS

Education
2001 – University of Kansas (Journalism)

Previous Positions
Web Services Manager for Orlando Magic
Advanced Media Manager for ATP World Tour

1. What "type" of social media content gets the most interaction (likes, comments, retweets, views, etc.) from the public? As a follow-up, is interaction the ultimate goal or are aspects like activation or click-throughs more important?

When we are discussing our content strategy, we try to focus on developing the human side of our team. We know big moments on the ice are going to generate a lot of social buzz. It's the moments that are captured off the ice that tend to define our brand. And by human side, I mean assist our fans in understanding the core of what's important to our franchise and who are players are when they are not on the ice. Fans want that intimate relationship with their favorite players. They watch them on TV, follow them on social media, and as a professional sports team, we can open doors with content they cannot find anywhere else.

For instance, we recently had a player that bid on a team trip at a charity auction for a good sum of money. At the time, most didn't know what he intended to do with the prize. But later we found out that he purchased the trip to give to an 11-year-old cancer patient that he met a few years back. We shot video of the surprise to this young girl in front of the entire team and that video reached more than 12 million people on social media.

Interactions with our fans are an extremely important part of our social media strategy. Activations with corporate partners, pushing of vital ticket messaging, and click-throughs to our digital properties are of course crucial pieces of our business, but social is meant to be a two-way conversation. We focus on trying to keep fans engaged with content, while also giving them an opportunity to demonstrate their level of fan-dom. It's not uncommon to see our account engaging in playful banter with a fan on Twitter, pulling in fan generated content via Facebook or utilizing Snapchat and Instagram to try and allow fans to show off how passionate they are for our team.

2. There is a debate among some if WiFi at stadiums is ultimately a good idea. In your experience, what are the positives and negatives of WiFi in stadiums?

The most important aspect of whether WiFi is needed in stadiums and arenas ultimately boils down to connectivity. Fans want to access info, post content, and interact with in-venue capabilities more than ever, and your mobile infrastructure should be in a place to make sure fans are getting a very reliable connection to the major cellular carriers.

In our particular building, fans had trouble finding signals if they were not a subscriber of the one carrier that was linked to our DAS (Digital Antenna System). It was important that we implemented WiFi as a way of assisting those fans with better connectivity if they were not getting a strong enough signal from their carrier.

The biggest positive of WiFi beyond connectivity for our fans is data collection. With fans sharing tickets, purchasing on the secondary market, etc., it is tough to really know who is in your venue on a nightly basis. By utilizing WiFi, we are able to provide it on a complimentary level to those in attendance in exchange for some very basis info such as email address, zip code, etc. In the future, these data collection efforts may also come from developing partner offers or in-venue exclusive access to content, in addition to tie ins with rewards/loyalty programs.

The initial negative each venue has to explore when looking at WiFi is investment. It's a considerable amount of money to pour into your infrastructure if connectivity isn't the biggest issue or you don't have a great plan on how to use it. Coming up with a solid model for monetization of WiFi at stadiums and arenas is another obstacle that many are still trying to overcome. The potential for a successful model is there, but development on that front seems to be ongoing.

3. What is one digital campaign you've championed that was especially innovative and/ or successful?

During my Orlando Magic tenure (2005–2008), the team held its summer league games at the practice facility and invited five other teams to town to participate. This was way before NBA TV was televising every game and summer league was a big deal. These games were not open to the public, so it's mainly just team personnel that attended.

Initially, there was going to be no way for fans to watch the games. A couple of weeks before, we had streamed a real-time video of our "war room" on NBA Draft night. That was successful, so we discussed internally and decided that we'd simply stream from the camera that was going to record the games for each team, but the only audio that would be picked up would be audio coming from the court (buzzers, sneaker sounds, etc.). So at the very least, fans would be able to go to the Magic website and watch the action — albeit in a far from sophisticated fashion.

On the day our first games were going to be streamed, our TV/radio sideline reporter and one of our PR guys decided they'd "call" the action. Summer league games tend to feature 1-2 Draft picks per team, along with a bunch of players most fans wouldn't know unless you follow the college game very, very closely. So our two TV commentators did a very loose call of the action and put together a fun broadcast where they would discuss anything from a particular player's hairstyle, the meal that was being served at the event, a nickname they just gave to a player because his last name was too hard to pronounce, things that were being witnessed on the sidelines, etc. — oh and a play-by-play of the action on occasion. It was amateur comedy hour meets the D-League, and fans were eating it up.

Before we knew it, the message boards everywhere (this was before social media really took off — unless you count MySpace) were lighting up about this streaming broadcast and the other five teams were also linking to our site for the stream. In a matter of hours, our website was getting traffic numbers it wasn't even seeing during the regular season.

Those fun summer league broadcasts happened for several more seasons before the NBA eventually started airing most summer league games on NBA TV. It ended up spawning a weekly video podcast with our two newfound commentators and led to other NBA teams reaching out asking a lot of questions about our streaming setup and successes.

4. You're clearly still a Jayhawk fan. Do you have any traditions or superstitions you follow when watching KU games?

I'm an obsessed KU fan and never miss watching a football or basketball game. My passion for the Jayhawks started with the 1986 Final Four when I was seven and only grew stronger and stronger with the 1988 National Championship team, followed by the Roy Williams era.

One of my superstitions that started during the 2008 National Championship game is closing my eyes when the opposing team is shooting free throws during tight games. With 1:15 left and the Jayhawks down 62-58, Memphis' Chris Douglas–Roberts went to the free throw line. I closed my eyes and he missed the shot and we went down and scored. Douglas–Roberts again went to the line with :16 left and missed both free throws. Then with :10 left, Derrick Rose missed 1-of-2 from the charity stripe, putting us down three in the final seconds. And we all know how that one ended!

5. When developing social media messages, how do you determine what is "edgy" and what is "too far?" Can you give an example of an instance where your team misjudged this line?

We try to make sure our messages spark conversation, not controversy. The biggest thing we try to think about with each post is making sure it still represents our brand. It's great to engage in some fun banter with another team or with fans, as long as you're voice is staying on brand. Most of our more playful content is deployed on Twitter. I always say that Twitter is our "mullet" approach to social media. It has that business in the front mentality, but the fun of the platform allows you to also show-off that party side. We are an entertainment brand, so it should always remain a priority to keep our accounts fun and playful.

Fortunately, I don't think we've gone too far with our content to the point that it has stirred up too much controversy. We've had a few occasions where our content has been questioned and a few posts we've ended up deleting. But by making sure our team understands what our brand voice should be through our social channels, we've been pretty consistent with our messaging.

6. Describe the favorite parts of your job and give some specific examples if possible.

Sports and technology are two of my biggest passions in life. So having the opportunity each and every day to join these passions together as my career is truly a blessing. In two different professional sports team settings now, I've been able to help build and shape a Digital Media department. Technology helps change our world and those experiences begin to take shape within sports all the time. Finding ways of integrating innovation into the product we deliver to our fans becomes more and more important as days pass by. Just in the last 10 years, we've gone from a website and email-focused digital environment, to embracing social media, adapting to a smartphone-first mentality and now all of those strategies are starting to emerge into the venue experience. The look forward to watching evolve how technology will next help shape the relationship between sports teams and their fan bases.

One of the favorite parts of my job is Opening Night and the first home game of the Playoffs. You put a ton of work into those events in particular. To go out on the concourse as fans file into the arena and see their excitement is what makes all that hard work worth it. Often times, I try to imagine myself as the fan when working on a strategy. I think about those moments when you still feel like a little kid when something gets you excited. I think about the moments that make me the happiest when I'm attending an event for my favorite teams. The chill you feel when that opening video plays or you hear that amazing rendition of the National Anthem. Those are moments you want to capture with each fan that walks through those doors. Those are the moments that make you pinch yourself.

But to do something you love every day and call it "work" is something that will never get old.

Name: _____   Section: _____   Date _____

HSES 289
Introduction to Sport Management

In-Class Quiz and Activity Sheet

Name (or names if done in a group)

Answer #1

Answer #2

Answer #3

Chapter 13

Sport Marketing

Matthew J. Bernthal • *University of South Carolina*

KEY TERMS

Fan identification

Marketing plan

Market segmentation

Positioning

Relationship marketing

Sport marketing

Icon Sportswire/Getty Images

"To satisfy the customer is the mission and purpose of every business. The question: 'what is our business?' can, therefore, be answered only by looking at the business from the outside, from the point of view of the customer and the market. What the customer sees, thinks, believes, and wants, at any given time, must be accepted by management as an objective fact and must be taken as seriously as the reports of the salesperson, the tests of the engineer, or the figures of the accountant. And management must make a conscious effort to get answers from the customer herself rather than attempt to read her mind." (Drucker, 1973)

—Peter F. Drucker, Management Expert

"Don't find customers for your products, find products for your customers." (Godin, 2009)

—Seth Godin, Author

"Make your customer the hero of your story. In other words, don't make your brand the hero, but really put your customer into the company itself. Talk about everything you do through that customer lens." (Gorgone, 2014)

—Ann Handley, Chief Content Officer, MarketingProfs

Introduction

Sport is big business. In today's marketplace, this statement appears somewhat obvious. Fox, CBS, and NBC will pay the NFL $27.9 billion in broadcast rights fees from 2014 through 2022, with the NFL earning an average of $3.1 billion in these fees per year, an increase from the $1.9 billion per year earned over the 2007 through 2013 time frame (Futterman, Schechner, & Vranica, 2011). Lebron James earns $42 million annually in endorsement revenue from Coca-Cola, Samsung, Nike, and others (Badenhausen, 2014). The Minnesota Vikings are building a new stadium at a cost of $1 billion, partially funded through tax dollars (Olson, 2014). Sport fans spend large amounts of their resources, both money and time, on the "consumption" of their favorite athletes and teams. Average paid attendance was over 30,000 fans for 2013 Major League Baseball games (Brown, 2013), while over 18,000 fans, on average, attended Major League Soccer games in 2013 (Prindiville, 2013). It is not unusual for over 100,000 fans to fill a stadium to watch a college football game. New product offerings, from mixed martial arts events to professional bass fishing events and everything in between, have expanded the options available to sport spectators. It seems that if there is a sport event to be held and/or broadcast, there is a market for it. Identifying that market, reaching it, and convincing the consumers that comprise it to spend their money on the sport product is the job of sport marketers.

So, what exactly is sport marketing and what is the main characteristic of successful sport marketers? The answer is surprisingly simple. When most students beginning an introductory sport-marketing class are asked to define sport marketing in their own terms, the two words that are most typically used are *advertising* and *sales*. That is, sport marketing is viewed, rather logically, as the advertising and selling of sport products. This view of marketing is rather typical, yet somewhat narrow. Indeed, good sport marketers must wield many tools successfully, including

One of the goals of sport marketers is to determine the best methods to utilize to attract customers.

Source: Mark Nagel

advertising, personal selling, social media, pricing, and public relations, among other things. However, at its foundation, successful sport marketing is bigger than these instruments that fill the marketer's toolbox. Consider the following questions:

- How does a marketer of a poorly performing baseball team drawing poor attendance design pricing packages and communication strategies that lead more consumers to attend more games?
- How does a marketer of a professional bass fishing event convince consumers to pack a 15,000-seat arena simply to watch fish being weighed?
- What can a golf course do to encourage more play on its course?
- How does a sport team maximize sponsorship sales and sponsor satisfaction?

The answers to these and similar questions must begin with the central component to successful marketing—*understanding the customer.* Successful marketers of any product, including sport, understand that they must think like their customers think, and understand their customers' wants, needs, and dislikes. A marketer of the losing baseball team understands that even losing teams can satisfy a consumer's desire for an affordable family outing, and as a result develop advertisements that appeal to the consumer's desire to spend quality time with family and construct family pricing packages that communicate value to the consumer. Through an understanding of sport consumers, a successful sport marketer would realize that when it comes to attending sport events, females are generally less motivated by winning than are men, leading to an allocation of a higher percentage of the advertising budget to media vehicles that reach women. The marketer of the professional bass fishing tournament will understand that some of the motivations drawing spectators to this event are the desire to view and purchase products and the desire to learn successful techniques used by the professionals. This leads the marketer to develop and market a product exposition along with the weigh-in where consumers can view and purchase the latest and greatest in fishing tackle as well as learn techniques from clinics given by those fishing in the tournament. A marketer for a golf course determines that to increase course play, she would benefit from developing a marketing program that includes rewards for both quantity of play and for consistent play throughout the year (see section on Relationship Marketing later in this chapter for an expanded example of this). The sponsorship marketer knows that in order to maximize sponsorship sales, sponsorship packages must be tailored to meet the specific business needs of various potential sponsors. Through researching and talking with potential sponsors, this marketer will develop sponsorship packages that focus on increasing brand awareness for one, sampling new products to consumers for another, and for yet another, allowing the sponsor to entertain potential clients and reward valuable employees through hospitality at the event(s).

This chapter began with quotes from Peter Drucker, Seth Godin, and Ann Handley, none of whom work in sport marketing. So why do they lead this chapter? For the sole reason that successful marketing in any industry must center on what these three individuals and others like them recognize: understanding and satisfying customer wants and needs. It matters not whether the product is a sport event, a sporting good, a sport franchise, a sanctioning body such as NASCAR, or a sport access facility such as a fitness center or golf course. A focus on the customer, from product development on, is paramount. Chuck Steedman, Fenway Sports Group Executive VP, illustrated this when he commented about determining which concerts to hold in the Boston Red Sox's Fenway Park: "While I'd like to have Megadeth play Fenway, it doesn't appeal to our season-ticket holders" (Coast to Coast, 2009, p. 29). As sport marketers, it does not necessarily matter how we would like to see our product advertised or how much we might be willing to pay for it. What matters is designing products, brands, marketing communications, and prices that will appeal to our customers. Only by thoroughly understanding our customers will our marketing avoid the pitfall of so many unsuccessful and/or inefficient marketers: throwing ideas (ad campaigns, sales promotions, etc.) against a wall and seeing if they stick. By being in touch with customers, good marketers have a much better understanding of the marketing strategies that are likely to stick, as well as the ones that are likely to fail.

Definitions of Marketing and Sport Marketing

Considering the prior discussion, it should come as no surprise that when definitions of marketing and sport marketing are examined, there is a central component common to each: the customer. The American Marketing Association (AMA) defines *marketing* as "the activity, set of institutions, and processes for creating, communicating, delivering, and exchanging offerings that have value for customers, clients, partners, and society at large" (Dictionary, 2014a). Philip Kotler, one of the foremost experts in marketing, has defined the term as "the science and art of exploring, creating, and delivering value to satisfy the needs of a target market at a profit (Kotler, 2014). While many definitions of sport marketing exist, the vast majority share this focus on the customer either directly or indirectly. Shank defines sport marketing as "the specific application of marketing principles and processes to sport products and to the marketing of non-sport products through association with sports" (Shank, 2009, p. 3). While not directly mentioning the customer, one needs only to look at the AMA definition of marketing itself to see that "applying marketing principles and processes to sport products" means creating, communicating, and delivering value to sport customers and managing sport-customer relationships. Fetchko, Roy, and Clow's (2013, p. 6) definition of sport marketing directly adapts the AMA definition of marketing specifically to sport, in that sport marketing is "the use of marketing for creating, communicating, delivering, and exchanging sports experiences that have value for customers, clients, partners, and society. Fullerton (2007, p. 3) defines **sport marketing** as "the proactive efforts that are designed to influence consumer preferences for a variety of sport products and services." Mullin, Hardy, and Sutton (2007, p. 11) put an even greater focus on the consumer by defining sport marketing as "all activities designed to meet the needs and wants of sport consumers through exchange processes." With its simplicity and its focus on the consumer first and last, this definition is one that students of sport marketing would be wise to adopt.

Sport Marketing
All activities designed to meet the needs and wants of sport consumers through exchange processes.

Market Segmentation

While successful sport marketing centers on meeting the needs and wants of sport consumers, it is clear that not all sport consumers want and need similar things from their sport products. Through market segmentation, sport marketers determine which groups of consumers provide the greatest sales and marketing opportunities (Shank, 2009). **Market segmentation** can be defined as "the process of dividing a large, heterogeneous market into more homogeneous groups of people, who have similar wants, needs, or demographic profiles, to whom a product may be targeted" (Mullin et al., 2007, p. 130). By grouping consumers into relatively similar groups, marketers can increase their efficiency and success through the knowledge that consumers with similar wants and needs will respond similarly to specific marketing efforts. A market is segmented utilizing bases of segmentation. While numerous bases of segmentation exist, common bases include demographics, psychographics, benefits, geographics, and geodemographics.

Demographics include such common variables as gender, age, family size, income, and ethnicity. Since such variables are so easily understood and available (one can obtain the demographic breakdown of a geographic market from any number of sources, including www.census.gov), they tend to be one of the most common ways a market is segmented. As an example of demographics, consider the efforts many sport properties have engaged in to reach females. Many collegiate athletic departments as well as NFL teams offer "classes" designed to teach women the basics of football. At these classes women learn rules and basic strategies, and meet coaches and players. The obvious hope is that the more women learn about the game, the more likely they are to become fans of it and, of course, by extension, consumers of the home team. In attempting to connect with more women, some Major League Baseball (MLB) teams have had wine-tastings at the ballpark. Yet others have featured their players with their own families in team advertisements in the hope that showcasing the players as "good family men" will resonate with women.

As another example, many sport properties have increasingly recognized the importance of attracting the millennial generation (born between 1980 and the early 2000s) in order to strengthen their future fan base, and have engaged in specific strategies that they hope will resonate with them. The Toronto Raptors, for example, have hired Canadian rapper Drake to help develop a new look and logo for the team that will appeal to this generation (Mickle, 2014). Drake has also lent his voice to the Raptors marketing communications. Stadium/arena Wi-Fi connectivity is extremely important for this generation, and sport teams wanting to attract them are increasingly updating facility connectivity. After determining that millennials desire special experiences to a greater degree than do older generations, the Philadelphia 76ers now hold breakfasts for 20 season-ticket holders and the team coaching staff in the locker room every Friday (Mickle, 2014). Finally, realizing that many millennials are likely to engage in "second-screen viewing" (i.e., engaging with their phone, tablets, often via social media) while watching a sport event, smart sport properties are increasingly leveraging this behavior to better connect with this generation.

Other uses of demographic segmentation can be seen with virtually every sport property. For example, many teams have gameday promotions that target a specific age group (dollar beer night for a minor league team in a college town, autograph night to target families with children, etc.). A fitness center might offer special classes designed specifically to appeal to senior citizens, and free childcare to help attract those consumers with young children.

Another basis of segmentation, *psychographics* can essentially be described as lifestyles or activities, interests, and opinions (*AIO dimensions*) (Wells & Tigert, 1971). Psychographics involves segmenting on activities such as what consumers do for a living, what they do for fun, what types of media they utilize most often, their political opinions, their religious beliefs, the social causes that they support, and the like. If marketers can understand their consumers at this level, they will better be able to predict their product preferences and tailor marketing efforts to appeal to them. For example, the U.S. Open tennis tournament has recently advertised on food websites to attract "foodies" (Kaplan, 2013), those individuals with a strong interest in cooking and/or eating. The ubiquity of "food TV" in today's society has created a strong and growing interest in food for pleasure, and smart sport marketers are leveraging this cultural phenomena. The West Michigan Whitecaps minor league baseball team and their home, Fifth Third Ballpark, were featured on an episode of the TV show "Man vs. Food" due to their "Fifth Third Burger Challenge" where a fan is challenged to eat a four-pound hamburger between the seventh-inning stretch

Drake has been utilized by the NBA's Toronto Raptors to help build their brand.

© John Steel/Shutterstock.com

© nicosann/Shutterstock.com

and the end of the game (winning a t-shirt and their picture on a wall of fame if the challenge is completed). Increasing numbers of teams in many sports are also simply adding more high-end, gourmet concessions to enhance fan experience and appeal to foodies.

As another example of psychographic segmentation, many sport teams are marketing to Christians with Christian-themed events. Third Coast Sports, in fact, is a Nashville company that provides religious themed promotions to sport teams. Such promotions exist in both minor and major leagues and across a spectrum of sports over the entire country. A typical promotion might have a team give away Bibles and religious figure (e.g., Noah, Goliath) bobbleheads to attending fans, entertain the fans pre- and/or post-game with a Christian rock band, and have the players give testimonials about the importance of faith in their lives. These types of psychographic promotions have become extraordinarily successful in attracting large numbers of new consumers to ballgames.

Psychographic segmentation can also be useful in attracting sponsors. For example, Old World Industries (owner of the brand Peak Antifreeze and Peak Motor Oil) recently signed sponsorship deals with Michael Waltrip Racing and the National Hot Rod Association (NHRA). The company's strategy is to increase its market share through attracting more "do-it-yourself" consumers to their Peak brand. Given the large number of "do-it-yourself" consumers who follow NASCAR and NHRA, these sponsorships are an ideal marketing strategy for Old World Industries (Mickle, 2012).

A third common method of segmentation, *benefit segmentation* is based on the realization that different consumers may seek different benefits from the same product. As an example outside of sports, think of the brand Excedrin pain reliever. One might find it surprising that Extra Strength Excedrin has the same exact active ingredients, in the same amount, as Excedrin Migraine. Why would the makers of Excedrin market a brand extension that has the exact same ingredients as one of their existing brands? They understand that there is a segment of consumers that has a specific need from their product: relief from debilitating migraine headaches. They knew that clearly communicating that their product could provide this benefit by creating a brand extension that labeled it as such would increase their overall sales as opposed to if they had continued to market only Extra Strength Excedrin. In other words, consumers see Excedrin Migraine as specifically designed for relief of migraine pain, and not the same as any other pain reliever, not even Extra Strength Excedrin. Successful sport marketers learn from companies like this and recognize that their product can often fulfill a variety of benefits sought by a variety of market segments. For example, through research, suppose a sponsorship salesperson for a spectator arena finds that a potential sponsor is having trouble with high rates of employee turnover. This salesperson might then make the connection that this potential sponsor could benefit from entertaining valuable employees in a luxury suite, and emphasize such a benefit in a sales presentation. On the other hand, this same salesperson discovers that another potential sponsor is seeking more brand awareness in the community, so arena signage is highlighted in a sponsorship presentation pitched to that potential sponsor.

As another example of benefit segmentation, think about the marketing of youth sports. Often, parents and children are seeking very different benefits from participation in youth sports. When communicating with parents, a marketer trying to increase participation in a local youth soccer league, for example, might emphasize the parent-sought benefits that youth soccer provides: it is relatively inexpensive, it emphasizes participation, it is safe, a child does not have to have a great deal of initial skill to begin playing, and it provides great exercise and an "energy-drain" from children participating. On the other hand, imagine the same marketer making a presentation to young children only (i.e., without their parents) in a school assembly. It is highly unlikely that the marketer would focus on benefits such as safety, inexpensiveness, or how soccer can help the children "drain energy" so that they will be easier for their parents to manage. Rather, the marketer would be wise to simply focus on the benefits more likely to be sought by children, such as fun, cool uniforms, more time spent with friends, camaraderie through outside events such as trips for pizza after the game, and the like.

Benefit segmentation is ubiquitous in the sporting good market. Many sporting good product categories base their segmentation primarily on this basis. Running shoes are segmented, in part, based on whether a runner is seeking more stability or more cushioning, more ground feel or less ground feel, comfort over long distances or lightness over short distances. ASICS markets several of their running shoe models and running apparel in "Lite-Show" versions, with enhanced reflective technology designed for runners who run outdoors in the dark and need greater visibility to oncoming vehicles. Tennis racquets are marketed to various specific benefit-seeking segments: players seeking more control, those seeking more power, those seeking a racquet that is particularly suited to net play, etc. Sport apparel is marketed toward consumers seeking clothing that wicks sweat away from the body during athletic participation, those seeking clothing that blocks wind, those seeking clothing that improves aerodynamics, those wanting more "fashionable" sport apparel, and the like.

A fourth basis of segmentation, *geographic segmentation* involves creating market segments that are based on geographic location. Marketing to different geographic segments often necessitates different marketing strategies for each. This could be due to geographic differences in things such as weather, culture, and demographics. For example, sporting good retail outlets such as Golf Warehouse might have several different geographic segments, and treat each differently in relation to marketing strategies such as pricing and promotion. In a northern state, for example, prices for Golf Warehouse's clubs would likely fluctuate much more during the course of a year than they would in a state such as Florida. The reason is that demand for golf clubs in Florida remains relatively consistent throughout the year due to the warm weather, while demand for clubs in northern states drops during the long winter months, simply because consumers are less likely to buy clubs when they know they will not be playing for a while. How can a retailer like Golf Warehouse adjust to this drop in demand in northern states? Through strategies such as price promotions (e.g., sales) and non-price promotions (e.g., buy a set of clubs over a certain price and get a free putter and/or a certain number of free rounds at a local golf course). Strategies such as these help the retailer keep sales much more stable throughout the course of the year than they would be otherwise. The greater demand for golf equipment in general in Florida versus a northern state such as Minnesota would also likely lead to a retailer such as Golf Warehouse investing in more locations in Florida.

A final basis of segmentation that is commonly used in sport marketing is *geodemographic segmentation*, so named because it reflects a synergy of geographic and demographic targeting. It also builds in psychographics, however. It is based on the simple notion that people tend to live around other people that are similar to themselves. What does this mean for marketers? It means that if a marketer can demographically and psychographically identify the type of person that is a likely consumer of their product, they can be located and marketed to with relative efficiency.

One of the most widely known geodemographic segmentation systems is Nielsen's PRIZM system. PRIZM defines every U.S. household in terms of 66 demographically and psychographically distinct segments (Nielsen PRIZM, 2014). Think back to our marketer of youth soccer. It is likely that he or she can envision the typical target segments. Perhaps one segment sounds something like this: "Upper-middle-class, suburban, married couples with children—that's the skinny on Kids & Cul-de-Sacs, an enviable lifestyle of large families in recently built subdivisions. With a high rate of Hispanic and Asian Americans, this segment is a refuge for college-educated, white-collar professionals with administrative jobs and upper-middle-class incomes. Their nexus of education, affluence and children translates into large outlays for child-centered products and services" (Segment Explorer, 2014). Kids & Cul-de-Sacs is one of the 66 PRIZM clusters, and its description certainly sounds like a demographic and psychographic profile of a likely target for youth sports. Once our youth soccer marketer has identified Kid's & Cul-de-Sacs as a likely consumer of his or her product, things become easier. Direct mail pieces, for example, can be targeted to zip codes that have been identified as having high numbers of Kids & Cul-de-Sac households. From the PRIZM data, the marketer can learn which magazines and newspapers these likely consumers read, which television shows they watch, and which websites they frequent. This information can help in placing advertisements for the youth soccer league. PRIZM can also help sport marketers identify which of the 66 segments are the most likely to buy their products. While it is beyond the scope of this chapter to describe exactly how this is accomplished, it is important for the introductory sport-management student to know that such services exist and can greatly enhance the sport marketer's chances of success.

Geodemographic systems such as PRIZM can also assist in new business feasibility or location analysis. For example, if Gold's Gym were scouting several markets in which to locate a new facility, what kind of market segments do you think the company would look for in the various proposed locations? One segment likely to be consumers of Gold's Gym is Young Influentials. This cluster, according to Nielsen, "reflects the fading glow of acquisitive yuppiedom. Today, the segment is a common address for young, middle-class singles and couples who are more preoccupied with balancing work and leisure pursuits. Having recently left college dorms, they now live in apartment complexes surrounded by ball fields, health clubs and casual-dining restaurants" (Segment Explorer, 2014). One consideration for Gold's Gym, then, when deciding among the various proposed locations, would be the relative numbers of likely consumers (e.g., Young Influentials and other PRIZM clusters who are reasonable targets for Gold's Gym) within a reasonable drive time of the various locations.

PRIZM and systems like it are widely used by major sport marketers such as the National Association for Stock Car Auto Racing (NASCAR), and major live entertainment marketers such as Feld Entertainment. Acquiring such data obviously costs money. However, geodemographic systems such as PRIZM help these marketers determine segments that are likely to purchase their products, and locate and reach these segments much more effectively and efficiently.

The Interconnectedness of Segmentation Bases

It is important to realize that while it is expedient to discuss each of the bases of segmentation in isolation, they rarely operate independently from one another. It does little good for a marketer, for example, to target women without understanding and appealing to the psychographics of this segment. The NFL, for example, has engaged in a strategy to increase sales of licensed merchandise to women by utilizing "style lounges" (Lefton, 2012). These lounges are temporary stores at NFL stadiums that include DJs playing music, manicurists, and fitting rooms with mirrors. Understanding that many women are used to shopping at department stores and boutique retailers, the league sought to create more of this environment at their stadiums in order to better appeal to the psychographics of female fans.

As another example of the interconnectedness of segmentation bases, imagine that the United States Tennis Association (USTA) attempts to increase both young adult single and senior citizen participation in its adult leagues across the country through a direct mail promotional piece and a television advertising campaign. Young adult singles and senior citizens are simply two demographic segments. However, should the USTA market the leagues to both segments using the exact same message? Based on their *psychographics,* these two *demographic* segments might be attracted to league play because of very different *benefits.* For example, young adult singles might be convinced to try league play because of the social opportunities it affords, while senior citizens might place more emphasis on the health and psychological benefits that come from staying physically active. Ideally, marketing communications geared toward each segment would then reflect this.

Relationship Marketing

Relationship Marketing
Marketing with the conscious aim to develop and manage long-term and/or trusting relationships with customers, distributors, suppliers, or other parties in the marketing environment.

An increasingly common concept embraced by sport marketers is referred to as **relationship marketing**, defined as marketing with the conscious aim to develop and manage long-term and/or trusting relationships with customers, distributors, suppliers, or other parties in the marketing environment (Dictionary, 2014b). Within the sport industry, marketers have become increasingly aware that to consistently succeed over the long term, satisfactory relationships with consumers must be created and *sustained.* It matters not whether the consumers are fans, sponsors, league participants, retail customers of a sporting goods store, members of a fitness center, or some other type of sport consumer. The bottom line is that sustained, satisfactory relationships with customers are paramount. To illustrate a main reason why, consider the concept of the lifetime value of a customer. *Lifetime customer value* represents the value, in dollars, that one customer is worth to a particular company over his or her lifetime. Let's imagine that you spend an average of $5 per week at McDonald's, and have since the age of 10. That means that since you were 10 years old, you've spent an average of $260 per year at McDonald's. That's probably not a stretch for some of you! If McDonald's can keep this relationship with you as a customer for the remainder of your life expectancy, they will have had you as a customer for 66 years if you are a male, and 71 years if you are a female (the average life expectancy in the United States is 76 years for men, and 81 years for women [Painter, 2014]). This means that you are worth $17,160 (male) or $18,460 (female) to McDonald's in direct revenue over the course of your life. For McDonald's, it certainly pays to keep you as a customer by delivering a satisfactory product and customer service, providing incentive to return, and simply making you feel valued as a customer! Sport marketers should approach their customers with the same mindset. How much is each individual fan, sponsor, fitness center member, and so on worth to the marketers of those products? Not the dollar value of an individual game ticket, a single event sponsorship, or the price of a year's membership at a fitness center. Rather, they are worth what they would have spent on the product over a reasonable lifetime as a customer. Viewing them as such will generally lead to increased efforts at customer satisfaction (e.g., putting on exciting, well-run events) and effective relationship marketing programs.

A relationship-marketing program generally consists of one or both of two primary strategies: financial bonding and social bonding. In general, *bonding* refers to the creation of a unified commitment that holds those in the relationship together (Fullerton, 2007). *Financial bonding* is a type of business practice designed to enhance customer loyalty through pricing incentives (Berry, 1995), while *social bonding* involves creating personal ties to develop buyer-seller relationships through interpersonal interactions, friendships, and identifications (Chiu, Hsieh, Li, & Lee, 2004). Consider a hypothetical local public golf course in Central Florida (a highly competitive market with many public courses) that decides to implement a relationship-marketing program in order to build long-term relationships (and thus revenue!) with players. The course, Baytree, establishes the free Baytree Buff program and collects basic information from those who join. Such information includes contact information, demographics such as gender, age, marital status, presence of children in the household, birthday, anniversary, and other information such as favorite restaurants (from a list of partnering restaurants). This information is used to create a database that serves as a tool to implement the program. A simplified version of the Baytree Buff program might look like that shown in Table 13.1.

With this program, Baytree is well on its way to developing sustained, valued relationships with local players, and gains a competitive advantage over the many competing courses in its market that are not aware of the value of relationship marketing.

Relationship marketing programs can be constructed in any number of ways, limited only by the marketer's creativity and/or resources. They may be based primarily on social bonding, financial bonding, or (as in our Baytree example) both. Many are relatively simple. Dick's Sporting Goods, for instance, has a simple financial bonding program called ScoreCard. Shoppers sign up for the program and receive a barcoded ScoreCard that they present to the cashier every time they purchase something at Dick's (if shopping online, the related ScoreCard number is entered). One point is earned for every dollar spent. Every time the customer accumulates 300 points, they are mailed a $10 gift certificate to Dick's. Dick's regularly mails members added incentives to reach the 300 points, such as a coupon for 100 or even 200 ScoreCard points with the customer's next purchase at Dick's. This encourages members to visit Dick's more often and make more purchases than they otherwise might. Further, it encourages Scorecard members to avoid shopping at Dick's competitors. The regular mailings also simply keep Dick's Sporting Goods top-of-mind with members.

Sport teams in various leagues regularly employ relationship-marketing programs to help build **fan identification**, defined as the personal commitment and emotional involvement customers have with a sport organization (Sutton, McDonald, Milne, &

Fan Identification
The personal commitment and emotional involvement customers have with a sport organization.

TABLE 13.1 Relationship Marketing Program for Baytree Golf Club

Strategy	Goal	Type of Bonding
One round of free golf for every five rounds played	• Encourage more rounds played by each customer than they might have otherwise • Discourage play at competing courses	Financial
Play at least once every month and at least 18 times for the year and receive unlimited play during one week of the following summer	• Encourage consistent play throughout the year • Discourage play at competing courses • Reward increases course usage during the slower summer season, enhancing atmosphere and ancillary revenue (food/beverage, clubhouse merchandise)	Financial
Program members are invited to annual party at clubhouse	• Social gathering for members, thanking them for their patronage	Social
Course partners with local restaurants to provide gift certificates to members on their birthdays. Certificate is mailed to members by the course with a birthday card. In exchange, each participating restaurant receives a hole sponsorship (name on tee box sign).	• Regular reminder to members that Baytree appreciates them • Provides opportunity for creating relationships/partnering with local businesses	Social and Financial
Baytree Buff League: Members form two-person teams for Friday afternoon 9-hole competitions. Teams pay flat yearly fee amounting to a per-9-hole rate heavily discounted from the regular rate.	• Encourage social activity, friendships, and competition among players in the context of Baytree • Encourage regular play at Baytree • Increase ancillary revenue	Social and Financial

Cimperman, 1997). Think of a sport team that you are very passionate about. Perhaps you consider yourself a die-hard fan of the Boston Red Sox. You would be considered to have "high identification" with that team. The reasons sport marketers want high fan identification are relatively obvious. Such fans generally attend more games, support the team through good seasons and bad, and buy and wear/display more team merchandise. Through helping fans feel a sense of belonging and staying actively involved with a franchise, relationship-marketing programs strengthen two factors identified by Sutton et al. (1997) as antecedents of fan identification: affiliation and activity. Such programs help fans build a sense of connection with the team and stay actively involved with the team. The San Diego Padres have one program called Compadres Fan Rewards. Members are automatically enrolled in the program when they purchase at least a partial-season ticket. They then earn points for purchasing tickets, attending games, using e-cash (a form of payment for purchases in the ballpark), and the like. Points can be redeemed for rewards such as ticket upgrades, game-used and autographed items, and special fan experiences. Further, they receive 10% off concessions and merchandise, as well as 5% cash back for e-cash use. In addition, members can choose one of four types of membership based on their lifestyle (family, business, fanatics, social), and they then are able to participate in team-sponsored activities that fit into that lifestyle. For example, members choosing the "family" membership type can have their children participate in a postgame Q & A with players, a family trip day on the field at Petco Park, etc. In these ways, the Padres show a clear understanding of how financial and social bonding can be an integral part of team marketing strategy. Such relationship marketing programs, combined with other bonding strategies (e.g., a strong presence on social networking sites such as Facebook) increase the likelihood of teams generating high identification with a core group of fans.

Sport marketers also value the establishment of strong, sustained relationships with sponsors, engaging in strategies to help sponsors feel valued and connected to the sport property (team, event, etc.). In fact, the word "partner" is increasingly used in place of sponsor, as partner suggests a two-way, mutually beneficial relationship between sport property and sponsor. That is, sport properties develop relationships with sponsors through caring about each sponsor's needs, and tailoring sponsorship packages to fit these needs, as briefly described earlier in this chapter. They also develop relationships with sponsors by providing each with *fulfillment audits*, post-sponsorship reports that illustrate and highlight how the sport property fulfilled their corporate needs. For example, a sponsor might sponsor a sport event primarily to entertain valued clients (and prospective clients) in a large, catered, hospitality tent provided as part of their sponsorship package. The sport property that recognizes the value of a sustained relationship with this sponsor would be wise to provide them with a fulfillment audit that contained (among other things) pictures, and perhaps even video, of the clients enjoying themselves in the hospitality area. In short, sport marketers develop sustained relationships with sponsors by *caring about their business needs, developing sponsorship plans to satisfy these needs, and documenting for them how these needs were satisfied.*

Branding and Positioning

Another extremely important aspect of sport marketing is branding and the related concept of positioning. The American Marketing Association dictionary defines a *brand* as a name, term, design, symbol, or any other feature that identifies one seller's good or service as distinct from those of other sellers (Dictionary, 2014c). Having a strong sport brand helps that brand create what is termed *brand equity,* the marketplace value that a brand contributes to a product (Shank, 2009). To illustrate, think of consumers wishing to purchase a few new t-shirts in which to work out. They go to the apparel section in their local department store and find a three pack of generic t-shirts and a three pack of Nike t-shirts. The package of generic shirts costs $12, while the package of Nike t-shirts costs $39.99. Do you think some of these consumers would purchase the more expensive Nike t-shirts? Now add in the information that the shirts are exactly the same, except for a small Nike swoosh in the upper right corner of the Nike t-shirts. Do you still think that many consumers would purchase the more expensive Nike shirts? The answer to each question is an absolute yes! The value of the Nike brand, in the visual representation of the name and the logo and all of the perceptions ("fashionable," "reliable quality," etc.) that go with it, adds significant value to the products on which it is placed. Quite simply, significant value resides in the Nike name and swoosh.

Other powerful brands having strong brand equity exist across the sport product spectrum. Others in the sporting good and apparel arena include brands such as Adidas and Under Armour. Some apparel companies have strong equity within a specific sport (for example, Asics and Brooks in running). The NFL as a league has strong brand equity, as do a number of individual teams within the league (e.g., Dallas Cowboys, Pittsburgh Steelers). University athletic programs can benefit from strong brand equity, as evidenced by brands such as the University of Texas Longhorns, the University of Florida Gators, and the like. In these cases, winning certainly helps, but also important are the strong and valued brand symbols themselves (the Cowboy's star, the University of Florida's popular gator head logo, etc.). Strong brand equity helps these teams generate everything from ticket and sponsorship revenue to significant licensed merchandise revenue. Gold's Gym is a fitness center that benefits from the strong brand equity it has created. Many athletes benefit, in the form of product endorsement revenue, from creating (often with the help of their agents) strong brand equity, with themselves as the brand. The New York Yankees have such extraordinary brand equity that because of the power of their brand, they decided against selling naming rights to their stadium and thus bypassed the revenue that would have resulted. Yankees COO Lonn Trost said "You would not rename the White House and you would not rename Grant's Tomb or the Grand Canyon. We will not rename Yankee Stadium" (Trost, 2008). Such a statement is a powerful testament to the brand equity that team enjoys.

Positioning

Establishing a brand's image in the minds of consumers.

Brands that have high brand equity are usually well-positioned. **Positioning** is essentially establishing a brand's image in the minds of consumers. It may be thought of as establishing a brand's "personality." Many things contribute to a brand's positioning, such as the brand name, logo, colors (e.g., team colors), price, and advertisements, to name but a few. To illustrate positioning, think back to the XFL, a professional football league created by World Wrestling Entertainment (WWE) head Vince McMahon. While the league folded after its inaugural 2001 season, it provides a clear and classic example of the concept of positioning. The WWE was in charge of branding for the league and for each of the league's individual teams, and did many things in an attempt to position the brand as a differentiated alternative to the NFL. First, the name of the league itself, XFL, was part of a positioning attempt. The letter X represents specific meaning to many in our society: extreme, edgy, hardcore, violence, sex. Therefore, its use next to the "FL" communicated to consumers that this meaning was part of the XFL's personality. Second, team names were chosen in an effort to build on this personality. Teams had names such as the Rage, Demons, Hitmen, Outlaws, Maniax, and Xtreme (note the use of the letter X in the spelling of the latter two). Third, team logos were chosen to build on this personality as well. For example, the Orlando Rage's logo represented an enraged, red, Hulk-like figure, while the Los Angeles Xtreme's logo represented what appeared to be a ninja-throwing star. Fourth, the football used by the XFL itself was designed to contribute to the positioning of the league in that its colors were black and red as opposed to the traditional brown. Much like the letter X represents meaning in our culture, so do colors. Dependent upon the context of their use, black and red in combination can communicate meaning such as powerful, fast, violent, and fearsome.

Source: Jeff Nycz

Fireworks are a popular entertainment activity that is often incorporated into sporting events.

Fifth, the league created rules in order to position themselves as a more fun and "extreme" league as compared to the NFL. For example, players were allowed to place nicknames on the back of their jerseys in place of their last names. A game rule allowed no fair catches on punts (potentially leading to violent hits). Another required only one foot in bounds on catches. Halftimes were only 10 minutes long, ostensibly to keep the pace of the entire event experience from lagging. Finally, microphone and camera use during the broadcasts attempted to position the league as more extreme than the NFL. Microphones were placed in a myriad of places (e.g., huddles, locker rooms, coaches) to provide the television viewer with new and unique access to the game that they had not experienced before. Cameras were placed in numerous positions to provide the viewer with new viewing angles. There are numerous reasons postulated as to why the XFL did not survive past its first year of play, and one primary reason relates to positioning. It might be hypothesized that fans saw too much of the WWE (WWF at the time) "sport-entertainment" personality in the XFL, and simply did not desire this personality for their professional football. In other words, it might be contended that while the XFL successfully differentiated its image from that of the NFL, it did a poor job predicting the extent to which fans desired to consume that image within the sport of football.

The concept of positioning is important not only for professional leagues and teams, but for many types of sport products, whether they be sport equipment brands, collegiate athletic programs, access facilities such as fitness centers, spectator facilities, or athletes themselves. For example, Brooks Sports, a company that makes running apparel, has effectively utilized positioning to become one of the leading marketers of running shoes. Decades ago, Brooks used to sell shoes and apparel for multiple sports (e.g., running, tennis, basketball, football). In 2001, Brooks repositioned their brand solely as a running brand, and focused on distributing their brand in specialty running stores (Badenhausen, 2013). In doing this, CEO Jim Weber repositioned Brooks as a more specialized running brand when compared to companies that continued to operate across a plethora of sports (e.g., Nike, Adidas). Brooks further positioned its brand in the minds of consumers by communicating an image of a "fun," "happy" running brand. The brand slogan is "Run Happy," and it creates fun and almost whimsical experiences for runners who compete in events that it sponsors. For example, as a sponsor of the popular Rock 'n' Roll Marathon & Half-Marathon series, Brooks has created unique sponsorship activation at the series' health and fitness expos (the product expositions associated with each race where vendors and sponsors market to the racers). The activation involves "Run Happy Island" where racers (and others attending the expo) can watch light-hearted entertainers dancing and singing around a volcano (named Mount Crackatoe-A), ride a large mechanical Brooks shoe (much like riding a mechanical bull), compete with other attendees in a running-in-place contest that moves each person's small mountain climber up the volcano, and the like. Of course, Brooks employees are on hand to educate the consumers about Brooks running shoes. CEO Weber compares Brooks to the Volkswagen automotive brand: both brands have superior engineering yet also convey a sense of fun (Badenhausen, 2013). In consumers' minds, this image helps set the Brooks brand apart not only from goliath brands such as Nike, but from other brands that are perceived, like Brooks, as specialty running brands (such as Asics or Saucony).

When one considers University of Oregon football, they might have the image of "sleek," "modern," and "flashy," while when one considers University of Alabama football, adjectives such as "traditional," "classic," and "no-nonsense" are likely to come to mind. In part, these images are fostered through the branding of the two teams via their respective uniforms (Oregon with bright neon colors and seemingly endless uniform combinations, and Alabama with a relatively plain, "old-school" look). Seeking to target the fitness novice that is relatively self-conscious about his or her body and inexperienced with fitness center use, a fitness center might position its brand as welcoming, "non-judgmental," and "non-intimidating" by having (among other things) no mirrors in the workout room(s), instructors who are skilled and encouraging with beginners, and the majority of its classes and programs predominantly designed for such beginners. An agent marketing Dennis Rodman in the twilight of his NBA career might have found success marketing him to teams struggling in attendance by positioning him as an entertaining, flamboyant, "character" who could provide somewhat of a boost to ticket sales and media attention. In any case, whether it is in relation to leagues, teams, equipment brands, facilities, or athletes, strategic positioning is an extremely important skill for the sport marketer to master.

External Contingencies

It is important to understand that sport marketers do not operate in a vacuum. The environment in which they operate contains many factors beyond their control. These factors, which can be termed *external contingencies*, include the economy, technology, competition, physical environment, cultural and social trends, the political and legal environment, and demographics (Shank, 2009). Such contingencies can present both opportunities and threats to sport marketers as they develop strategies to market their products. To illustrate the necessity of sport marketers' attention to these factors, consider the economy and technology.

The state of the economy affects both the amount of money consumers have to spend on sport products, as well as their willingness to spend the money that they do have. This applies to both individual consumer spending on sport products and corporate spending on sponsorship. As an example of this, the U.S. economy experienced an economic downturn beginning in late 2008. The stock market plunged, unemployment rose, and wages for those employed stagnated. Further, people were bombarded on a daily basis with media messages reminding them how bad the economy was. This resulted in an economic climate that had individual consumers more hesitant to spend their money on non-necessities, and corporations less willing to allocate tight dollars to sport sponsorship. One obvious way this affected marketing strategy was in pricing. In down economies, sport marketers must pay particular attention to their pricing strategies and must often adjust prices to meet reduced demand. This may mean ticket price reductions, special ticket promotions, or simply avoiding ticket price increases in a down economy. The NFL, for example, introduced a limited number of lower-priced tickets ($500) to the 2009 Super Bowl in response to the poor economy. Further, and perhaps more illustrative, most NFL teams kept ticket prices the same for the 2009 season in response to the down economy. Eighteen NFL teams held prices steady, while three teams reduced prices. Much of this pricing strategy can be attributed to the poor economy (Team Marketing Report, 2009b). For example, the Chicago Bears senior director of sales and marketing said his team's decision to keep ticket prices flat was a "good decision in a tough economic environment" (Team Marketing Report, 2009b). The economy contributed to teams in other leagues following suit. For example, in Major League Baseball, while only six teams held prices steady or increased less than 1% over the 2008 season, a full ten teams actually reduced ticket prices, with several teams also offering cheaper concession options (Team Marketing Report, 2009a). As the economy has slowly rebounded since 2009, the prices charged to attend sporting events has generally increased (see Table 13.2). The FCI is a standard index used to track the price of attending events within the four major U.S. professional leagues, and represents the average price for a family of four to attend one of these events. The index includes four averaged-priced tickets (for two adults and two children), four hot dogs, four small soft drinks, two small beers, two programs, two hats, and parking. The average FCI for the four major U.S. professional leagues is provided in Table 13.2.

As noted, the economy can also affect sponsors' ability and willingness to sponsor sport events. A major industry survey found that 51% of those companies surveyed said that their sponsorship spending would decrease in 2009, and another 36% said their spending would remain relatively unchanged (Klayman, 2009). In this same survey, 47% of companies even reported that they would be seeking to get out of current sponsorship deals. It is quite clear that in poor economies,

TABLE 13.2 2009 and 2014 Fan Cost Index for NFL, MLB, NBA, NHL

League	Average Ticket Price (2009, 2014)	FCI (2009, 2014)
NFL	$74.99, $81.54	$412.64, $459.65
MLB	$26.64, $27.93	$196.99, $212.46
NBA	$49.47, $52.50	$291.93, $326.60
NHL	$49.66, $61.62	$288.23, $359.17

Source: Team Marketing Report, Chicago, IL.

sponsors become hesitant to sign new deals because of economic uncertainties, as well as because of fears that consumers will see the spending as wasteful at a time when the sponsors may, for example, be laying off workers. This can affect sport marketers in a number of ways. Realizing that sponsorship revenue might suffer in poor economic times, wise sport marketers pay particular attention to the investigation of new revenue streams. For example, the NBA recently reversed a longstanding (1991) ban on courtside advertising by liquor brands in an attempt to increase revenue during the period following the 2009 economic crash (Lombardo & Lefton, 2009). Poor economic conditions also present a challenge to the sport marketer with regard to sponsorship sales. In economic downturns, sport marketers must increasingly seek to put together sponsorship proposals that directly address the specific needs of each individual potential sponsor and must be particularly cognizant about sponsorship pricing. In addition, they must seek improved leveraging opportunities for their sponsors. *Leveraging* (sometimes referred to as *activation*) refers to the utilization of various marketing strategies to improve sponsor value. For example, in order to leverage a sponsorship of a college football team, a local auto dealer, along with team marketers, might develop a "Youth Captain of the Week" program to leverage the sponsorship. This program might entail having those who test-drive a car during a certain time frame at that dealership enter a child of their choice to win the opportunity to be a "youth captain" of the team for a game during the season, whereby the winning child gets to meet coaches, be on the field for player warmups, enter the stadium with the team, and remain on the sidelines during the game. Through this leveraging/activation program, the sponsor receives customer prospect data through the entry form and directly encourages more test drives among local consumers.

Technology is another external contingency that has had significant recent impact on sport-marketing strategy. Where beneficial, sport marketers look to technology with an eye toward how it can help them better market their product and improve the fan experience. For example, the University of California has adopted marketing automation technology (which has been used in professional leagues for some time) that allows its ticket department to better target ticket offers to potential buyers. The technology tracks where potential customers visit on the athletic department's website (e.g., a specific sport's page), and responds with ticket offers based on this behavior (Smith, 2013). The Dallas Cowboys are utilizing technology to collect fan satisfaction data from fans in real time (i.e., while they are attending Cowboys' games). A program called Express Feedback allows fans to use their mobile phones to select their seating section and rate their event experience across the four dimensions of entertainment, food and beverage, service and staff, and traffic and parking (Muret, 2013). The NFL has recently launched a partnership with a mobile app developer that allows fans to use their mobile phones to upgrade their in-stadium gameday experience. Through a mobile app, fans can purchase things such as upgraded seats, an in-seat visit from a cheerleader or mascot, or the ability to be on the field pre-game or in the post-game press conference (Kaplan 2013). Perhaps ironically, through adoption of this app, the league is combatting improving technology in the home-viewing experience in part through technology that enhances the in-stadium experience, hoping it gives fans one more reason to buy a ticket rather than stay home and watch the games on television.

Advances in video and broadcast technology have allowed sport marketers to offer enhanced products and enjoyment to fans. The Dallas Cowboys installed a $40 million high-definition video board in their new $1.15 billion stadium in Arlington, Texas. The board is four-sided, with a 160-foot wide by 71-foot high screen for fans on both sides of the stadium, and a 50-foot wide by 28-foot high screen for fans in both end zones. Such boards offer fans enhanced views of the action and replays, and offer increased value to sponsors through enhanced messaging opportunities. Sports broadcaster ESPN continues to blaze trails through the use of technology. It recently made a foray into 3D television with ESPN 3D. While ESPN 3D ultimately failed due to lack of consumer adoption, ESPN continues with its technologically forward thinking by advancing on other technologies such as 4K (ultra high definition) TV. ESPN is the first high-profile television content provider to announce a focus on this emerging technology (Pendlebury, 2013). Interestingly, the National Hot Rod Association (NHRA) has partnered with Guitammer Co. to capture sounds and sensations at races, and then transmit these sensations to viewers of NHRA events on ESPN through Guitammer's ButtKicker device. This device is installed under furniture by home viewers and receives signals that shake the furniture, allowing viewers to "feel" part of the event and experience it in a sensory-enhanced way. Guitammer has tested the device at NHL arenas also, and has plans to apply the product to other contact sports as well (Mickle, 2013).

Opportunities for sport marketers made possible through advancing technology are certainly not limited to advances in web tracking, mobile devices, or video and broadcast technology. Yet another strategy increasingly used by sport organizations combines technology with another external contingency—cultural and social trends. Specifically, smart sport marketers are increasingly taking advantage of social media. It is now standard for teams, sporting goods brands, individual athletes, access facilities such as fitness centers and golf courses, and virtually any other type of sport product to create a presence on social networking sites such as Facebook and Twitter. Related specifically to sport teams, these sites allow teams to build fan identification through connecting and involving the fan with the team and other fans. These sites accomplish this in a number of ways. For example, fans can communicate with other fans, find other fans in their geographic location with which to connect, post pictures, and the like. Teams can share information (such as player roster moves, news from training camp, etc.) that keeps the fans informed, and they can involve the fan in community dialogue by asking for responses to posts or tweets (for example, asking which player is likely to have the best upcoming season), among other things. Not only do such sites help teams build fan identification and community, but also through the process of participating in such sites, fans provide the team with information that can be used to target future marketing messages. While it is beyond the scope of this chapter to detail the marketing benefits and strategies associated with social media, it is clear that sport properties that fail to effectively capitalize on this technology in the current environment will fail to realize their full potential.

With regard to all external contingencies and the role that they play in shaping marketing strategy, the key lesson for sport marketers is to always pay close attention to all that is happening in the environment (cultural environment, technological environment, competitive environment, etc.) in which they operate. Such attention will illuminate both marketing threats and opportunities that less attentive sport marketers will, at their own peril, miss. Attention without action, however, does little. Marketers must respond creatively to their external environment. As a brief example, recall the surge of U.S. gasoline prices in 2007-2008. Understanding the "pain at the pump" consumers were experiencing, creative sport marketers took advantage,

turning this economic threat into an opportunity. Callaway Golf, for example, gave away gift cards worth $100 in free gas with the purchase of certain drivers (Ramde, 2008). For fans buying 2008-2009 season tickets, the New Jersey Nets offered 10% of the purchase price back in the form of free gas. While not offering a price promotion, the Detroit Pistons utilized the gas price surge as a public-relations tool, having Pistons players pump $20 of free gas per car during a 1.5-hour period at a local gas station. In each case, these organizations attended to a happening in the external environment and utilized it to their advantage.

The Marketing Plan

A **marketing plan** can be defined as the document containing an analysis of the current marketing situation, opportunities and threats analysis, marketing objectives, marketing strategy, action programs, and projected income (and other financial statements [e.g., budget]) (Dictionary, 2014d). Formulating a marketing plan guides the sport marketer in developing a strategic plan that increases the probability that the product will find success in the marketplace. The plan includes items such as a SWOT analysis, intended target markets, and strategies for promotion, pricing, and distribution. A marketing plan will also often include performance objectives, such as goals for a percentage increase in event attendance over the prior year, quarterly sales objectives, brand awareness objectives, and the like.

To illustrate the basics of a marketing plan, consider a plan for a February Philadelphia stop for the event "Monster Jam," a monster truck competition sanctioned by the U.S. Hot Rod Association. A brief summary of selected strategies of the marketing plan for the Monster Jam show is provided in Box 13.1. Not all strategies in the actual plan are presented, nor is every detail provided about the strategies that are presented. The summary is simply intended to give the reader a glimpse of the content of an actual marketing plan.

Marketing plans vary widely in their detail and thoroughness. For example, an expansion of the Monster Jam plan might provide additional demographic

BOX 13.1

Strengths/Opportunities

- Ticket prices remain affordable for a large portion of the overall population at $27, $22, and $5 for children.
- The Philadelphia market is focused on football, but it is unlikely the Eagles will be in the playoffs and thus take focus away from show promotion or consumer's disposable income allocated to entertainment.

Weaknesses/Threats

- The show has been in the market for several years and is thus in need of fresh marketing ideas.
- The marketing budget has not increased over the last two years.
- No big names are part of the show.
- Normally snowy and cold weather hurts the possibilities of doing a PR event outside.

Target Audience

- Primary target market: Males 18–44
- Secondary target market: Children 6–11

Ticket Prices

- Adult: $27, $22
- Child: $5
- Discounts: Group Tickets for 20+ people: $14 per ticket
- Boy Scouts 12 or older: $13
- Early Bird purchases: $22, $17
- Adult coupon: $22, $17

Promotions

Radio
- WWMR (rock), WXTU (country)
    —WWMR sponsors a truck
    —WWMR runs ride to work/school in a monster truck with the morning show promo
    —Fifteen 10-second advertisements
    —Hourly Monster Jam on-air promotions during weekend of event
    —Advertisements on WWMR.com
    —Live mentions by on-air personalities
- For the following stations, seek to provide tickets in exchange for on-air ticket giveaways, on-air mentions, website inclusion, email blasts, and distribution of Monster Jam promotional material at station events: WJSE, WJBR, WMGK, WSTW, WZZO, WTHK, WPST, WRDW, WIOQ

Outdoor Advertising

- Ads on 60 bus backs on suburban bus routes
- 12 billboards

Internet

- Monster Jam logo and web page link on every partnering radio station website
- Email blasts in early December to database lists, including Tony Hawk, Boom Boom, HuckJam, WWE, Motocross, Incubus, Linkin Park, Beastie Boys, prior Monster Jam shows, American Idols Live, Van Morrison, Red Hot Chili Peppers, Barenaked Ladies, Panic at the Disco, Wachovia Complex Cyber Club
- A presence on MySpace, Facebook, and Friendster will be created to help reach the younger crowd
- Sixers, Flyers, Phantoms, and Kixx to send discount email to members promoting Monster Jam

Television

- KYW-TV 3 (CBS)
  —The Early Show (M–F, 5 am–7 am)
- WPVI-TV 6 (ABC)
  —TGIF (Friday during news 5 pm–6:30 pm)
  —Fast Forward (last Saturday of each month)
  —Visions (Saturday at 7:30 pm)
- WCAU-TV 10 (NBC)
  —10! Show (M–F, 10 am–11 am)
- WTXF-TV 29 (FOX)
  —Good Day Philadelphia (Weekdays 5 am–9 am)
- Comcast SportsNet
  —Daily News Live

Partnerships

- Wendy's
  —Tray liners in-store mid-through-late December
- Bally's Total Fitness
  —Prominently displayed promotional information at front desk of all area locations
  —Promotional offer and show information in all Bally print advertising
  —"Bally Total Fitness Discount" to Monster Jam displayed on Ballytotalfitness.com with direct link to purchase tickets
  —Monster Jam information included in Bally's e-blast
  Monster Jam marketing plan information provided courtesy of Feld Motor Sports, Inc.

and psychographic detail about the target markets, including income levels, areas of geographic concentration, other activities of interest, types of media that they consume, and the like. This can provide insight into how to reach the targets with various marketing messages. It might also include budgetary information such as the amount allocated to each media outlet (e.g., radio station, television station). However, the idea behind each plan is the same. The process of formulating the plan is an exercise that assists marketers in thinking strategically about how to best market their product, and the resultant plan essentially acts as a marketing "recipe" to follow. A marketing plan does not guarantee success, but it certainly increases its probability.

Conclusion

Sport marketing is a fascinating and growing industry. It is impossible to fully describe or even briefly discuss everything that sport marketing entails in one chapter. The purpose of this chapter, rather, has been to highlight and emphasize the foundation upon which sport marketing, and indeed all of marketing, is built: understanding and satisfying customer wants and needs. Through this, you have been introduced to the key related topics of sport marketing, market segmentation, relationship marketing, branding and positioning, external contingencies, and the marketing plan. There are many interesting and important aspects of sport marketing that have not been either directly addressed or addressed in great detail here. For example, there is much more to learn about pricing, sponsorship, public relations, advertising, and marketing research, to name but a few. There are indeed a myriad of tools in the marketer's toolbox, and the person who is an expert at using each has yet to be found. However, if in using each one of the tools of the trade, the marketer keeps the customer front and center, his or her chances for success increase exponentially.

Study Questions

1. This chapter has defined good sport marketing as being customer-focused. Explain what this means and provide an example of a sport marketer (can be an individual, franchise, league, etc.) that you believe has a strong customer focus.
2. Give an example of a sport marketer who you believe has a relatively weak customer focus and has suffered because of it.
3. Describe what is meant by fan identification. What are the various reasons that we want highly identified fans?
4. What businesses do you frequent outside of the sport industry that use relationship-marketing strategies? What are the various financial and/or social bonding strategies they use? Do you believe that you have spent more money with some of these businesses and/or have been a customer of theirs for longer than you would have otherwise due to these marketing efforts?
5. Describe the concept of lifetime value.
6. A key to successful sport marketing is staying tuned in to external contingencies (competition, technology, social/cultural trends, etc.). This chapter has very briefly illustrated the external contingencies of the economy and technology.

What are some examples of how other external contingencies can affect the strategies of sport marketers?

7. What are the major components of a marketing plan?

8. What are the major bases of market segmentation?

9. What is meant by positioning? What are some sport brands that you believe position themselves well? What are some sport brands that you believe could be positioned better?

10. What is included in the Fan Cost Index (FCI), and what is the average FCI for the NFL, NBA, MLB, and NHL?

Learning Activities

1. You are the marketing director for a minor league hockey team in a city of your choice. Using each of the bases of segmentation discussed in this chapter, identify five distinct market segments that you will target. Develop 10 gameday promotions (autograph night, discount beverage night, etc.), with each segment that you have identified being targeted by at least two of them. Try to be creative with your promotions. Now, develop other marketing strategies that you might use to target each of your five segments. Your strategies should include, but not be limited to, advertising and pricing.

2. Working for the PGA, you have been charged with developing marketing strategies that will take advantage of the millennial generation's tendency to engage in second-screen viewing while watching television. The goal of these strategies, as a whole, is to make the viewer feel more involved in the PGA event that he or she is watching and more connected to others watching the event. What specific strategies would you suggest?

3. You work in marketing for a Major League Baseball team. You have been charged with developing a relationship-marketing program for the team, a program to increase fans' involvement with the team throughout the year. What might your relationship-marketing program look like? Be sure to include elements of both social bonding and financial bonding.

4. "Like" on Facebook and/or "Follow" on Twitter two sport franchises of your choice, or pick two that you have already Liked/Followed on these sites. Keep a log of how these franchises utilize both sites in their marketing efforts every day over the course of at least two weeks (preferably longer). How does each franchise utilize this medium to build fan community? What does each franchise do to build fan identification? After analyzing your log, which franchise do you think better utilizes social media in its marketing efforts and why? What suggestions for improvement do you have for each franchise?

References

Ad Spotlight. (2004, February 6). *Team Meeting Report.*

Badenhausen, K. (2013, May 20). Brooks running shoes hit their stride. *Forbes.com.* Retrieved June 13, 2014 from http://www.forbes.com/sites/kurtbadenhausen/2013/05/20/brooks-running-shoes-hit-their-stride/

Badenhausen, K. (2014, January 22). Lebron James' endorsements breakdown: By the numbers. *Forbes.com.* Retrieved June 4, 2014 from http://www.forbes.com/sites/kurtbadenhausen/2014/01/22/lebron-james-endorsements-breakdown-by-the-numbers/

Berry, L.L. (1995). Relationship marketing of services: Growing interest, emerging perspectives. *Journal of the Academy of Marketing Science, 23*(4), 236–245.

Brown, M. (2013, October 3). The good, the bad, and the ugly about MLB's 2013 attendance. *Forbes.com.* Retrieved June 4, 2014 from http://www.forbes.com/sites/maurybrown/2013/10/03/the-good-the-bad-and-the-ugly-of-mlbs-2013-attendance/

Chiu, H., Hsieh, Y., Li, Y., & Lee, M. (2004). Relationship marketing and consumer switching behavior. *Journal of Business Research, 58*(12), 1681–1689.

Coast to Coast. (2009, December 22–28). Coast to coast. *Street and Smith's SportsBusiness Journal,* 29.

Dictionary. (2014a). Marketing. *ama.org.* Retrieved on June 9, 2014 from https://www.ama.org/resources/Pages/Dictionary.aspx?dLetter=M

Dictionary. (2014b). Relationship marketing. *ama.org.* Retrieved on June 12, 2014 from https://www.ama.org/resources/Pages/Dictionary.aspx?dLetter=R

Dictionary. (2014c). Brand. *ama.org.* Retrieved on June 12, 2014 from https://www.ama.org/resources/Pages/Dictionary.aspx?dLetter=B

Dictionary. (2014d). Marketing plan. *ama.org.* Retrieved on June 13, 2014 from https://www.ama.org/resources/Pages/Dictionary.aspx?dLetter=M

Drucker, P. (1973). *Management: Tasks, responsibilities, practices.* New York: Harper & Row Publishers.

Fetchko, M., Roy, D., & Clow, K. (2013). *Sports marketing.* Upper Saddle River, NJ: Prentice Hall.

FFA. (2008, January 14). FFA fundraiser night at the Blazers. *Business Wire.* Retrieved on January 4, 2009 from http://www.businesswire.com/portal/site/google/index.jsp?ndmViewId=news_view&newsId=20080114006248&newsLang=en

Fullerton, S. (2007). *Sports marketing.* New York: McGraw Hill.

Futterman, M., Schechner, S., & Vranica, S. (2011, December 15). NFL: The league that runs TV. *The Wall Street Journal.* Retrieved on June 4, 2014 from http://online.wsj.com/news/articles/SB10001424052970204026804577098774037075832

Godin, S. (2009). First, organize 1,000. Retrieved on June 4, 2014 from http://sethgodin.typepad.com/seths_blog/2009/12/first-organize-1000.html

Gorgone, K.O. (2014). Battling mediocrity in content: Ann Handley talks to marketing smarts [Podcast]. Retrieved on June 4, 2014 from http://www.marketingprofs.com/podcasts/2014/25029/writing-content-ann-handley-marketing-smarts

Kaplan, D. (2013, September 9-15). DDB helps Open sharpen digital strategy. *Street & Smith's SportsBusiness Journal,* 17.

Kaplan, D. (2014, March 24-30). NFL ups fun factor via technology. *Street & Smith's SportsBusiness Journal,* 1.

Klayman, B. (2009, October 28). Over half of firms to cut sponsorship spend: Study. Retrieved on November 3, 2009 from http://www.reuters.com/article/idUSTRE52969320090310

Kotler, P. (2014). Dr. Philip Kotler answers your questions on marketing. Retrieved on June 9, 2014 from http://www.kotlermarketing.com/phil_questions.shtml#answer3

Lefton, T. (2012, October 1-7). Marathon starts campaign; NFL effort targets women. *Street & Smith's SportsBusiness Journal,* 13.

Lifestyle. (2010). Lifestyle and behavior segmentation: Nielsen PRIZM. Retrieved on January 7, 2010 from http:// enus.nielsen.com/etc/medialib/nielsen_dotcom/en_us/documents/pdf/fact_sheets.Par.69269.File.dat/PRIZM_US_SS_n8006.pdf

Lombardo, J., & Lefton, T. (2009, January 19-25). NBA cans ban on liquor ads. *Street & Smith's SportsBusiness Journal,* 1, 26.

Mickle, T. (2012, September 17-23). New deals for Old World brands. *Street & Smith's SportsBusiness Journal,* 6.

Mickle, T. (2013, September 30-October 7). NHRA broadcasts will rock the sofa. *Street & Smith's SportsBusiness Journal, 41.*

Mickle, T. (2014, March 24-30). Industry looks for right recipe to attract fans among millennials. *Street & Smith's SportsBusiness Journal,* 1.

Mullin, B., Hardy, S., & Sutton, W. (2007). *Sport marketing* (3rd ed.). Champaign, IL: Human Kinetics.

Muret, D. (2013, October 7-13). Cowboys plug feedback tool into app. *Street & Smith's SportsBusiness Journal,* 10.

Nielsen PRIZM. (2014). Nielsen PRIZM: Overview. Retrieved June 11, 2014 from http://www.claritas.com/MyBestSegments/Default.jsp?ID=70&&pageName=Learn%2BMore&menuOption=learnmore

Olson, R. (2014, February 8). Personal seat licenses will raise $100 million for new Vikings stadium. *StarTribune.* Retrieved on June 4, 2014 from http://www.startribune.com/politics/statelocal/244270481.html

Painter, K. (2014, May 15). Life expectancy up worldwide; Japanese women live longest. *USA Today.* Retrieved on June 12, 2014 from http://www.usatoday.com/story/news/world/2014/05/15/world-life-expectancy/9123889/

Pendlebury, T. (2013, June 12). ESPN to drop 3D channel in 2013. *CNET.* Retrieved June 10, 2014 from http://www.cnet.com/news/espn-to-drop-3d-channel-in-2013/

Prindiville, M. (2013, October 29). Seattle Sounders break MLS attendance record, average 44,038 fans per game. *ProSoccerTalk.* Retrieved June 4, 2014 from http://prosoccertalk.nbcsports.com/2013/10/29/seattle-sounders-break-mls-attendance-record-average-44038-fans-per-game/

Ramde, D. (2008, June 8). Companies offering free gas to attract business. *USA Today.* Retrieved on June 8, 2008 from http://www.usatoday.com/money/economy/2008-06-08-2344632439_x.htm

Segment Explorer. (2014). Segment explorer. Retrieved June 11, 2014 from http://www.claritas.com/MyBestSegments/Default.jsp?ID=30&menuOption =segmentexplorer &pageName=Segment%2BExplorer&id1=1027

Shank, M. (2009). *Sports marketing: A strategic perspective* (4th ed.). Upper Saddle River, NJ: Prentice Hall.

Smith, M. (2013, September 16-22). Cal uses tech to track potential ticket buyers. *Street & Smith's SportsBusiness Journal,* 4.

Sutton, W., McDonald, M., Milne, G., & Cimperman, J. (1997). Creating and fostering fan identification in professional sports. *Sport Marketing Quarterly, 6*(1), 15–22.

Team Marketing Report. (2009a, April). Team marketing research. *Team Marketing Report,* 6–7.

Team Marketing Report. (2009b, September). Team marketing research. *Team Marketing Report,* 8–9.

Team Marketing Report. (2013a, September). Are you ready for some FCI: Rising prices in the NFL. *Team Marketing Report.*

Team Marketing Report. (2013b, November). Buck handling: NHL prices increase in 2013-2014. *Team Marketing Report.*

Team Marketing Report. (2013c, December). Alley oop: NBA ticket prices on rise. *Team Marketing Report.*

Team Marketing Report. (2014, March). 2014 MLB fan cost index. *Team Marketing Report.*

Trost, L. (2008, December 22–28). They said it. *Street and Smith's SportsBusiness Journal,* 29.

Wells, W., & Tigert, D. (1971). Activities, interests, and opinions. *Journal of Advertising Research, 11,* 127–135.

Suggested Sources

Street and Smith's SportsBusiness Journal—www.sportsbusinessjournal.com

Team Marketing Report—www.teammarketing.com

American Marketing Association—www.ama.org

Sport Marketing Quarterly, Morgantown, WV: Fitness Information Technology.

Duffy, N., & Hooper, J. (2003). *Passion branding: Harnessing the power of emotions to build strong brands.* West Sussex, England: John Wiley and Sons, Inc.

Martin, A. (2012). *Renegades write the rules: How the digital royalty use social media to INNOVATE.* San Francisco, CA: Jossey-Bass.

Newman, T., Peck, J., Harris, C., & Wilhide, B. (2013). *Social media in sport marketing.* Scottsdale, AZ: Holcomb Hathaway.

Ries, A., & Ries, L. (1998). *The 22 immutable laws of branding: How to build a product or service into a world-class brand.* New York: HarperCollins.

Ries, A., & Trout, J. (1993). *The 22 immutable laws of marketing: Violate them at your own risk.* New York: HarperCollins.

Jayhawks in the Field

Hunter Lochmann

Senior Vice President of Marketing and Brand Strategy for
Monumental Sports (Washington Capitals, Washington Wizards)

Hometown
Andover, MA

Education
1994 – University of Kansas (Sport Management)

Previous Positions
Senior Vice President of Marketing for Phoenix Suns
Chief Marketing Officer for University of Michigan Athletics
Vice President of Marketing for New York Knicks

1. How important are star/recognizable players when marketing teams in a crowded sports market?

Having a star player can only help elevate your team brand, especially depending on the sport. For instance, in the NBA, players are arguably much more identifiable than most athletes – due to not being behind a helmet, being a global game and the NBA being on the forefront of social media. That is why in today's sports world, you read more about LeBron, Curry, and Westbrook – their marketability is 2-fold when you add their personalities on top of their talent. When you have a player that transcends the sport as one of the current greats—like Alex Ovechkin of the Capitals—then their star power can lift an entire team (and city) by itself. Their connection to the community/city is what is going to cut through the crowded marketplace.

2. If an organization want to changes their image or brand to the public, what are some best practices in that transition (i.e., the NBA after the Artest melee)?

First, the situation needs to be identified and any mistakes made are going to need to be learned from and a plan developed and communicated as to why it won't happen again. Then, the team needs to listen to its key stakeholders – sponsors, season ticket holders, fans – to understand what they hold near and dear to the team. By understanding the brand history and framework, teams can decide what is the best direction to alter any negative thoughts from the past. It could be simple communication of a plan. It could be new leadership or a new voice. It could be a complete re-brand if

the problem was just too big to overcome with a few simple tactics. It really is a case-by-case situation but listening and acting are the two non-negotiable results.

3. What is one marketing or branding campaign you worked on that you're especially proud of and why?

During my brief time in Phoenix, the Suns were a team in flux. While the long-standing and storied franchise in the Phoenix professional sports scene (almost 50 years), the team was starting to lose its connection with their fans due to a number of non-playoff years as well as other disconnects with the team and the city. Similar to the previous answer, we did some deep research internally on what made the brand tick and what we needed to communicate. We decided upon a campaign called "WE ARE PHX," a simple statement used by many other schools and pro teams in general marketing campaigns but this was one that would manifest itself in how we acted. We wanted to reconnect to the storied past (which we did), we wanted to introduce and connect our current players to the community (which we did) and finally, we wanted to re-connect the brand to the community (which we did). It was a multi-year campaign that would grow with as the team grew in opportunity (including the just completed 2016–17 season).

4. If you could relive one year of your college life at KU, which one would it be and why?

Junior year. By that point I was knee deep in the Sport Management major and also working for the KU Football team as a student manager, traveling with the team, and learning how a Division I Football program worked. On the fun side, I was rush chairman at my fraternity and enjoyed every minute of college life. The realities of the real world were still a year away!

5. Monumental Sports and Entertainment oversees multiple teams and venues. What about this organizational structure appealed to you and what are the advantages and disadvantages when compared to working for an individual team?

We all learn from each other each and every day with the diverse make up of teams and properties. We have an NHL team (Capitals), an NBA team (Wizards), a WNBA team (Mystics), two

Arena Football Teams (Washington Valor, Baltimore Brigade), and even an e-sports relationship with Team Liquid. In addition, we have the first Over The Top (OTT) network of its kind owned by a professional sports entity – Monumental Sports Network. Every day we learn something new across each team and property and are able to share best practices. Additionally, having this diverse portfolio allows for our various sales and marketing teams greater opportunity to fit the needs of potential clients. What makes it even more unique is the city of Washington DC – global, powerful, and a "super city" which expands over the Mid-Atlantic region from Baltimore to Richmond. I personally oversee the marketing for the Capitals and Wizards and it's fun to toggle between two leagues and two very different sports and properties. As they are in the same season, it's also very busy! (at least I'm learning that in my first year here).

6. Describe the favorite parts of your job and give some specific examples if possible.

What I love about my job is the creativity that comes with marketing. We can roll out marketing campaigns, sales ideas, etc. and sometimes they work and sometimes they don't. This constant feedback loop—especially with social media—not only keeps you honest and on your toes but also makes you better. But my favorite part of my job is at the end of the day, I work for properties that people care very passionately for. What we take for granted—working in an arena—others find so interesting and want to read about us and consume everything about our brand every day. Not every brand can say that. And it never fails—when you surprise a fan with something small (e.g. a seat upgrade at a game) the looks on their faces and the memories you are making is what makes the hard work and long hours satisfying.

Name: _____ Section: _____ Date _____

HSES 289
Introduction to Sport Management

In-Class Quiz and Activity Sheet

Name (or names if done in a group)

Answer #1

Answer #2

Answer #3

Chapter 14

Sport Facility and Event Management

Farah Jiries Ishaq • *University of Kansas*

© Taya Ovod/Shutterstock.com

Introduction to Sport Events

In 2019, the North American sport industry is estimated to be valued at $73.5 billion, up from $60.5 billion just 5 years prior in 2014 (Heitner, 2015). This valuation illustrates the magnitude of industry's economic impact across the continent and the world. While sports media rights are the primary contributor to this growth, it is important to gain an understanding of the history and development of sports, particularly sport events, throughout the years.

While the earliest depictions of sport date back to 15,300 BC in the form of cave paintings in southwestern France (GOUNESCO, 2016), organized sporting events and competition began in Olympia, Greece, in the year 776 BC. This sporting event is now commonly known as the Olympic Games. According to the IOC, once originally consisting of one running event, the Olympics now draw over 10,500 athletes from over 200 countries in 41 summer and winter sports. Although the Olympic Games are one of the oldest institutionalized sporting events in the world, sport events continue to contribute to the growing industry in a multitude of ways. This chapter will explore the types of sport events, aspects of a sport event, careers in sport facility and event management, the three phases of the event cycle, and current issues, challenges, and trends in facilities and event management.

Contributed by Farah Jiries Ishaq. © Kendall Hunt Publishing Company.

© Anastasios71/Shutterstock.com

Types of Sport Events

As the sport industry has grown, so have the types of sport events that are organized, ranging from a neighborhood 5Ks to international, mega events like the FIFA World Cup. This section will explore the different sport events, including community participation events, large spectator events, mega events, youth events, and adaptive and disability sport events, which all vary in size and scope. It is important to understand that regardless of the size and scope, "an event is a carefully crafted experience delivered to make an impact on the person in attendance" (Greenwell, Danzey-Bussel, & Shonk, 2014, p. 7). Ultimately, the goal for the event is to deliver a well-run program that provides a sense of entertainment for the participants and spectators while being able to strategically plan, manage time effectively, and understanding the resources, budgeting, and financing involved in doing so (Greenwell et al., 2014).

Without a doubt, many types of events can take place in the realm of athletics. Indoor events often take place in arenas while outdoor events take place in stadiums, fields, and facilities equipped for multiple events. It is important to note that facilities primarily used for athletic events are often used for other events, including concerts or community programs. Prior to understanding the more well-known, global, mega events, it is important to develop a perspective that illustrates a broader approach to what sport events consist of, including the smaller, local, often community-based participation events.

Participation Events

These participation events typically include running events, cycling events, endurance events, and community sport and recreation events. Often with much smaller attendance than larger spectator events or mega events, community events are meant to drive participants to be active within their communities. Examples of such events include 5ks or similar running events, triathlons, cycling road races, or even community swim events. These events likely draw higher participation than spectator attendance. Athletes participate in these events for a variety of reasons, including for physical fitness or to support a community cause or charity.

Large Spectator Events

Large spectator events include events associated with the major professional sport leagues, including the NFL, NBA, MLB, NHL, and MLS. These major professional sport leagues often draw thousands of fans each and every game. The average attendance varies across each league; however, within the United States, the NFL is king, averaging 67,405 fans in the stands (Statista, 2018). While fans can travel to these large spectator events, typically the fans in attendance include local or regional fans of the particular teams, versus sport tourism seen in large mega events.

Mega Events

Mega events consist of sport event know across the world, including the FIFA World Cup and the Olympic competitions, involving elite athletes competing in front of large crowds. According to Hiller (2000), "mega-events are short-term, high-profile events like Olympics and World Fairs that always have a significant urban impact" and often "stimulate urban redevelopment and . . . promote economic growth" (p. 439). These events draw crowds even if they will not be attending events. Events like the Olympics, or even the Super Bowl, draw crowds for the experiences, including festivals, parties, or meetings that occur specifically surrounding the event (Greenwell et al., 2014). After hosting a mega event, the city will likely continue to draw fans who are interested in seeing the sites where it took place and enjoy the legacy surrounding the city or host site. While mega events likely create a lasting impact across the host cities, it does not come without a cost, especially to host the Olympic Games. With infrastructure costs ranging from $5 billion to over $50 billion, estimated costs are often well below the final costs, resulting in financial burden lasting years for the host cities (McBride, 2018). Mega events are likely to involve sport tourism, which includes traveling to experience a sport event specifically.

Youth Events

The youth sports industry in the United States is now a $15.3 billion market that has grown 55% since 2010 (Gregory, 2017). This statistic illustrates the magnitude of the youth sport industry and how big a role it plays in sport events. Cities are now moving away from trying to attract minor league teams to participating in a "facilities arms race once reserved for big colleges and pros" (Gregory, 2017, para. 26) in hopes of attracting large youth tournaments at these "play-and-stay mega-complexes" to lift the local economy. One example of such mega complexes is Disney's ESPN Wide World of Sports Complex located in Orlando, Florida. At this 220-acre site, over 350,000 athletes come through the gates every year completing in a variety of sports, including baseball, basketball, cheerleading, football, soccer, softball, and volleyball, among many others (ESPN Wide World of Sports, 2018a; 2018b). Youth sport governing bodies involved in such competitions include Amateur Athletic Union (AAU), Little League Baseball, Pop Warner, U.S. Youth Soccer, USA Football, USA Hockey, and others (Greenwell et al., 2014).

Adaptive and Disability Sport Events

Several sports and sport events exist specifically for people with physical or cognitive disabilities. For example, the Paralympic Games occur after the Olympic Games in the same city location. In 2018, the PyeongChang Paralympic Winter Games set a record with 567 athletes from 49 delegations competing in six sports across 80 medal events (International Paralympic Committee, 2018). According to Greenwell et al. (2014), 26 sports are offered across the summer and winter Paralympic Games, including adaptive traditional sports like wheelchair basketball and sledge hockey, or disabled-specific sports like goalball. Furthermore, "six different classifications exist according to their disability: amputee, cerebral palsy, visual impairment, spinal cord injuries, intellectual disability, and a group that includes all those who do not fit into the aforementioned groups" (p. 14). Other events for adaptive and disability sport participants include the Deaflympics, Extremity Games, and Special Olympics with upward of 2.5 million athletes competing (Greenwell et al., 2014).

Aspects of Sport Events

As previously mentioned, the goals of sport events typically involve an understanding of revenues, resources, time management, and strategic planning; however, all this is not possible without the knowledge of several areas and departments involved in the successful planning and implementation of sport events. Primary departments involved in a successful event include facilities, ticket sales, concessions, operations/event management, parking/transportation, security, marketing/communications, game entertainment, sponsorship, and medical, among others. According to Kaplanidou and Vogt (2010), "participants attribute meanings related to organizational, environmental, physical, social, and emotional aspects of the sport event experience" (p. 544), meaning that the overall sport event relies on several factors throughout the sport experience to be successful. Typically, managers in these areas will rely on the four functions of management, including planning, organizing, leading, and evaluating in order to ensure and shape positive event outcomes, leadership, and management throughout the process (Chelladurai, 2014).

Facilities

In sport, a wide variety of facilities exist. Facilities are described as, "all public and private facilities designed to accommodate people wishing to assemble for a common purpose" (Russo, Escklisen, & Stewart, 2009, p. 4). These types of assembly places range from indoor facilities, like arenas, to large, outdoor stadiums accommodating thousands of fans and spectators. Typically, the largest venues across the world are those of motor racing and horse racing. The Indianapolis Motor Speedway is the

TABLE 14.1 Top 10 Biggest Sport Stadiums in the World by Capacity

Stadium Name	Capacity	Location
Rungrado May Day Stadium	114,000	Pyongyang, North Korea
Michigan Stadium	113,065	Ann Arbor, Michigan, USA
Beaver Stadium	110,753	University Park, Pennsylvania, USA
Ohio Stadium	104,944	Columbus, Ohio, USA
Kyle Field	102,733	College Station, Texas, USA
Neyland Stadium	102,455	Knoxville, Tennessee, USA
Tiger Stadium	102,321	Baton Rouge, Louisiana, USA
Bryant-Denny Stadium	101,821	Tuscaloosa, Alabama, USA
Darrell K. Royal Texas Memorial Stadium	100,119	Austin, Texas, USA
Melbourne Cricket Ground	100,024	Melbourne, Australia

Source: The Daily Telegraph

largest sport facility in the world with 235,000 permanent seats, which was reduced from the world record of 257,325 seats in 2013 (Cavin, 2004). If we specifically look at the largest sport stadiums in the world by capacity, eight of the top ten stadiums are surprisingly university football stadiums located in the United States (Wright, 2017). Table 14.1 lists the top 10 biggest sport stadiums in the world by capacity.

While the size and use of these facilities may vary depending on the sport, facilities staff play a vital role in the management and upkeep of these stadiums, arenas, or other special event facilities involved in the sport event. Facility managers and their staff are responsible for the overall operation and maintenance of the facility, ensure a safe facility capable of hosting the sport event, establish budgeting and forecasting for current and future facility projects, and utilize space management to maximize use and comfort of the sport facility (Fried, 2015). Depending on the facility, the staff may also be responsible for the custodial crew, security, and parking facilities. Some job titles in this area include facilities operations coordinator, facilities manager, coordinator of athletic facilities, sport facility director, athletics facility intern, and facility graduate assistant, among others.

Ticket Sales

The ticket sales team has a role in the overall revenue generation of the sport event and is the financial "backbone." If we specifically look at the National Collegiate Athletic Association (NCAA), ticket sales revenue accounted for more than 25% of overall income for Power Five schools (Hobson & Rich, 2015). Figure 14.1 illustrates the growth in revenue sources over the past decade for NCAA Power Five universities.

FIGURE 14.1 Revenue Source Comparison at NCAA Power Five Level

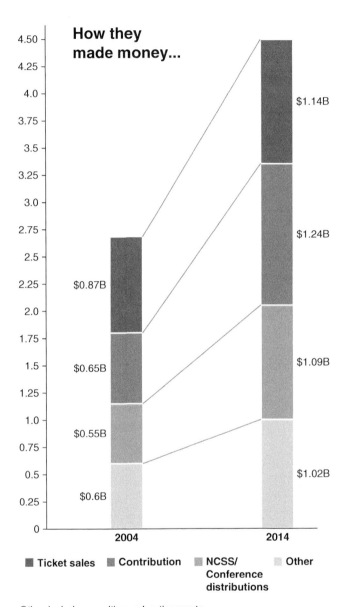

Other includes royalties, advertisements,
sponsorships, concessions and sports camps.

Source: NCAA financial reports, Washington Post analysis

The responsibilities of the ticket sales staff include managing box office operations, maintaining ticket sales records, selling tickets through outgoing or incoming call campaigns, event promotion, managing ticket accounts, and answering to ticket-related issues or questions. While ticket sales are one of the top revenue sources in sport events, according to a report by PricewaterhouseCoopers, media rights are set to surpass ticket sales "as the North American sports industry's largest revenue stream" by the end of 2018 (Broughton, 2015, para. 1). Table 14.2 illustrates

TABLE 14.2 North American Sports Revenue by Segment (in millions)

	2013	2014	2015	2016	2017	2018	2019
Gate revenue	$17,372	$17,707	$18,251	$18,637	$19,385	$19,717	$20,122
Sponsorship	$13,900	$14,689	$15,309	$16,140	$16,822	$17,635	$18,306
Media rights	$12,262	$14,595	$16,366	$18,427	$19,150	$19,949	$20,630
Merchandising	$13,144	$13,493	$13,672	$13,861	$14,042	$14,252	$14,464
Total	**$56,678**	**$60,484**	**$63,598**	**$67,065**	**$69,399**	**$71,553**	**$73,522**

Source: PricewaterhouseCoopers

the North American Sports Market by Revenue (in millions) since 2013. Recent data suggest that the National Football League (NFL) has the highest ticket price average cost at $92.98 per ticket, followed by the National Hockey League (NHL) at $62.18 per ticket, the National Basketball Association (NBA) at $55.88 per ticket, and Major League Baseball (MLB) rounding out the big four leagues at $31.00 per ticket (Statista, 2017). The New England Patriots are owners of the highest ticket prices with an average upward of $120 for a seat in Gillette Stadium (Brennan, 2017). Positions in ticket sales include ticket sales representative, box office manager, director of ticket sales, interns, and graduate assistants at the collegiate level

Concessions

While concessions do not make up the largest portion of revenue like we see with ticket sales and media rights, it plays a vital role in overall guest and fan experience at the sport event. According to Greenwell et al. (2014), "it is rare to find any large events that do not have some type of meal function. Food and beverage operations at an event are vitally important and can be a significant source of revenue" (p. 171). Significant source of revenue does not always mean raising prices. For example, in 2018 in the NFL's Atlanta Falcons brand new Mercedes-Benz Stadium, concession prices were decreased by 50% from their previous Georgia Dome home. This decrease in costs led to 16% more food and beverage spending by fans, thus leading to additional revenue for the organization (Belson, 2018).

While the Atlanta Falcons have taken this unorthodox approach, the cost at the concession stands continue to rise with the average price for a beer at $7.40 and a hot dog more than $5.00 at an NFL game (Lancaster, 2016). Event management and concession managers can use this opportunity to develop strategic plans to create a revenue inflow as seen with the Atlanta Falcons. Furthermore, at sport events, managers must take into account the number of fans who will be in attendance, the amount of purchase points across the facility, concession outsourcing, and the overall need and sophistication of the event (Greenwell et al., 2014). Concession operations are often outsourced to companies like Aramark, U.S. Foods, and Levy Restaurants, who maintain and run these operations across a wide variety of sport facilities. Food and beverage staff is typically responsible for the food safety health requirements, the preparation and selling of concession items, filling, reporting and

© Gregory Moyer/Shutterstock.com

maintaining proper inventory, monitoring money, and maintain a clean workspace. These positions typically include a director of food and beverage, concession manager, and food service workers.

Operations/Event Management

The operations and event management team is responsible for several areas throughout the sport event experience. These areas include custodial staff, safety and security, guest services, and, often times, parking. Custodial staff is primarily responsible for the overall cleanliness of the facility, including concourses, restrooms, seating areas, and trash disposal areas. While housekeeping services are often overlooked when it comes to event planning, it is vital to maintain a satisfactory guest experience (Bass, 2017). This includes before, during, and after the event has concluded. Before the event, the custodial crew ensures there are enough cleaning supplies, trash bins, and fully stocked restrooms. During the event, the custodial crew must maintain this cleanliness and respond to any cleanup calls. After the event, the staff is responsible for cleaning up after the guests in the stands, concourses, restrooms, suites, and beyond. While often unnoticed, the fans expect to enjoy the sport event in a clean environment.

While custodial care does go unnoticed, safety and security staff often have a clear presence at sport facilities. While each sport event offers a unique experience, it is important to understand the factors that play a role in the overall safety and security of fans. These factors include fan demographics, the number of spectators, rivalries, alcohol consumption, and beyond (Hall et al., 2012). While the threat of terrorism is relatively low, the security team still plays a crucial role in crowd management before, during, and after the event, as well as the security bag searches prior to entering the facility and assist with any medical calls or disturbances in the stands. A key aspect of sport event safety and security is the proper training of employees, whether part of the security staff or not. According to Stacey Hall of Security Magazine, "Training should center on incident management strategies, risk management practices, safety and security plans, policies, protective measures, and business continuity and recovery principles" and answering questions like what, why, and how? Like custodial staff, security can either be an in-house or third-party operation.

Parking is an area that involves revenue possibilities. Whether fans purchase season parking passes or an individual game pass, the prices tend to vary across venues and events. For example, the Chicago Bears offer six official parking lots on game days at Soldier Field, ranging from $35 to $121, depending on the location of the lot (Chicago Bears, n.d.). Other NFL, NBA, MLB, and NHL teams also offer a variety of official lots to choose from with price ranges. According to ParkWhiz, Boston Red Sox fans paid the highest parking costs for baseball games during the 2017 season and paid, "57 percent more than New York Yankees fans, and 215% more than Philadelphia Phillies fans during the regular season" (Ahlander, 2017, para. 3), likely due to popularity and short supply. While parking is seen as a revenue source, it also has its implications when it comes to fan experience as well as safety and security. Event managers must use properly trained staff and efficient parking lot management in order to create the most convenient and effective parking experiences for the guests. As many of these lots may be used to tailgate prior to the games, crowd management and security presence is essential, especially when alcohol is involved at tailgates.

Besides custodial, security, and parking staff, the operations and event management team assist with in-game operations from staffing needs, setup and teardown of ancillary events, home and visiting team assistance, among other day-to-day operational needs. Furthermore, the operations and event management staff is typically responsible for space management and schedule of outside events and activities taking place at the

© Branislav Nenin/Shutterstock.com

venue. Positions in operations and event management include director of operations, athletic directors for game operations and event management, game day manager, assistants, interns, game day staff, custodial, security agents, and other game day necessary staff.

Three Phases of the Event Cycle

While the different aspects of a sport event each play a vital role in the overall planning, organizing, and implementation of the sport event, it is important to understand how they play a role within the event cycle. The event cycle consists of three steps within the sport event management process, including pre-event, main event, and post-event. An event manager and related departments must understand and successfully navigate each step in the cycle in order to create positive outcomes for the sport event. This section will discuss the role of the event manager in the pre-event, main event, and post-event stages.

Pre-Event

Especially for first-time spectators or participants at your event, the pre-event provides an opportunity to maximize positive first impressions and maintain a positive guest experience from the start. As an event manager, you would likely arrive at the venue several hours prior to the start of the event in order to ensure that all event aspects are ready to go. The pre-event will likely include meetings with staff to go over any special promotions, guests, changes in the schedule, or other event management and operation-related information or issues. Although the event manager will be there hours ahead of the sport event, fans may arrive hours earlier to tailgate or wait in line, depending on the event. For example, during NFL or college football games, fans are

© Monkey Business Images/Shutterstock.com

likely to attend pre-game tailgates. For successful college basketball programs, fans may wait hours or days "camping" prior to the start of the event in order to get the best seat possible. For instance, at the University of Kansas, this occurs throughout the basketball season. According to Scola (2016), this is "an ancillary event called KU basketball camping, which is a ritual that allows students to obtain the best seats in the student section . . . by 'camp[ing] out' in Allen Fieldhouse throughout the entire basketball season" (p. ii). Similar pre-events can be found across the country, including Texas A&M's yell practice that occurs the night before a football game day (Scola, 2016).

An event manager must be prepared for pre-event action and be able to determine how to make fans and guests feel comfortable and welcomed while meeting their pre-event needs. Furthermore, early arrivers provide a potential for additional revenue sources for the facility and event (Bass, 2018). Whether it's sponsorship areas, food and beverage sales, limited giveaways or on-field pre-game experiences, the opportunity to maintain event experience while obtaining additional profit can be an essential part of the pre-event process. While fan experience is vital to the overall success of the event, pre-event entertainment should not exceed what takes place during the main event as fans should still want to purchase tickets to attend the game (Bass, 2018). Lastly, one major policy change to understand relating to the pre-event is the implementation of clear-bag policies across both professional and collegiate sporting events. According to Emily Attwood of the Athletic Business Journal,

> Clear-bag policies had been enacted at 31 of 65 universities comprising the Power 5 conferences, with four universities in the Big Ten (Ohio State, Michigan, Michigan State and Penn State) taking an even stricter stance by prohibiting bags altogether. Under the clear-bag policy, modeled after that used throughout the NFL, fans are allowed either a clear tote bag no larger than 12 by 6 by 12 inches or a one-gallon plastic freezer bag (para. 2–3).

Figure 14.2 illustrates the extent of clear-bag policies across the NCAA Power Five conferences. With policies and procedures that are often reviewed yearly, it is essential that event managers are properly training workers in understanding any changes that may affect the overall event experience. Furthermore, new policies and procedures often can result in unhappy fans and guests, so it is vital for employees to be trained in the handling of unruly or unhappy fans (Bass, 2018). As the pre-event wraps up, once the event begins inside the arena or stadium, it now becomes the main event.

Main Event

The main event begins once the fans or guests enter the stadium or arena in which the sport event is taking place. The primary concerns for the event manager during the main events include issues like comfort, safety and security, fan experience, and overall event efficiency (Bass, 2018). Although extreme cases are not likely to occur, improper event and crowd management has led to dire consequences, including death at sport events. In 1989, 93 fans lost their lives after being crushed to death at a central England soccer match, "when thousands of spectators without tickets gained last-minute entry to an enclosed viewing section already overcrowded

FIGURE 14.2 Clear-Bag Policies in Power 5 Conferences

CLEAR- BAG POLICIES IN POWER 5 CONFERENCES

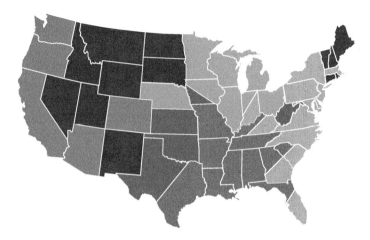

35% of the Big Ten	75% of the Pac-12	40% of the Big 12	64% of the SEC	40% of the ACC
BIG TEN	Pac-12	BIG 12	SEC	ACC
Northwestern University	Arizona State University	Texas Christian University	University of Alabama	Clemson University
University of Iowa	University of Colorado	Texas Tech University	Acburn University	Florida State University
University of Minnesota	University of Arizona	Kansas State University	University of Florida	North Carolina State University
University of Maryland	University of California Berkeley	Iowa State University	Louisiana State University	Virginia Tech
Rugers University	UCLA		University of South Carolina	University of Pittsburgh*
	University of Southern California	ALTERNATIVE BAG POLICIES	University of Tennessee	University of Miami*
ALTERNATIVE BAG POLICIES	Stanford University		University of Mississippi	*Games played in NFL venues, utilize NFL security policies
	University of Washington	University of Kansas	Mississippi State University	
Purdue University		Oklahoma State University	Texas A&M	ALTERNATIVE BAG POLICIES
University of Nebraska	ALTERNATIVE BAG POLICIES	Baylor University		
University of illinois		West Virginia University	ALTERNATIVE BAG POLICIES	Wake Forest University
University of Wisconsin	Washington State University	University of Texas at Austin*		Syracuse University
Indiana University	University of Oregon	University of Oklahoma*	Vanderbilt University	University of Virginia
Ohio State University*	Origon State University		University of Arkansas	University of Notre Dame
Penn State University*	University of Ultah		University of Missouri	Georgia Institute of Tech
University of Michigan*			University of Georgia	University of Louisville
Michigan State University*			University of Kertucky	University of North Carolina
				Duke University
				Boaton College

* No bags at all permitted

Source: Athletic Business. Map © MisterEmil/Shutterstock.com

with paying customers" (Fisher, 1989). Event managers must be aware of crowd movement and crowd control throughout the main event and beyond to prevent such tragedy. Event managers will be keeping a keen eye on anything that can affect the overall impact on the fan experience, including transportation, food and beverage, restrooms, cleanliness, entertainment, and disturbances, among others. Once the event has concluded, the post-event process begins.

Post-Event

After the conclusion of the main event comes the post-event. Within the post-event comes the issue of crowd management and parking control associated with fans leaving the stadium/arena and parking lots (Bass, 2018). It is vital to have proper communication among the parking and facility operations team during the post-event. Although the event has concluded, the exiting of the facility is still part of the overall fan experience; therefore, any issues faced in the parking lot, including wait times to exit, affect the overall experience and attitudes of attending the sport event next time (Bass, 2018). If this remains an issue, fans may start to leave the sport event early in anticipation of parking lot hassles, which would affect not only the experience inside the arena, but outside of it as well.

Furthermore, the post-event allows for the event manager to reflect on and evaluate the planning, organizing, and execution of the event from start to end. This allows the event manager to prepare for future events that might require similar planning, while adjusting to issues that occurred or utilize aspects that went well. Even as the event wraps up, many event managers begin the preparation process for events that directly follow the event that has just concluded (Bass, 2018). As facilities are adding more and more events to their calendar each year to maximize their revenues, the post-event process illustrates the vital role of event managers in space management and flexibility of their specific facilities (Bass, 2018).

Challenges and Trends in Facilities and Event Management

As technology has continued to develop in society, it has affected the sport industry as well. In fact, new technology has played a significant role in sport events across the United States. For instance, many sport events now use metal detectors to ward off gun users. In addition, many establishments have taken to electronic ticket scanners at the entry gate for events. These are just some of the trends currently within the sport event management field. This section will discuss additional trends, including sustainability, increased security, digital services, and fan experiences, and how they play a role in the current realm of sport events.

Sustainability

In recent years, the idea of creating sustainable stadiums and fan experiences had grown more and more into a priority rather than a trend (Trendafilova, Kellison, & Spearman, 2014). For example, the Chicago White Sox became the first MLB team to ban the use of plastic straws with beverage purchases and, instead, will provide biodegradable straws upon request from the fan (Kane, 2018). This is part of an initiative with Chicago's Shedd Aquarium titled "Shedd the Straw" in an effort to "highlight the dangers plastic straws pose to aquatic life" (Kane, 2018, para. 2). The White Sox anticipate keeping 215,000 out of the trash over the 2018 MLB season. Similarly, Folsom Field at the University of Colorado has begun zero-waste efforts by offering recyclable, compostable, and refillable food and beverage packaging inside their stadium, while offering a special tailgating zone with compostable tailgate supplies (Green Sports Alliance, 2016). While these initiatives have been added to existing venues, new facilities have also been built to be green and sustainable.

For example, the Sacramento Kings' Golden 1 Center became the "first indoor sports venue to earn an LEED Platinum designation . . . the highest level of global recognition for environmentally conscious buildings and organizations" (Golden1

© Adam Vilimek/Shutterstock.com

Center, 2016, para. 1). With 17,500 seats, the venue is completely powered by solar energy and primarily offers food and beverage options that are sourced within 150 miles of the arena (Golden1 Center, 2016). While efforts like these require significant financial resources and can prevent financial challenges, these amazing new sustainability advances will continue to set an example and provide great opportunity for future facilities. Furthermore, it will allow for organizations to be more visible and recognize their sustainability efforts as a priority.

Increased Security

As security issues across the country are becoming all too common, event planners must begin to establish safety and security as their number one priority in the fan experience. As security threats are becoming more and more sophisticated, so are the security solutions in sport venues across the world. Times have changed across all major sporting venues across the world as bag checks and metal detectors have become the standard; however, some sport organizations have taken it a step further as, "companies have begun offering biometric and other tools to create the equivalent of express security lanes like those in airports" (Levin & Levin, 2017, para. 3). Teams like the NBA's Miami Heat use a special entrance line for fans opting in to finger print scanners for entrance (Levin & Levin, 2017). Technology like these that are new to the sport industry combined with global security collaboration and social media monitoring can contribute to the overall safety and security of fans (Global Sports Jobs, 2017). While this is a trend, it also becomes a challenge to balance safety and security with the overall enjoyment and fan experience at the sport event.

Digital Services

With increase smartphone technology and utilization of applications, digital tickets and services are becoming more and more common with some organizations going as far as banning paper tickets. In an effort to combat ticket fraud cases, in 2016, the New York Yankees banned the use of PDF print-at-home tickets in favor of hard paper tickets and digital ticketing (New York Yankees Mobile Ticketing, n.d.). Organizations are likely to continue to shift away from paper tickets in favor of more digital ticketing and services. Other digital services include concession ordering apps like FanFood that allow you to order concessions from your seat to avoid long lines or have your items delivered to your seat for an upcharge (Levine, 2017). As smartphone usage continues to rise, industries must begin to adapt to digital services as part of the overall fan experience.

Spectator Experiences and Engagement

As the at-home viewing experience becomes more and more appealing to the fan experience, "it is getting harder for sports and entertainment properties to complete for fans' leisure time and entertainment spend" (Cisco Vision for Sports and Entertainment, 2018, para. 1). As at-home technology improves, it is important for sport facilities and venues to keep up with these technological improvements. Companies like Cisco System, Inc. are creating cost-effective ultra-high-definition viewing experiences within stadiums, allowing for a more appealing in-game experience with opportunities to maximize fan engagement through customized experiences, camera views, marketing opportunities, and promotions (Cisco Vision for Sports and Entertainment, 2018). As the at-home technology makes it more and more difficult to compete with, technologies like Cisco Vision must continue to promote and discover in-game opportunities that still make fans want to purchase a ticket and enjoy the in-game atmosphere.

© Oleksii Sidorov/Shutterstock.com

Different Fan Base

Leagues, like the NFL, are gearing more and more of their programming toward women. While women still are the minority at 45% of the league's fan base, viewership grew a sizable 26% between the years 2009 and 2013, contributing to the shrinking of the male–female viewership gap (Hampton, 2017). At the 2017 Super Bowl in Houston, the NFL organized a women's summit as part of the festivities as a place for "young women to discuss how to achieve goals, prepare for challenges, and utilize tools critical for personal and professional development" (Shortsleeve, 2017, para. 9). This trend in attracting greater female viewership has even translated in organizational behavior with an increase in female coaches, officials, and NFL staff (Hampton, 2017). While the NFL has led the way with this initiative, it will be important to follow the progress among other sport leagues moving forward.

Summary

As the sport industry continues to grow in value, in becomes important to establish what opportunities are available in the industry and understand the importance of sport events and event management. The chapter was able to explore the types of sport events, aspects of sport events, careers in the field, the three phases of the event cycle, and current issues, challenges, and trends in event management. In order to further your understanding of sport event management, industry spotlights, case studies, and activities have been provided.

References

Ahlander, R. (2017). Which sports fans pay the most for parking? *ParkWhiz*. Retrieved from http://blog.parkwhiz.com/which-sports-fans-pay-the-most-for-parking

Bass, J. R. (2017). Facility/Event Management [PowerPoint slides].

Belson, K. (2018, January 25). In Atlanta, concession prices got down and revenue goes up. *The New York Times*. Retrieved from https://www.nytimes.com/2018/01/25/sports/football/nflconcessions.html

Brennan, A. (2017). The American big four need to stop pushing up ticket prices like English football has. *Forbes*. Retrieved from https://www.forbes.com/sites/andrewbrennan/2017/01/31/the-american-big-four-need-to-stop-pushing-up-ticket-prices-like-english-football-has/#30d21be54b1e

Broughton, D. (2015, October 19). Media rights to trump ticket sales by 2018. *Sports Business Daily*. Retrieved from https://www.sportsbusinessdaily.com/Journal/Issues/2015/10/19/Research-and-Ratings/PwC.aspx.

Cavin, C. (2004, May 27). Take a seat: Study puts Indy's capacity at 257,325. *USA Today*. Retrieved from http://usatoday30.usatoday.com/sports/motor/irl/indy500/2004-05-27-attendance-count_x.htm

Chelladurai, P. (2014). *Managing Organizations for Sport and Physical Activity* (4th ed.). Abingdon, United Kingdom: Routledge.

Chicago Bears. (n.d.) Parking and Transportation Guide. *Chicago Bears*. Retrieved from http://www.chicagobears.com/tickets-and-stadium/parking-transportation.html

Cisco Vision for Sports and Entertainment. (2018). *Cisco*. Retrieved from https://www.cisco.com/c/en/us/solutions/industries/sports-entertainment/ciscovisionsports.html

ESPN Wide World of Sports. (2018a). Events. Retrieved from https://www.espnwwos.com/events

ESPN Wide World of Sports. (2018b). Sports. Retrieved from https://www.espnwwos.com/sports

Fisher, D. (1989, April 16). 93 killed in soccer game crush: Victims trampled at English stadium; 200 reported hurt. *Los Angeles Times*. Retrieved from http://articles.latimes.com/1989-04-16/news/mn-2494_1_soccer-game-crush-european-football-assns-ban-on-english-teams

Fried, G. (2015). *Managing Sport Facilities* (3rd ed.). Champaign, IL: Human Kinetics.

Global Sports Jobs. (2017). Five trends for 2017 in sports events and operations. *GlobalSportsJobs*. Retrieved from https://www.globalsportsjobs.com/article/five-trends-in-sports-events-and-operations-for-2017-

Golden1 Center. (2016). Sacramento Kings new arena is first indoor sports venue to earn LEED Platinum designation. *Golden1 Center*. Retrieved from https://www.golden1center.com/news/detail/first-indoor-sports-venue-earn-leed-platinum-designation/?ref=kings

GOUNESCO. (2016). Wrestling—the oldest combat sport in the world. *United Nations Educational, Scientific and Cultural Organization*. Retrieved from https://www.gounesco.com/wrestling-oldest-combat-sport

Green Sports Alliance. (2016). Eco-products, University of Colorado turn stadium green on the inside and the outside. *Green Sports Alliance*. Retrieved from http://greensportsalliance.org/eco-products-university-of-colorado-turn-stadium-green-on-the-inside-and-the-outside

Greenwell, T. C., Danzey-Bussell, L. A., & Shonk, D. J. (2014). *Managing Sport Events*. Champaign, IL: Human Kinetics.

Gregory, S. (2017). How kids' sports became a $15 billion industry. *Time*. Retrieved from http://time.com/4913687/how-kids-sports-became-15-billion-industry

Hampton, L. (2017). Women comprise nearly half of NFL audience, but more wanted. *Reuters*. Retrieved from https://www.reuters.com/article/us-nfl-superbowl-women/women-comprise-nearly-half-of-nfl-audience-but-more-wanted-idUSKBN15J0UY

Heitner, D. (2015). Sports industry to reach $73.5 billion by 2019. *Forbes*. Retrieved from https://www.forbes.com/sites/darrenheitner/2015/10/19/sports-industry-to-reach-73-5-billion-by-2019/#10629041b4b9

Hiller, H. (2000). Mega-events, urban boosterism and growth strategies: An analysis of the objectives and legitimations of the Cape Town 2004 Olympic bid. *International Journal of Urban and Regional Research, 24*(2), 439–458.

Hobson, W., & Rich, S. (2015, November 23). Playing in the red. *The Washington Post*. Retrieved from http://www.washingtonpost.com/sf/sports/wp/2015/11/23/running-up-the-bills/?noredirect=on&utm_term=.dae58fb76382

International Olympic Committee. (2018). National Olympic Committees. *International Olympic Committee*. Retrieved from https://www.olympic.org/national-olympic-committees

Kane, C. (2018, April 20). White Sox are 1st MLB team to ditch single-use plastic straws. *Chicago Tribune*. Retrieved from http://www.chicagotribune.com/sports/baseball/whitesox/ct-spt-white-sox-plastic-straws-20180420-story.html

Kaplanidou, K., & Vogt, C. (2010). The meaning and measurement of a sport event experience among active sport tourists. *Journal of Sport Management, 24*(5), 544–566.

Lancaster, E. (2016, September 16). Check out the outrageous beer and hot dog prices at each NFL stadium. *Food Beast*. Retrieved from: https://www.foodbeast.com/news/check-out-the-outrageous-beer-and-hot-dog-prices-at-each-nfl-stadium

Levin, A. & Levin, J. (2017, January 1). Sport stadiums and arenas increase high-tech security tools. *Chicago Tribune*. Retrieved from http://www.chicagotribune.com/sports/breaking/ct-stadium-security-spt-20170101-story.html

Levine, M. (2017, November 14). This Chicago startup lets you order snacks to your seat. Can it compete with entertainment giants? *Chicago Tribune*. Retrieved from http://www.chicagotribune.com/bluesky/originals/ct-bsi-fanfood-product-launch-20171114-story.html

McBride, J. (2018). The economics of hosting the Olympic Games. *Council on Foreign Relations*. Retrieved from https://www.cfr.org/backgrounder/economics-hosting-olympic-games

Russo, F. E., Escklisen, L. A., & Stewart, R. J. (2009). *Public assembly facility management: Principles and practices* (2nd ed.). Coppell, TX: International Association of Assembly Managers.

Scola, Z. (2016). A qualitative examination of the motivations behind participating in KU basketball camping. (Master's thesis). Retrieved from University of Kansas, ProQuest Dissertations Publishing (10130146).

Shortsleeve, C. (2017). What the NFL is doing to reach women. *Teen Vogue*. Retrieved from https://www.teenvogue.com/story/nfl-reach-women

Statista. (2017). Average ticket prices in the major sports leagues in North America in 2015/16 (in U.S. dollars). *Statista*. Retrieved from https://www.statista.com/statistics/261588/average-ticket-price-major-us-sports-leagues

Statista. (2018). National Football League average per game attendance from 2008 to 2017. *Statista*. Retrieved from https://www.statista.com/statistics/249372/average-regular-season-attendance-in-the-nfl

Trendafilova, S., Kellison, T. B., & Spearman, L. (2014). Environmental sustainability in sport facilities in East Tennessee. *Journal of Facility Planning, Design, and Management, 2*(1), 2331–2351.

Wright, D. (2017, January 17). The 20 biggest sport stadiums in the world ranked by current capacity. *The Daily Telegraph*. Retrieved from https://www.dailytelegraph.com.au/sport/more-sports/the-20-biggest-sport-stadiums-in-the-world-ranked-by-current-capacity/news-story/80518908e2555e277565b87fd019e462

Field Interview

Jacquelyn Luedtke

Special Events Manager at U.S. Ski & Snowboard Association

Jacquelyn Luedtke studied Event Management at Iowa State University and proceeded to work in a fast, exciting sport management industry by being a part of the "Team behind the Team" for the United States Olympic Committee and U.S. Ski & Snowboard. In her short four and half years with Olympic & Paralympic movement, she has experience of two Olympic Games, one Para Pan American Game, and has coordinated over 350 programs and events all over the world that have had a direct impact on Olympic & Paralympic athletes. Outside of the Olympic movement, Jacquelyn's interests include planning weddings, rodeos, and anything else that needs planning.

1. As an event planner within the sport industry, what have you noticed as emerging trends?

There are several trends within the industry primarily focusing on the "greening" of events and the overall fan experience. Such trends include sustainable events, virtual and social fan engagement both at the events or at home, unique venues that create memorable statements, and sensory engagement of our guests and fans. While these are trends within the sport industry, I still believe the biggest and most important trend is focusing on creative and innovative ways to improve event safety and security for fans, athletes, and staff.

2. How did you become interested in working in event management?

I became interested in event management by getting involved with the Recreation Department at my university. They help foster a love for people, events, and planning that I didn't know could turn into a career. It is never too early to get involved in event management even as an undergraduate at a university recreation department.

3. What are some essential skills to be successful as an event planner?

While there are plenty of skills that are useful in the overall successful planning of a sport event, I think event planners must exhibit characteristics like organization, creativity, and selflessness.

Furthermore, it is especially important to be a team player and exhibit a strong attention to detail.

4. How is the sport industry unique versus non-sport events when it comes to event management?

The sport industry is something amazing. No matter what language athletes speak, no matter where they come from, or who they are, they understand the language of sport and once they step on that field of play, that's all that matters. It unifies and unites people whose paths otherwise may not have crossed. There is a major sense of pride that goes along with sporting events when you see the good that it can do.

5. Throughout your time working in sport events, how has the industry changed?

It is constantly evolving. Venues have become high tech, television time has become more valuable, so you have to add in elements outside of just the sporting event to gain the attention you want. It also is evolving with more policies and regulations around Safe Sport and Anti-Doping, especially with Olympic sports like ski and snowboard.

6. What is one piece of advice you would give to current undergraduate students in sport management who are interested in working in facility and event management?

Go after that amazing sports internship, apply for those jobs that maybe out of reach, because once you land those, your life will forever be changed by the positive impact the sports world can bring to you and your experiences.

7. What aspects does the planning process entail for your events? How long does it take to plan?

It varies depending on the scope of the event. For the Olympics, it takes 4 years to plan and execute. That is everything from four to five site visits, to finding lodging, ticketing, transportation, uniforming, restaurants, to naming the team. The planning process includes a lot of meetings, starting with vision, goals, that leads to trying restaurants, driving routes, and everything and anything in between. This is a small task and it takes a lot of working groups and people to make it happen.

8. What do you enjoy most about working in sport event management?

The ability to be able to be a part of something bigger than myself. Events are meant to create lifelong memories for people and knowing that I have a small part of being the team behind the team to create that memory is what brings me so much joy in event management.

9. What is the most challenging aspect of being a sport event manager?

Recreating a different experience for events time after time. There will always be a championship between two schools or two pro teams but how do you make that event so desirable for people to come back year after year? What do you do to push those events to better year after year?

Field Interview

Emily Fiorini

Assistant Festival Manager for Spartan Race

Emily Fiorini has been working at Spartan Race since 2015. She began her career as a weekend event staff person and is now the Assistant Festival Manager for the Central Team. Emily graduated with a Master's degree in Sport Venue and Event Management from Syracuse University and currently resides in Orlando, FL.

1. What are your roles and responsibilities as a festival coordinator for Spartan Race?

My role focuses on the setup, management, and teardown of the festival from beginning to end. I travel to a city the week before the race (on Thursday) with a handful of people including my festival manager. Together we unload the trailers, move everything out into Festival, and with the help of a few other staff members we set up Registration, Bag Check, Finish Line, etc., while the build crew sets up the obstacles. On race day we have event day staff who work in these zones and my job is to oversee and support them. I make sure they have volunteers, I am there to answer questions, and I help them put out fires as things happen during the day. At the end we tear it all down, load it into the trailers, and head to the next venue.

2. How do you think your role differs from working with a professional sport team or at a large, spectator event?

A major difference is that the people who set up and manage the event are the same people. We do have race planners who work in the office and make sure we have a venue, a plan for where things go, and the supplies and equipment we need, but once we get there it is our event. When I worked for runDisney, we had event management staff who worked through the event, but all of the setup was done by Walt Disney World Operations. I think that is true of most venues in professional sports. They have a facility operations team and an event team and at Spartan those are all the same people. So, the blue shirts you see along the course as you run, built the obstacles as well.

Another big difference is that we travel. With professional sports teams and large spectator events, the facilities people are always working in the same venue. The event they are producing might be different (concert, sporting event, etc.) but they use the same venue, so they have their equipment and a central storage place. We are a mobile event. Everything we take out to set up also needs to be put back and accounted for. A lot of people think we

don't want to innovate to make new obstacles at each race, or have new shirts, but really, we don't have any more room on our trailers and to ship things from race to race when you have 52 races a year can get pretty pricey.

3. What unique challenges do you face while planning, organizing, and executing endurance sporting events?

The first problem we have no matter where you go is weather. Rain creates the most problems. A lot of our audio equipment and shirts can't get wet. The access roads to get around become slippery. Machines have to be ready on race day to pull cars out of parking lots. The ground is slippery and creates more injuries while people are running, and honestly it is just not fun to work in all day. Wind is another concern. A lot of things in festival (tents, trash cans, fencing) all tend to blow away and create more work. The temperature is a major factor as well. If it is too hot, medical help needs to be ready to cool people down and we need to have extra water sources. It also means the lines at showers will probably be very long. If it is too cold, people get hypothermia and we need to be prepared with Mylar blankets and things that will warm them up.

Travel can be a challenge as well. We tend to do pretty well working with our travel coordinators, but things do happen. In 2017, we had a race in Vermont and some of the people on our team lived in Florida. Because of Hurricane Irma, the airports shut down and they could not get out for a week. This left the team on-site short staffed and made for some long hours to make up the difference.

Another unique challenge that we face is the fact that we rely so heavily on volunteers. When most of your workforce depends on whether or not people feel like coming out to help that day can be stressful. Especially on race day, when there are lines in festival and long waits to help people, it usually means we do not have enough volunteers. We all want our racers to be happy and satisfied but volunteers are number one.

4. How did you become interested in a career in endurance sports?

I have always liked the endurance event side of sports because your customers are also your athletes. If I worked in sales, it is much easier for me to sell someone on the idea of coming out to an event and trying something that is going to make them feel good about themselves and maybe give them a sense of accomplishment. With professional sports teams, you are selling someone on the idea of coming to an event to watch complete strangers play game. Now I love being one of those people who watches sporting events, but I wouldn't be able to convince someone else that they should spend their money on it.

We do have elite racers at Spartan and plenty of people like to watch them come across the finish line, but I like the people in the middle or the end of the day. The guy who has spent the past year losing 30 pounds, so he can come out and show people he can finish a race. The woman who just had surgery and came out because she wants to run with her son. Those are the stories that make me come back to this job.

5. What advice can you give to undergraduate sport management students who may be interested in a career in endurance sports?

To work in endurance events you need to be ok with working long hours and sleeping for very few. We have about a week to set up an event and about 2 days to tear it down. In addition to that, we have race days which are a minimum of 15 hours. This was the most shocking thing to me when I started. Unless you are already doing it, there is no way to prepare. You do get used to it but in the meantime just get your tasks done and keep a positive attitude.

You also need to be flexible. The race planner comes out about 3 months before and does a site visit, but things may change, and you have to be able to adjust accordingly. Not to mention you are working on a team. These people will need help at times and so you need to be willing to do things that aren't within your job description. You will be happy you did when the time comes that you need help.

The other thing about this job is you are not at home very often during the peak of the season (May–October). It is normal to get homesick once in a while but if you cannot handle being away from your loved ones for very long, this is not the job for you. We work on teams which means we travel with the same people to each event, so they do become your second family if you let them. You get to travel and meet a lot of amazing people, but you miss a lot of things at home and that can be hard.

6. What other areas or departments of Spartan Race do you work with during the event?

So, my department is Festival. The department I work the closest with is Build which just means the people who build the obstacles while I build festival. We call ourselves the field staff and are both under the overall umbrella of production, so it feels like we are the same department most of the time. We also work very closely with Sponsorship, Merchandise, Procurement, Registration, and lately Social Media. Many of these people work in the office in Boston or from home and are not always on-site with us. So, they communicate to us any sponsorship activations, deliveries, or branding we need to put out to satisfy those needs.

7. How does your clientele affect the overall participant experience? What makes Spartan Race unique in that sense?

The cool thing about Spartan is that we have three different distances. We get a lot of first-time racers and bigger groups at our shorter races. And at the longer races you will see a lot of familiar faces and you will see a lot more people who are anxious because this is something they never thought they would try (especially 13 miles on the side of a mountain). It is cool to see the range of beginners to veterans in that aspect. The obstacle course racing community in general is also such an interesting clientele. These are not the people who train for months and months to finish a marathon. They are people who go around and do all of these races and are so committed that they have versions of these obstacles in their own yards to practice. I don't think this is unique to Spartan, but to obstacle course races in general.

8. What are some ways you attempt to create a positive participant experience throughout the event?

We try very hard to have little to no lines at the event. Registration works to make sure their systems are in place that people have a flawless time registering online to then picking up their bibs on-site. We work a lot with racer flow. We want bag check to be close to the start line, so you don't miss your wave, but also close to the rinse station and the changing tents for after you finish. We try to do these things without anyone realizing we did them on purpose. We also try to have our branding look clean and lines straight so that everything looks put together and presentable. We also make sure our guest-facing staff are friendly and knowledgeable, so people feel comfortable asking questions.

9. Are there any trends that are occurring within the endurance sport event industry?

I have not recently looked at what other companies have been doing but this year Spartan is really focusing on our kids race. We made our Kids Race Leads full time, so they are with us from start to finish. We have awards now that is on the same podiums as the adult awards ceremony, and we are working on making it its own brand that mimics the adult brand. It is cool how people are reacting to it and kind of funny how serious these kids can get.

We are also really pushing social media. We want people to be able to take photos on-site and immediately post them. Most times with racing companies we have event photographers and a couple days after the event you check your bib number and see all the photos they took. We still do that, but we are also looking at more immediate ways to get photos of racers online.

Name: _____   Section: _____   Date _____

Event Management Trends Case Study

Cisco Vision for Sports and Entertainment

Cisco Systems, Inc. is a technology company located in San Jose, California. Specializing in the design, manufacturing, and selling of information technology and communications, Cisco has created a Cisco Vision for Sports and Entertainment. According to Cisco, "This innovative solution helps you distribute video and digital content. Use Cisco Vision to centrally manage customized video, team and sponsor promotions, and relevant event information, and target delivery to monitors throughout your venue. Drive fan engagement and create revenue-growth opportunities for you and your business partners (Cisco Vision for Sports and Entertainment, 2018)." As technology enhancements and fan viewing experience continue to grow as trends in the industry, watch the video to see how Cisco is "captivating crowds with digital experiences." Watch the video (https://www.cisco.com/c/en/us/solutions/industries/sports-entertainment.html) and answer the following questions.

1. How is Cisco using Cisco Vision for Sport and Entertainment to visually captivate fans at the stadium or arena? As an event manager, how does this affect the overall event management experience for fans?

2. What are the possible benefits to organizations that utilize this technology?

3. Explore the Cisco Vision for Sport and Entertainment website (https://www.cisco.com/c/en/us/solutions/industries/sports-entertainment/ciscovisionsports.html). Which sport organizations have utilized this technology and what outcomes were seen?

4. If you were a sport manager for a professional sports team in charge of deciding whether or not to use this technology, would you purchase this? Why or why not? What factors would play a role in your decision-making process? Would working for a minor league or semiprofessional team change your purchase decision? Why or why not?

Name: _____   Section: _____   Date _____

Event Management Trends Case Study

Hockey Club Davos Rink Bingo

Hockey Club Davos is a professional ice hockey team located in Davos, Switzerland. HC Davos is a perennial championship contender in the National League and has won 31 Swiss championships. This club specifically is highly dependent on merchandise and food and beverage sales for revenue. In 2016, HC Davos implemented a Rink Bingo promotion in attempt to increase overall revenues. Watch the video titled HCD Rink Bingo (https://www.youtube.com/watch?v=ZNSHKSnQawo) and answer the following questions?

1. What benefits did HC Davos see from the implementation of Rink Bingo at their facility?

2. How does this promotion affect the overall fan experience at the arena?

3. Overall, how did HC Davos capitalize on this idea? Was it successful and should it continue to be implemented?

4. Should this idea be implemented at the National Hockey League level? Why or why not?

5. If you were a sport manager for a professional sports team in charge of deciding whether or not to implement such a promotion, what factors would play a role in your decision-making process?

Name: _____   Section: _____   Date _____

Event Management Activity

Sport Facilities

Select two sport facilities (ballpark, stadium, or arena) that you are interested in learning more about. The purpose of this activity is to research specific aspects of these facilities that best illustrate key information and characteristics. Once the sport facilities are chosen, research the following key information regarding each facility. Organize the information into the chart in order to easily compare and contrast each facility that you chose. Once you complete the chart, answer the questions that follow.

Key Information	Name of Facility #1:	Name of Facility #2:
City in which facility is located		
Year built plus any renovation years		
Current tenants		
Owner/Operator of the facility		
Seating capacity		
Funding: Public or private?		
Parking availability		
Food and beverage options		
Ticket options and costs (general admission, suites, club, etc.)		

1. What were the key similarities between the two facilities that you chose? What were the key differences that you discovered?

2. What was the most interesting information you researched on each of the facilities?

3. Throughout your research, what information surprised you the most?

4. Were there any special/unique features to these facilities?

5. What information was the most difficult to find?

Name: _____ Section: _____ Date _____

Event Management Activity

Three Phases of the Event Cycle—Auburn v. Alabama Iron Bowl

You are an event manager working at the annual Southeastern Conference batter between the Auburn Tigers and Alabama Crimson Tide in Tuscaloosa, Alabama. This in-state rivalry draws large crowds, tailgating starting hours before kickoff, and added security before, during, and after the game. Based on the responsibilities in each of the three phases of the event cycle—Pre-Event, Main Event, and Post-Event—make a short checklist illustrating what your primary tasks are as an event manager for this event.

Pre-Event

- _____
- _____
- _____
- _____
- _____
- _____

Main Event

- _____
- _____
- _____
- _____
- _____
- _____

Post-Event

- _____
- _____
- _____
- _____
- _____
- _____

Name: _____   Section: _____   Date _____

HSES 289
Introduction to Sport Management
In-Class Quiz and Activity Sheet

Name (or names if done in a group)

Answer #1

Answer #2

Answer #3

Chapter 15

Sport in the Community and Recreation Context

Peyton Stensland • *University of Kansas*

"Do you know what my favorite part of the game is? The opportunity to play."

—Mike Singletary, American football coach and former professional player

Contributed by Peyton Stensland. © Kendall Hunt Publishing Company.

Introduction

Although community sport has been defined in various ways, the current textbook will use this phrase as an umbrella term for the segment of sport that largely involves "direct participation" by consumers. Unlike fans, who engage in indirect consumption by watching the event, the "customer" directly consumes the event through participation. In the following sections, readers will examine community sport through participation trends, motivations, and barriers. They will also evaluate the similarities and differences that have emerged between nonprofit and for-profit recreation programs/facilities.

Participation

Every year, the Physical Activity Council (PAC) conducts a study that tracks the participation of individuals in various sports and fitness activities. This study provides a broad overview of activity levels including recent trends, which are used by sport organizations and recreation programs throughout the country. In a general sense, the 2017 report showed that 72% of the U.S. population (aged 6+) was active. Although this number has remained steady compared to past years, the level of activity and frequency of activity has decreased. By examining the recent trends, sport and recreation leaders could understand the motivations and constraints individuals experience in regard to sport and activity participation.

Trends

Most notably, the highest participation numbers (63.8% of U.S. population over the age of 6) have been focused around fitness sports. These sports include activities such as running, jogging, high intensity training, rowing machines, swimming, step machine, kickboxing, cycling, etc. The second highest category by participation rate was outdoor activities, which includes outdoor bicycling, hiking, kayaking, rafting, trail running, and rock climbing. For other participation rate categories and percentages, see Figure 15.1, which includes data from the 2017 PAC report.

Furthermore, the 2017 PAC report discovered differences between generations in regard to general participation in recreational activities and activity categories.

FIGURE 15.1 Participation Trends by Category

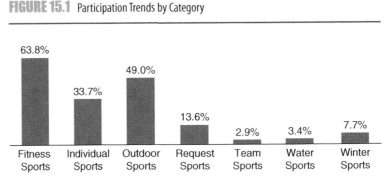

Source: 2017 PAC Report; Graph created by Peyton Stensland

FIGURE 15.2 Participation Trends Among Different Age Groups

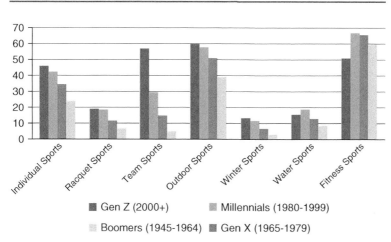

Gen Z (2000+) Millennials (1980-1999)

Boomers (1945-1964) Gen X (1965-1979)

Source: 2017 PAC Report; Graph created by Peyton Stensland

Generation Z (year 2000+) tended to be more active overall. They also were more likely to participate in team sports and outdoor sports. Although the Millennials (1980–1999) had very similar numbers as Generation Z, some key differences emerged in terms of team sports and fitness sports. Finally, Boomers (1945–1964) were more interested in fitness sports that had low impact levels. For the complete data set, see Figure 15.2, which includes data from the PAC report.

Assignment 1 - 'Trends: So What?'

- Using the charts above (and data from the PAC report), describe how these trends could impact programs within a Parks and Recreation department.
- As a Parks and Recreation Director, how would you utilize these trends to your advantages?

Motivations

Although most individuals' level of physical activity starts to decrease after high school, community recreation sport programs exist to counteract this trend. By understanding the reasons individuals participate in recreational sport, individual leagues and programs can be tailored toward personal motivating factors to increase overall participation. In general, three motivating factors have been listed as reasons individuals participate in adult recreational leagues: social, physical, and psychological. These factors are not surprising considering physical activity in general has been linked to increased benefits in all three categories. Other commonly cited motivational factors that influence community recreational participation are aesthetics and skill acquisition. Aesthetic motivation occurs when individuals are attracted to the beauty and grace of the individual sport (Gantz & Wenner, 1995). Skill acquisition involves the mastery of sport skills and sport related-knowledge (Schrag, 1992).

In addition to specific motivating factors that impact participation, two types of motivation emerge: extrinsic and intrinsic. Extrinsic motivation is influenced by outside factors and the individual is typically engaged in behaviors as a means to an end (Deci, 1975). Relating to recreational sport/activities, individuals with extrinsic motivation are likely to participate to improve their physical appearance, lose weight, gain social recognition, or play for league championships. The other type of motivation, intrinsic motivation, is based on internal factors where an individual participates in an activity for the pleasure and satisfaction derived from simply performing the task (Deci, 1975). People who are intrinsically motivated will perform the behavior voluntarily regardless of any external rewards given. In terms of recreational sport/activities, individuals with intrinsic motivation will join a league/team for the simple satisfaction of participating. They may also be motivated to participate in order to learn something new or achieve a particular goal. (See Boxes 15.1 and 15.2 for strategies to increase participants' perceptions of success based on their motivation type and questions for consideration.)

Barriers to Participate

Although participation in recreation activities has been generally increasing throughout the years, particular groups of individuals are becoming inactive. These groups of people experience similar barriers that influence their participation and involvement in community recreation programs. The most common constraint cited was income level, which supports the findings that inactivity has increased for individuals who have household incomes under $50K (PAC, 2018, p. 12). Additionally, income level affects the facilities, events, and clubs a person may try to join. Because for-profit recreation programs require membership fees, some individuals are not allowed to participate strictly because of their lack of finances.

Other barriers that affect participation activity levels strictly deal with social aspects. For instance, many individuals do not want to participate alone, but they do not have someone to take part with. This feeling of isolation is a commonly cited reason for why individuals choose not to participate or sign up for recreation programs. Another cited constraint to participation is time. Many individuals have other commitments, such as family, school, and work, which take priority over participation in a sport or recreation activity. A final barrier to participation is the

BOX 15.1 DIFFERENCES IN STRATEGIES BASED ON PARTICIPANTS' MOTIVATION

Strategies to Increase Participants' Perceptions of Success (Russell & Jamieson, 2008)	
Extrinsic Motivation	**Intrinsic Motivation**
• Emphasize the status of the activity	• Match skill levels of the participants
• Provide membership cards, mugs, uniforms, T-Shirts, bumper stickers, etc.	• Use verbal and nonverbal praise
• Employ well-planned & controlled competition	• Involve participants in decision making
• Capitalize on people's desire to be a part of a group	• Share the power with participants
• Offer prizes and rewards associated with the activity	• Be sure participants have the knowledge and skills needed to participate in the program

BOX 15.2 IDEAS TO CONSIDER IN CHAPTER 15

Questions for Consideration

- As a Parks and Recreation director, how do you account for the various motivations participants have for joining a recreation program?
- When strictly considering motivations to participate, how would your marketing strategies differ between promoting a senior pickleball league and an adult slowpitch softball league?
- How would you address any of the barriers individuals may experience when deciding to participate in a local community recreation sport league?

local environment in terms of the space available for recreational activities, the distance to recreation facilities, and the quality of equipment (Gomes et al., 2016). While all of these factors may surface as individual barriers to participation, they are not mutually exclusive and in many cases impact each other.

Nonprofit Community Recreation

Sports and recreation programs promote a partnership with individuals and their local communities. Many parks and recreation departments across the globe create these programs for the purpose of building a stronger, healthier, happier, and safer local community. Because these community recreation programs and facilities operate as nonprofits, they are typically financed through general obligation bonds, park dedication fees, grants, real estate transfer fees, user fees, nonprofit partnerships, philanthropy, etc. Additionally, due to the positive associations between community members and recreation programs, municipalities have begun to actively market their community recreation offerings to attract new residents. These offerings have emerged in the form of recreation facilities/events and natural spaces (including walking/biking trails and event spaces).

Recreation Facilities and Hosting of Events

Public sport and recreation facilities have emerged through the development of programs such as the Boys and Girls Club and YMCA. These national organizations have been vital in the development of children both athletically and socially for decades. The centers associated with these organizations were the first to appear in terms of local community recreation facilities. Since then, cities have built a number of local ballparks, gymnasiums, and multipurpose fields.

According to Project Play, many recreation facilities were originally built to "support quality of life, health, and community development as well as to provide low-cost access to sport and recreation programs." However, in recent years, cities have built these facilities to attract major events, which can bring in additional revenue through sport tourism. For example, the city of Lawrence, Kansas, recently built a $25 million Sports Pavilion, with the hope that it would be selected to host large sporting events. According to the Topeka Capital-Journal, the city of Lawrence was able to capitalize on their investment when the Sports Pavilion acted as one of the

BOX 15.3 LEARNING ACTIVITY TWO

Activity 2: Community Trail Routes

- As previously discussed in the chapter, trails and pathways are viewed as some of the most important amenities provided by the Parks and Recreation Department of a city.
- For this assignment, you will act as a Community Project Director for your hometown. You are tasked to create walking/running routes for a local club that meets on a weekly basis. The purpose of these routes will be to provide participants with same options depending on their abilities, experience, and fitness levels.
- Utilizing online resources (such as Google maps) create 5 routes that you could present to the local run/walk club. The first route should be an easy (flat and firm terrain) and short route. The second route should be an easy long route. The third should be a short route with medium difficulty. The fourth route should be a long route with medium difficulty. The final route should be quite strenuous with a sustained steep hill (if possible, may depend on hometown location).

major facilities in the 2017 Junior Olympic track championships. This event was said to provide a $1 million boost for the Lawrence economy as well as a $22 million impact on Northeast Kansas.

Natural Spaces

Another area of focus among city parks and recreation departments are the nature areas. These spaces include trails and greenways, backcountry trails, mountain biking trails, rowing lanes, water trails, wildlife management areas, beach volleyball, nature and education centers, and state and national parks (Project Play, 2017). The purpose of these nature areas is to provide opportunities for nature-based, outdoor recreation and experiential environmental education. Because they have little to no cost for users, the nature areas are a great place for the general public who would like to partake in outdoor recreational activities.

According to a community survey conducted by the Parks and Recreation Department of Cupertino, 80% of respondents said city trails and pathways were the most important amenity provided by the department. Additionally, when the respondents were asked to identify the most important improvements to existing facilities, 64% indicated completing the loop and adding connector trails. (See Box 15.3 for trail route activity.)

For-Profit Recreation

Unlike the aforementioned community recreation programs, for-profit recreation clubs and events operate exclusively for members by providing private sport and recreation facilities. According to the 2015 Project Play, the purpose of these clubs is, "to address the lack of inventory of recreation spaces through entrepreneurial investments." Because of the nature of the for-profit recreation clubs, they are financed through private investment and receive no public funding. Additionally, these clubs are owned and operated by private developers, who are not associated with city recreation departments. Due to the nature of these private and competitive establishments, the International Health, Racquet, and Sportsclub Association (IHRSA) research shows the number of for-profit clubs and members is at an all-time high (2017).

Country Club Sports and Health Clubs

Country clubs and health clubs exist to provide a group of individuals with a place to socialize and act upon a specific interest. Relating to their for-profit design, the purpose of these clubs is to operate as a successful business venture. Essentially, they are designed to return the owners the greatest net profit through membership fees. In addition to membership costs, many country clubs and health clubs offer daily access passes for a specific price. In fact, the average cost of an 18-hole round at a daily fee course can range anywhere from $15 to $150. These clubs also provide private facilities (such as pools, fitness centers, and restaurants) for an additional fee.

Despite operating in similar fashion, country clubs and health clubs are trending in opposite directions. The National Golf Foundation's 2017 annual report on golf participation showed a decrease by 1.2%, which is the lowest reported number in the Tiger Woods era. In contrast, the latest data from the IHRSA show the U.S. health club industry serves 70.2 million individuals with growth in membership by 33.6%. While both these numbers are notable, country clubs and health clubs must both continue to find innovative ways to engage consumers in the competitive world of sport and entertainment.

Amateur Leagues

Another area where for-profit recreation exists is in the context of adult amateur leagues. These leagues were developed to provide adults with the opportunity to participate in organized team sports at a competitive level. In fact, for-profit companies such as Valley Sports Leagues, USTA, and USSSA are popping up across the country. These leagues typically fall into one of three levels: local, regional, or national. Typically, the main differences between these levels are in the form of the structure and legitimacy of the league. However, regardless of the level, these companies are known to target Millennials because they are more likely to participate in team sports than any other generational category (SFIA, 2017).

Extreme Endurance Competitions

Extreme endurance competitions, such as Ironman, Spartan Races, ultramarathons, marathons, and triathlons, have become the fastest growing segment in recreational sport. In particular, this growth has been seen over the past decade in terms of increased participation numbers, especially among women. The organizations that host these competitions are consistently trying to elevate the customer's experience through unique branding and cultural aspects. For example, runDisney has created the Dopey Challenge where participants will run the 5K, 10K, Half Marathon, and *Walt Disney World*® Marathon back-to-back days. Despite the high cost ($560 in 2017), this challenge draws participants because of its direct connection to Disney, routes that go through the Disney parks, and finisher medals/gear.

Additionally, extreme endurance sport has created an avenue for sponsorships to emerge, which adds to overall marketing and promotion of the individual event. In fact, the 2015 IEG Sponsorship report stated that the sponsorship spent for endurance sport reached $118.8 million in 2015, which is an increase of 4.6% from 2014 (see Figure 15.3). Common company sponsors for these events are Nestlé, Anheuser-Busch, Clif Bar, and the most popular PepsiCo.

Youth Sports

As discussed in Chapter 7, there is a known shift occurring at the youth and high school level from *sport for play* to *sport for competition*. This transition is a new phenomenon, which is occurring based on the legitimacy, organization, and structure associated with club sports. These club or "elite" programs are in direct competition with the community recreation leagues, which has led to decreases in participation

FIGURE 15.3   Yearly Growth in Sport Sponsorship Sales

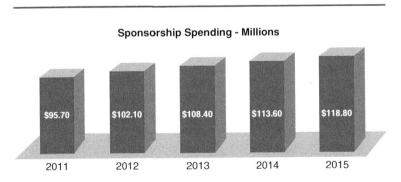

Source: 2015 IEG Sponsorship report; Graph created by Peyton Stensland

and funding at the local level. In addition, a further divide has been created between individuals who can afford to have their children participate in club sports and those who cannot. This for-profit mind-set adds to the divergence between groups and creates a perception of mediocracy at the community recreation level where children may be left behind.

Conclusion

In the previous chapter, it was made evident why the authors chose to define community sport as an umbrella term that largely involves "direct participation" by consumers. Because individuals continue to participate in recreational programs for a variety of reasons, it is important to understand the trends, motivations, and constraints that exist. Additionally, by understanding the differences and similarities between for-profit and profit recreation programs, participants are able to find a program/league/sport that works best for their lifestyle.

References

Deci, E. L. (1975). *Intrinsic motivation*. New York: Plenum Press.

Gantz, W. & Wenner, L. (1995). Fanship and the television viewing experience. *Sociology of Sport Journal, 12*, 56–74.

Gomes, C. S., Matozinhos, F. P., Mendes, L. L., Pessoa, M. C., & Velasquez-Melendez, G. (2016). Physical and social environment are associated to leisure time physical activity in adults of a Brazilian city: A cross sectional study. *PLoS ONE, 11*(2), e0150017.

PAC. (2018). 2018 participation report: The Physical Activity Council's annual study tracking sports, fitness, and recreation participation in the US. *Physical Activity Council.* Retrieved from http://www.physicalactivitycouncil.com/pdfs/current.pdf

Schrag, F. (1992). Conceptions of knowledge. In P. W. Jackson (Ed.), *Handbook of research on curriculum* (pp. 268–301). New York: Macmillan.

SFIA. (2017). 2017 Sports, fitness, and leisure activities topline participation report. *Sports & Fitness Industry Association.* Retrieved from https://www.sfia.org/reports/512_2017-Sports%2C-Fitness%2C-and-Leisure-Activities-Topline-Participation-Report-

Field Interview

Elizabeth Karr

Active Ad Astra Run Walk Lawrence Participant and Business School Advisor at the University of Kansas

1. Please describe the main purpose of the *Ad Astra-Lawrence* training programs?

Run Walk Lawrence (RWL) provides training programs using the Galloway Method (aka run/walk intervals, developed by Jeff Galloway) for completing various race distances such as 5K, 10K, half marathon, and full marathon. This program aims to reduce the risk of injury for runners while also making these race distances attainable for people of all different ages and skill levels. The program also aims to make running fun and enjoyable. Being able to train with a group of people keeps people accountable and is easier to stick to than training alone.

Another training program operated by Ad Astra in Lawrence is the Mass Street Milers. This program is a free weekly run that starts at Ad Astra Running on Mass St every Thursday at 6 p.m. The purpose is to bring the local running community together for a fun run every week. There are two to three distance options usually ranging from 2.5 to 6 miles. People of all paces and ages come together and they can choose to run in groups or at their own pace.

2. The *Ad Astra-Lawrence* training programs sound like a great opportunity for community members to get together. Given your experiences, how have these programs connected you to other individuals in the Lawrence area?

RWL and Mass Street Milers have introduced me to people I never would have met otherwise. I also now have a strong connection with a local running store where I know I can get good advice if I have running questions. I look forward to seeing my running partners every Saturday morning. We're able to motivate each other and making these connections has made training feel less like a chore. This year I'm now a pace group leader. While this current program has just started, the goal for the pace group leaders is to reach out to their group during the week to keep people motivated and occasionally organize a midweek run. I hope being a pace group leader will help me strengthen my connections with the people in RWL because we'll be communicating and training together more than just once a week.

3. If the *Lawrence Journal-World* newspaper were to write a feature story on these run/walk programs, what quote would you add to highlight your overall experience?

"RWL made training for a marathon less daunting. I didn't think I could complete this distance until I found a group of diverse people who believed in me. When I tell people not in the program how much fun I have training and running 20+ miles, they usually think I'm nuts, but the community within the program creates such a positive atmosphere that you can't help but have fun."

"Mass Street Milers provides such a laid-back environment that it's easy to commit to a weekly run regardless of the weather. Hot or cold, rain or shine, people show up and have a good time. I always leave feeling more relaxed and energized than I've been all week."

4. The motivations individuals have for participating in community recreational sport programs have been shown to vary between social, physical, and mental aspects. What would you say are the main reasons you participate in the *Ad Astra-Lawrence* training programs?

I started participating in RWL as a way to reach my goal of completing a full marathon. I keep going back because it keeps me in a regular exercise routine, so I can stay healthy and it also provides socialization while I'm training. I know if I was doing all my training alone, I wouldn't be able to stick to a routine. Now I have a variation of group and individual workouts during the week and that variation prevents the training from getting stale. It's also motivating to see everyone else's progress throughout the program and that inspires me to keep challenging myself.

I participate in Mass Street Milers because it's fun and it provides exercise for me and my dog. The routes are different every week so that keeps the runs from getting boring. Ad Astra also provides discounts on shoes for people who attend regularly so that motivates me to go every week. One of my favorite things about Mass Street Milers is that the run happens in all weather conditions, hot or cold, rain or shine (except when there's ice on the sidewalks because that's not safe). This means I'm training in various conditions so I'm prepared for whatever happens on race day.

5. What are some of the biggest differences you have noticed between training on your own and joining the *Ad Astra-Lawrence* training programs?

For both RWL and Mass Street Milers, the biggest difference is that I'm more motivated to stick to a training plan and I don't get burned out as quickly. Having a group of people that is fun to be around makes training a positive experience even if I'm not running well. I look forward to attending both programs every week.

After I finished my first marathon, I took a couple of weeks break from RWL so I could recover and I noticed it was hard for me to get up and exercise on those Saturday mornings when I didn't have a group of people expecting me to show up. I also noticed that I had a much more negative outlook on exercise in general. Now that a new marathon program has started, I'm already in a much more positive headspace and it's been easier to commit to Saturday morning group workouts.

6. Describe your favorite aspects of *Ad Astra-Lawrence* and give some specific examples, if possible.

My favorite aspect of RWL is our long training runs. With these runs, we're paired with two to three other people of a similar pace and we do a double-digit route at a pace 2 to 3 minutes slower than race pace. Having the other people around makes the long runs fly by since we can usually chat the whole time. This has allowed me to get to know the people in the program pretty well. I also enjoy the structured warmup and cooldown we do each week. I'm really bad at properly warming up and cooling down when I train by myself so this forces me to form good habits and helps prevent injuries.

I love that I can bring my dog to Mass Street Milers. Several other people bring dogs occasionally so that's good socialization for my dog. I also like that every few weeks they'll bring in a shoe company and do a test run. This is where you can test out a pair of shoes before purchasing. This allows people to find the perfect shoe. Usually these test runs are also paired with free refreshments and raffles. That contributes to the fun atmosphere created by the runs.

Name: _____ Section: _____ Date _____

HSES 289
Introduction to Sport Management

In-Class Quiz and Activity Sheet

Name (or names if done in a group)

Answer #1

Answer #2

Answer #3

Chapter 16

Fundraising

Zach Scola • *University of Kansas*

Icon Sportswire/Getty Images

The Beginnings and Rise of Fundraising in Athletics

Sport on college campuses began as student-run activities to break up the strict day-to-day schedules that a university provides (Flowers, 2009). Football, which was created as a mix of soccer and rugby, was an important galvanizing intracollegiate event by the early 1800s. Even though these matches were only played between men who attended the same colleges, often separated by their year in school, football and a sport closely resembling field hockey became incredibly popular campus activities (Flowers, 2009). Until the 1850s these student clubs only competed against their classmates; in 1852, Yale and Harvard participated in the first American intercollegiate event as their rowing clubs competed.

Despite only 1,000 spectators at the first intercollegiate event, it took only 7 years when there were 20,000 spectators in a rowing competition where Yale took on College Union Regatta (Flowers, 2009). As the popularity rose, so did the need for financial support. As universities moved west and competition for perspective students increased, the importance of college athletics rose. Even by the late 1800s, the presidents of both Princeton and Columbia made statements suggesting how important football was to their campus. Specifically, these men noted how valuable it was to beat the likes of the top schools, Harvard and Yale, at the time (Flowers, 2009). Even by the early 1900s it was felt that to be a legitimate university, a successful athletics program was necessary (Davis, 2007)

As the importance and popularity of college football rose, so did the spending. Even while they were still considered student-run organizations, alumni had influence (Flowers, 2009). Alumni were asked to donate to the clubs and at times allowed to coach. As alumni began putting money toward these clubs, winning and spectating became even more important. By the 1880s, schools were hiring professional coaches (Flowers, 2009) and charging spectators to watch collegiate football games (Smith, 1988). In 1904, Harvard saw revenues from football of 42,000 dollars and in response created the first permanent football stadium, which cost them 300,000 dollars. In 1914, Yale followed Harvard, arguably starting the arms race in college sport, building a 75,000-seat football stadium and by the 1930s, large football stadiums were commonplace on campus.

Through the growing popularity and importance of winning, college sport has found itself in an arms race to attract the best perspective student-athletes to their university. In doing so, colleges have become heavily reliant on fundraising, specifically from donors. Dating back to 1984, booster and donor groups made up 12% of athletics budgets at National Collegiate Athletic Association (NCAA) DI universities (Alfano, 1986). The same NCAA report also found that 87% of DI university presidents saw boosters as the biggest potential integrity problem in their athletics departments. Increasing the reliance on alumni donors can bring headaches to an athletics department and universities.

Athletics donations have been on the rise for many years. In 1990, the average reported donation for DI athletics departments was 1.55 million dollars; by 1999, that was up to 3.5 million dollars, more than doubling over 9 years (Fulks, 2002). In 2014, the Knight Commission found that 22% of DI athletics department revenues came from donor contributions and at the FCS and DI schools without football, donations only made up 8% of their total revenues. The revenues are skyrocketing, especially for universities in the Power 5 conferences.

Total revenues at these top athletics schools nearly quadrupled from 2005 to 2015 and are on pace to increase by nearly a billion dollars from 2015 to 2020.

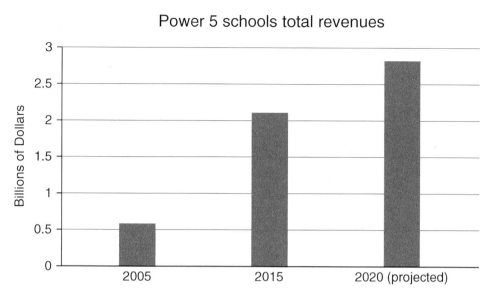

Power 5 schools total revenues

Finances of College Sports—
Knights Commission (n.d.)

Source: Graph created by
Zach Scola

As the arms race continues to accelerate and winning becomes more important, fundraising from alumni donors is of the utmost importance.

Benefits for Donors and Types of Donors

Donors can receive a magnitude of benefits from donating to college athletics programs, the most prestigious being naming rights. A recent example of this is at the University of Kansas, where David Booth gave a 50-million-dollar donation to kick-start a 350-million-dollar project. As a part of this donation, the school changed the name of their stadium from Kansas Memorial Stadium to David Booth Kansas Memorial stadium (Hancock, 2017). At the University of Connecticut, a former men's soccer player donated 8 million dollars to build a new soccer stadium. Rather than changing the name of the stadium, the school is calling the soccer complex (which includes the practice field and training grounds) the Rizza Family Soccer Complex (Goodnough, 2014). Naming rights are the greatest benefit a donor can receive, but there are other benefits, small and large, that donors may receive.

Those who donate because they are motivated by the tangible benefits they receive would be considered transactional donors. These donors' behaviors will be impacted based on what they can receive from their donation. Therefore, tier systems, where the more you donate the more you benefit, may be effective for these donors.

The other type of donor is motivated by how donating makes them feel, or the intangible benefits and they are called transformational donors. To connect with these donors, athletics departments can create booster clubs and focus on how their money will go to support the university and the student-athletes. There is often some overlap in donors, meaning donors may be motivated by both transactional and transformational benefits. It

List of Potential Benefits for Donors

- Naming Rights
- Tickets
  - Can be the way to access season tickets
  - Can allow donors to improve their seats
- Access
  - Sideline, VIP events
- Parking
- SWAG
  - University-branded materials (lanyards, posters, license plates, flags, etc.)
  - University-branded gear
- Tax benefits
  - New tax law changes in 2018

is likely that a big-time donor who donates millions of dollars and gets naming rights of a stadium has transformational feelings of doing good for their university as well.

> **Transactional donors**—motivated by tangible benefits, such as tickets, SWAG, or special access
>
> **Transformational donors**—motivated by the intangible benefits, like the good feeling one gets from donating because they like helping the students or the athletics department

Motivations of Athletics Donors

Figuring out why people donate to college athletics programs is of grave importance to athletics directors. One such study examined this question and found that the answer varied based on the structure of the athletics department donor fund (Gladden, Mahony, & Apostolopoulou, 2005). One important note from this study was that across all four of the schools examined, 48.5% or greater were motived to support and improve the athletics program, which has a transformational tone to it. Another study found that supporting the university, an attachment to the university and athletics department, the benefits associated with donating, and that their children were attending or participating in the athletics events were motivations for becoming an athletics donor (Bass, Achen, & Gordon, 2015). Further, it was noted that the primary reasons for discontinuing their donation were: financial, lost contact with the university, and losing satisfaction with their benefits of donating.

Understanding what motivates donors of athletics departments is crucial for fundraisers to be successful. Further, it is helpful to understand what demographics of people donate to athletics departments. Research has shown that a donor base is likely to be made up of highly identified fans; one study examined Power 5 schools and found that 96.2% of their participants were highly identified (Popp, Barett, & Weight, 2016). Additionally, it has been found that achievement, philanthropy, commitment, and tangible benefits were all significant motivators for donors regardless of the size of their contribution (Park, Ko, Kim, Sagas, & Eddosary, 2016). Highly identified fans may make up most athletics donors and regardless of whether they donate large or small gifts, they may have similar motivations. Creating highly identified fans at an early age could be beneficial in creating future athletics donors.

Intercollegiate Athletics Fundraising Campaigns

The type of fundraising conducted may vary upon the size of a university's alumni base and success of their athletics programs. Athletics departments can take numerous routes to attract alumni and community members to donate. For example, the athletics department at Duke is attached to the university's 7-year fundraising campaign called Duke Forward (Duke Sports Information, 2017). The university raised 3.85 billion dollars with this campaign, and 340 million dollars were contributed to the athletics department. Despite attaching to the university's fundraising campaign, they titled their campaign "building champions" and promoted how the money would go toward updating their athletics facilities. Another all-campus fundraising campaign "For All: The Bicentennial Campaign for Indiana University" began in 2016 and had a goal of 2.5 billion dollars (Varsity Club, 2016). The athletics department at Indiana attached a 170-million-dollar fundraising goal for various facility renovations. These two prestigious universities were able to put together multibillion-dollar campaigns and their highly successful athletics departments attached to the campaign to promote improving their facilities successfully.

Another way to attract donors is through a transformational campaign, where the donors are motivated by the feeling of helping the athletics department, rather than the process of receiving a tangible benefit. The University of Maryland athletics department was having trouble getting donations from their alumni; in fact, only 9% of their alumni had made donations to the athletics department in 2013 (Prewitt, 2013). The athletics department had cut seven teams in 2012, in part because of low donation totals. Therefore, in 2013, the athletics department changed their booster club name from the Terrapin Club to the Terrapin Club Scholarship Fund and their chief fundraiser Tim McMurray described their philosophical change stating: "In the past, it was a transactional operation. We need to communicate that it's transformational" (Prewitt, 2013, para. 17).

Another Big 10 school that has moved to a more philanthropic approach is Nebraska that created the Student-Athlete Experience Fund (Barfknecht, 2016). In 2014, the NCAA allowed Power Five schools to offer additional benefits to their student-athletes. In response to this, Nebraska awards each of their scholarship athletes: a laptop, up to 7,500 dollars to pursue an internship, study-abroad program, or graduate school upon graduation, and additional resources involving sport medicine and training. To help raise additional funds, Nebraska shifted their message to let donors to know they're donating to help student-athletes. Although many alumni still donate to receive tickets, Nebraska has seen a large increase in overall giving and attributes that to the new philanthropic donors (Barfknecht, 2016). If you tell donors where their money is going, they may be more willing to donate. Donors may be more motivated to donate to see a new track and field for their athletes than they would be to blindly throw money at the athletics department.

Transformational donors may be even more important at small schools. Fundraising for small school athletics departments can prove tricky, as they do not often have the prestigious athletics programs or high-end benefits to give donors. At smaller schools, fundraising coordinators need to get more creative. During the 2015–2016 school year, Drew University athletics, in Madison New Jersey, created the Blue & Green challenge. This challenged pitted alumni from their various sports against each other and the past student-athlete group that was most successful saw their sport get a "prize" which was a larger fundraising dollar amount given to improve that sport (Blue & Green challenge, n.d.). Another way smaller colleges may attract donors is to describe exactly how it will benefit a team and connect it to an important figure with that university. The University of Wisconsin La Crosse athletics department sought to improve their swimming and diving facility and created a campaign honoring their recently retired swimming coach. The Richard Pein pool fundraiser's goal was to earn 50,000 dollars, which would all go toward the swimming and diving team. If the goal was met, their swimming facility would be named after coach Richard Pein (Richard Pein Pool Fundraiser, n.d.). This fundraiser was transformational as it asked for donations specific to the swimming and diving team, but added to that by promising to change the name of the facility to a past great coach once the goal was met.

There are immense variations of campaigns conducted by university athletics departments. It is important to understand that smaller schools may not have the same alumni base or valuable offerings to get substantial donations to fund their athletics departments. When this is the case, fundraisers must get creative and frequently target those transformational donors discussed above. Creating these campaigns require a type of person who understands their alumni base and have a great deal of perseverance.

What It Takes to Be a Fundraiser

There are a handful of key skills one must possess to be a successful fundraiser. Raising money for an athletics department is a vital job that requires one to always be on the clock. Some of the most important skills to successfully raise money for an athletics department include:

- *Networking*—A fundraiser must be able to interact with many different types of people. Creating connections with alumni, faculty, coaches, and other decision makers is crucial. Obviously, the better a fundraiser networks, the easier raising money for the athletics department should be.
- *Patience and Persistence*—Being told "no" is often a part of the job. The best way to combat this as a fundraiser is to take your time with each potential donor and do your best to not take no for an answer. In any sales or fundraising job, the worst that may happen is someone decides they do not want to give you their money. A successful fundraiser can accept that, while continuing to pursue many potential donors, often following up with donors who said no.
- *Political Skill*—The term political skill has multiple facets, but is most simply explained by Ferris and colleagues (2005) as: "the ability to effectively understand others at work, and to use such knowledge to influence others to act in ways that enhance one's personal and/or organizational objectives" (p. 127). Political skill involves understanding

your situation and the people around you as well as being able to push forward whatever agenda you have. As a fundraiser, it is instrumental that one can work well with other people and influence them to move toward a common goal.

- ***Situational-Awareness & Always being "on"***—As a fundraiser, one must be able to not only network well but understand how to act around different groups of people. Successfully raising funds for an athletics department means interacting with people from various walks of life, including athletes, faculty, and staff, and if one is lucky, many wealthy individuals. Beyond understanding how to work well with all types of people, and adapting to one's situation, it is important for a fundraiser to always be "on." A fundraiser never knows where their next potential donor may be. Therefore, it is important that a fundraiser is always selling and always portraying the athletics department to others in a positive light.

Successful fundraisers have various backgrounds and strategies, but most will embody at least some of the skills discussed above. For a more detailed look at the happenings in college athletics fundraising we conducted a short Q&A with Ben Fraser of the University of Minnesota.

Field Interview

Ben Fraser

Director of Annual Giving and Premium Seating at University of Minnesota Athletics Department

1. In your eyes, what are the most important traits to being a successful fundraiser in college athletics?

Fundraising, in any area, is about relationships. Being able to build strong, positive relationships with prospects is an integral part of being a successful fundraiser. Work ethic is another key component to being successful in the fundraising in Intercollegiate Athletics. In Intercollegiate Athletics, you may be managing many, many prospects at one time and being able to be on top of their different interests and needs are important. The final skill that is crucial in fundraising is communication, being able to not only relate to donors, but be able to keep the looped in to the day-to-day operations of the department makes them feel important and a valued investor.

2. In your experience, what is the best way to connect with donors and what methods have been best for you to get lifelong athletics donors?

I like to talk to donors about investing into our program and most importantly into our student-athletes. I think if the donor truly feels part of the program and gets to develop relationships with student-athletes, that is the best way to build a lifelong passion of philanthropy.

3. What aspects of your job do you think would be surprising to most people?

I think that many areas within Intercollegiate Athletics are known for their long hours, and the quantity of work. I think sometimes Development is viewed as more a "lighter" role, but that is the exact opposite. I have donors contacting me at all hours of the day and reaching out different requests seven days a week. The demand to quickly either resolve a problem or provide information is crucial.

4. What advice would you give a student who wanted to work in college athletics and then more specifically, into fundraising for college athletics?

I would tell them to work on developing relationships. Working with people and developing positive relationships are the key to successful fundraising. I honestly believe that great fundraisers can come from many different areas within Intercollegiate Athletics, I always say "We are all in fundraising."

5. What are some of the current trends you see today in college athletics fundraising and do you see any specific changes coming in the near future?

One of the biggest, most recent changes, in Intercollegiate fundraising is the change in seat-related giving. The recent change in the tax law has made these donations no longer tax deductible which has/and will make a large impact on Annual Funds around the country as individuals contemplate their ticket-purchasing habits. Being able to get creative with driving annual donations as the student-athlete experience cost continues to raise will be crucial for departments to stay competitive.

Trends in Intercollegiate Athletics Fundraising

Fundraising has changed a great deal over time. As the expenses around college athletics have increased, so has the need for fundraising dollars. This need has caused changes in strategies, including offering naming rights for various aspects of the athletics department, moving from a pledge system to a payment plan, as well as creating student booster groups. On top of the new strategies, athletics departments are creating more support facilities which offers more donor opportunities and need. Additionally, the 2018 tax law has the potential to negatively impact donations as it takes away a key benefit for athletics donors.

New Strategies for Athletics Fundraising

To earn additional fundraising dollars, departments have been offering naming rights for basically anything and have been creating endowments for many unique positions. Cape Fear Community college, a member of the NJCAA, suggests potential naming rights on many unique things, stating: "Naming opportunities enables a donor to have their name, or that of a loved one, attached to a specific athletics facility, building, room, garden, brick walk, etc., for a specified amount" (Methods of giving, n.d., para. 20, n.d.). At the University of Boston, they offer athletics endowments as one of the prominent ways to donate, and they have endowed scholarships, programs, and coaching positions (Athletic endowments, n.d.). As the process of getting top recruits has intensified, athletics departments are getting more creative and one way is through support buildings like the DeBruce Center and McCarthy Hall at the University of Kansas, which were both privately funded. Both of these buildings are not exclusively for athletes, but the DeBruce Center feeds all athletes and is frequently closed for athletics events and McCarthy Hall houses only 37 people, 16 of them being basketball players.

The concept of building a facility to house athletes is not necessarily new. In fact, many major athletics programs have put together similar dormitories or apartments. These facilities are expensive and used as recruiting tools for top football and basketball programs. Some examples of these facilities include:

- Louisville's Bill Minardi Hall, which opened in 2003 and cost 4.5 million dollars. Thirty-eight students live here, and about half of them are men's basketball players.
- Kentucky's Wildcat Coal Lodge, which was constructed in 2012 at a price of nearly 8 million dollars. Nearly half of the residents are men's basketball players and only 32 students live in this residence.
- Auburn opened the South Donahue Hall in 2013. This facility was constructed for 51 million dollars and holds 209 students, including nearly the whole football team.
- Kansas's McCarthy Hall discussed above opened in 2014 and cost 12 million dollars.
- In August 2019, North Carolina State expects to have Case Commons constructed, which will be a 15-million-dollar dormitory primarily for their men's and women's college basketball players (Alexander, 2017).

The arms race of college athletics has led to many schools building luxurious and expensive living spaces for their athletes as well as other support services such as dining halls and additional academic services. These services cost a great deal of money, therefore requiring greater fundraising efforts. Beyond just offering up additional naming rights or endowments, schools have tried to make donating easier and allow small donors to have more importance by moving to payment plans and creating student booster groups.

Many athletics departments require a large donation to earn priority with basketball or football tickets. To allow more flexibility with donations, schools are offering payment plans where a donor can take the entire year and make their full donation in segments, instead of all at the time of their initial pledge. This targets donors who are transactional and motivated by the tangible benefits they can receive. Another way that athletics departments are trying to reach new donors is through booster clubs. A booster club is a way to connect all donors to the department, big or small. Additionally, a booster club can compile all the small donations and encourage alumni to give what they can, whether that is 10 dollars or 1,000 dollars. Clemson has a great example of a booster club, called IPTAY (I pay ten a year) club. This organization was started in the 1930s, and the goal was to get as many supporters to participate as possible and a 10-dollar minimum was viewed as reasonable for nearly all alumni (Blackman, 2000). Today, Clemson still has IPTAY and its focus has become the student-athletes, to reach the transformational donors. Booster clubs can fundraise millions of dollars by compiling many small donations, and Clemson's IPTAY was at the forefront of this movement.

Many schools are even creating student booster clubs, which may not require any financial donation, but they keep the student fan base connected to all the happenings in their athletics department. The goal of these programs is to increase the identification with the athletics department and in turn create a potential future donor. A student booster club may begin as a student fan club for your sporting events, but making a connection to the students early could have a great impact on their potential future donating behavior. These trends have been changing the landscape of college athletics fundraising, but a new law passed in 2018 may have an even greater impact.

Impact of the 2018 Tax Law

On January 1, 2018, the Tax Cuts and Jobs Act was enacted. This bill was generally in place to reduce corporate tax rates. In addition, this law had an impact on college athletics donors, particularly donations tied to receiving season tickets (Murschel, 2018). Prior to this law being enacted, donors could claim deductions on 80% of all charitable donations to athletics departments. Many schools require a donation before having the right to purchase season tickets and now this law no longer allows donors to claim these "licensing fees" donations as a tax deduction. When donors could claim 80% of their required donation for tickets as a write-off, making a four-figure donation for the right to season tickets was more manageable. Now that fans cannot claim any of that "donation" as a charitable act on their taxes, schools like North Carolina and Duke, who require 6,000 and 4,000 dollar donations respectively, to earn the right to purchase two season tickets may need to adjust their fundraising strategies (Smith, 2017). The impact of this new tax law may cause a great deal of issues in college athletics departments, as it may cost them millions of dollars.

As noted prior, in 2014, the total revenues of NCAA DI universities were very reliant on donation dollars. The Knight Commission found that donations made up 22% of the total revenues at Football Bowl Subdivision (FBS) schools. Although not all donations are connecting to receiving tickets or other benefits, even a small dip in total donations in response to this tax law could be disastrous. As the total revenues at FBS schools were just over 2 billion dollars in 2015, 22% would estimate that over 400 million dollars in revenue was contributed by donors. Even a 1% drop in total donations would see a 4+ million dollar decrease across FBS schools. This tax law will cause college athletics fundraisers a great deal of stress and should lead to some new creative fundraising strategies.

Conclusion

Beginning and Rise of Fundraising in Athletics

- Sport began on college campuses as a competition between classmates; as it became intercollegiate competitions, the need for funding increased.
- Yale and Harvard began the arms race in the early 1900s building spectator football stadiums on campus.
- The revenues in college athletics have skyrocketed over time as have the total donations to athletics departments, making up 22% of total revenues at FBS schools.

Benefits for Donors and Types of Donors

- Donors can receive many tangible benefits including: naming rights, tickets, access to special events, parking, SWAG (university-branded gear and items), as well as tax benefits.
- Transactional donors are motivated by the tangible benefits listed above.
- Transformational donors are motivated by intangible benefits, such as the good feelings they have about assisting the student-athletes or athletics department.

Motivations for Athletics Donors

- A clear majority of donors may be highly identified fans of the school's sports.
- Many donors may also be motived to support and improve the athletics program, therefore being more transformational donors.

Intercollegiate Athletics Fundraising Campaigns

- Athletics departments can connect with a university-wide campaign.
- Many schools are using a philanthropic approach, with campaigns supporting the students, and being more specific about telling the donors where their dollars are going.

What It Takes to Be a Fundraiser

- Key skills include networking, patience and persistence, political skill, and situational awareness/always being "on."
- Ben Fraser harped on the importance of building relationships, work ethic, and communication to be a successful fundraiser.

Trends in Intercollegiate Athletics Fundraising

- Naming rights and endowments are being offered for nearly anything, including athletics support facilities which are on the rise.
- Moving to an approach using booster clubs where potential donors are encouraged to donate whatever money they can, including student booster clubs which may create future donors.
- The new tax law may have an incredible impact on the landscape of college athletics fundraising.

References

Alexander, J. M. (2017). NC State joins a nationwide trend: A $15 million 'boutique' dorm for athletes. *The News & Observer*. Retrieved from http://www.newsobserver.com/sports/college/acc/nc-state/article175911846.html

Alfano, P. (1986). The college sports industry; power in purse strings. *The New York Times*. Retrieved from https://www.nytimes.com/1986/06/11/sports/the-college-sports-industry-power-in-purse-strings.html

Athletic endowments. (n.d.). *BU Changing the Game*. Retrieved from https://www.bu.edu/changingthegame/ways/athletic-endowments

Barfknecht, L. (2016, August 27). Since Nebraska began earmarking donations for benefit of athletes, giving has increased. *Big Red Today*. Retrieved from http://www.omaha.com/huskers/football/since-nebraska-began-earmarking-donations-for-benefit-of-athletes-giving/article_2d0c7d09-6c57-5ba9-a7b3-9759aef8104f.html

Bass, J. R., Gordon, B. S., & Achen, R. M. (2015). Motivations for athletic giving: Examining non-renewed donors. Applied Research in Coaching and Athletics, 30(2), 166-186.

Blackman, S. (2000, September 5). History of IPTAY. *Clemson Athletics*. Retrieved from http://www.clemsontigers.com/ViewArticle.dbml?DB_OEM_ID=28500&ATCLID=205524148

Blue & Green Challenge. (n.d.). *The Campaign for Drew*. Retrieved from http://www.drew.edu/oneandall/blue-green-challenge/?

Davis, R. O. (2007). *Sports in American life: A history*. Malden, MA: Blackwell Publishing.

Duke Sports Information. (2017, August 15). Athletics raises $340 million in Duke forward campaign. *Duke Athletics*. Retrieved from: http://www.goduke.com/ViewArticle.dbml?DB_OEM_ID=4200&ATCLID=211661442

Ferris, G. R., Treadway, D. C., Kolodinsky, R. W., Hochwarter, W. A., Kacmar, C. J., Douglas, C., & Frink, D. D. (2005). Development and validation of the political skill inventory. *Journal of Management, 31*(1), 126–152.

Flowers, R. D. (2009). Institutionalized hypocrisy: The myth of intercollegiate athletics. *American Educational History Journal, 36*(2), 343–360.

Finances of college sports (n.d.). *Knight Commission on Intercollegiate Athletics*. Retrieved from https://www.knightcommission.org/finances-college-sports

Fulks, D. L. (2002). Revenues and expenses of division I and II intercollegiate athletics programs: Financial trends and relationships-2001. *National Collegiate Athletic Association*. Retrieved from http://www.science.smith.edu/exer_sci/ESS200/Ed/Fulk2003.pdf

Gladden, J. M., Mahony, D. F., & Apostolopoulou, A. (2005). Toward a better understanding of college athletic donors: What are the primary motives?. Sport Marketing Quarterly, 14(1), 18.

Goodnough, K. (2014, October 13). UConn alum pledges total of $8 million for soccer complex. *UConn Today*. Retrieved from https://today.uconn.edu/2014/10/uconn-alum-pledges-5-million-match-for-soccer-complex

Hancock, P. (2017, December 20). KU football stadium to be renamed after donor David Booth. *KU Sports*. Retrieved from http://www2.kusports.com/news/2017/dec/20/ku-football-stadium-be-renamed-after-donor-david-b

Methods of giving. (n.d.). *Cape Fear Community College Athletics*. Retrieved from http://www.goseadevils.com/sea_devil_club/methods_of_giving

Murschel, M. (2018, February 17). New tax law could prove costly for college athletics. *Orlando Sentinel*. Retrieved from http://www.orlandosentinel.com/sports/college/college-gridiron-365/os-sp-college-athletics-tax-law-changes-0219-story.html

Park, C., Ko, Y., Kim, H., Sagas, M., & Eddosary, M. (2016) Donor motivation in college sport: Does contribution level matter? *Social Behavior and Personality, 44*(6), 1015–1032.

Prewitt, A. (2013, November 20). Terps athletics looks to give fundraising a shot in the arm. *The Washington Post*. Retrieved from https://www.washingtonpost.com/sports/colleges/terps-athletics-looks-to-give-fundraising-a-shot-in-the-arm/2013/11/20/2ece724c-513b-11e3-9fe0-fd2ca728e67c_story.html?noredirect=on&utm_term=.f18e9a501e5a

Popp, N., Barrett, H., & Weight, E. (2016). Examining the relationship between age of fan identification and donor behavior at an NCAA division I athletics department. *Journal of Issues in Intercollegiate Athletics, 9*, 107–122.

Smith, C. (2017, December 22). New tax law could cost top college athletic departments millions. *Sports Money Forbes*. Retrieved from https://www.forbes.com/sites/chrissmith/2017/12/22/gop-tax-law-could-cost-top-college-athletic-departments-millions/#7eba032babea

Smith, R. A. (1988). Sports and freedom: *The rise of big time college athletics*. New York, NY: Oxford University Press.

Varsity Club. (2016, March 6). IU athletics announces capital campaign as part of university wide "For all bicentennial campaign." *IU Athletics*. Retrieved from http://iuhoosiers.com/news/2016/3/6/varsity-club-iu-athletics-announces-capital-campaign-as-part-of-university-wide-for-all-bicentennial-campaign.aspx?path=varsityclub

Name: _____   Section: _____   Date _____

Discussion Questions

1. Discuss the difference between transformational and transactional donors. Which type of donor do you think is more important to focus on as a fundraiser?

2. If fundraising was not a viable option for athletics departments, what other revenues should they rely on? Do you think they would they be financially sustainable?

3. To be a successful fundraiser, which of the mentioned skills do you think is most important? Are there any skills you would add to the list that would help one to be successful?

4. With the new tax law, what adjustments do you think fundraisers need to make? Now that donors cannot write off any of their donations tied to receiving tickets, how can schools convince theses donors to continue offering their same contribution?

Name: _____   Section: _____   Date _____

Assignments

---

1. You are the new fundraising coordinator for a DIII university with a small alumni base in a small city. Your AD has tasked you with creating a new fundraising campaign focusing on student-athlete alumni. To complete this, you must do the following:

   a. Describe your campaign, what will be the focus, when and how will you reach out.

   b. Explain why this will work. What about this campaign will motivate the alumni to donate.

   c. Explain how this campaign would differ if you were targeting general student alumni and not former student-athletes.

---

2. As the fundraiser at a large DI university, you feel your alumni base is tapped out and cannot offer more fundraising dollars. Your next move is to try to fundraise with community members. List and describe three ways in which you will try to entice community members (who are not necessarily alumni) to donate to your athletics department.

Name: _____   Section: _____   Date _____

HSES 289
Introduction to Sport Management

In-Class Quiz and Activity Sheet

Name (or names if done in a group)

Answer #1

Answer #2

Answer #3